D0753310

"Perfectly Able: How to Attract and Hire Talented People with Disabilities is full of insight and practical help for both job applicants and employers [that] is utterly compelling and convincing. This book is a wonderful example of putting into practice the idea that dignity is a universal right, applicable to both sides of every hiring decision. Every employer in the world should have a copy on his desk."

—ROBERT W. FULLER
former president of Oberlin College
and author of *Somebodies and Nobodies:
Overcoming the Abuse of Rank* and
*All Rise: Somebodies, Nobodies
and the Politics of Dignity*

Perfectly Able

Perfectly Able

How to Attract and Hire Talented People

with Disabilities

Lighthouse International

Compiled and Edited by Jim Hasse

American Management Association

New York • Atlanta • Brussels • Chicago • Mexico City • San Francisco
Shanghai • Tokyo • Toronto • Washington, D.C.

Bulk discounts available. For details visit:
www.amacombooks.org/go/specialsales
Or contact special sales:
Phone: 800-250-5308
E-mail: specialsls@amanet.org
View all the AMACOM titles at: www.amacombooks.org

eSight, eSight Careers Network, and Blindstorming
are trademarks of Lighthouse International,
111 East 59th Street, New York, NY 10022.

Library of Congress Cataloging-in-Publication Data

Perfectly able : how to attract and hire talented people with disabilities / compiled and edited by Jim Hasse.
    p. cm.
  Includes index.
  ISBN-13: 978-0-8144-1564-1 (hardcover)
  ISBN-10: 0-8144-1564-4 (hardcover)
  1. People with disabilities—Employment—United States. 2. Employees—Recruiting—United States. 3. Corporate culture—United States. I. Hasse, Jim.
  HD7256.U5P398 2011
  658.3'11087—dc22

                                                            2010014281

About AMA
American Management Association (www.amanet.org) is a world leader in talent development, advancing the skills of individuals to drive business success. Our mission is to support the goals of individuals and organizations through a complete range of products and services, including classroom and virtual seminars, webcasts, webinars, podcasts, conferences, corporate and government solutions, business books, and research. AMA's approach to improving performance combines experiential learning—learning through doing—with opportunities for ongoing professional growth at every step of one's career journey.

Printing number

10 9 8 7 6 5 4 3 2 1

Contents

Foreword

▲

Roads More Easily Traveled

I'M MORE CONVINCED THAN EVER there are basic misunderstandings on the part of both employers and job seekers with disabilities about what each other needs. These misunderstandings are holding back progress in dramatically improving the employment rate of individuals of working age with disabilities.

Why are there gaps in understanding between job seekers with disabilities and potential employers? Many of us may have simply taken roads more easily traveled than those we often bypass because we believe they're perhaps more dangerous. Yet, those bypasses, we sometimes forget, can be more rewarding.

Here are some concrete examples.

As cited later in this book, more than four of ten respondents to the first-ever national study of self-employed people with disabilities said they chose the entrepreneurial route because they "needed to create their own job." A similar number also said they had chosen self-employment with its flexible hours and working conditions "to accommodate a disability."

These are just two findings from a study conducted by the National Institute on Disability and Rehabilitation Research's Research & Training Center on Rural Rehabilitation Services, connected with the University of Montana–affiliated Rural Institute on Disabilities.

"Research has shown that there are nearly as many people with disabilities who own their own business as who work for federal, state, and local governments combined," says Rural Institute research director Tom Seekins. "When you consider the extraordinary difficulty that people with disabilities have had finding employment, starting one's own business makes good sense."

I've recently heard that same logic about the 180,000 or so veterans who have come home from Iraq and Afghanistan with disabilities since 2003. Government and private support people are encouraging these vets to start their own businesses instead of jumping into the job market, because it simply may be easier.

It's true that these vets have probably acquired many valuable skills that may be immediately transferable to establishing small businesses. But many individuals with disabilities (with and without military service) lack the work experience either in a job or as a volunteer necessary to establish a small business. They may lack the track record people often need to establish access to capital and/or credit, and they may also lack a customer base. They must have credible offerings of goods and/or services and, it is hoped, a ready source of potential clients. Even for people without disabilities, that often takes years of working on the job for someone else. And what seems like an easier road ends in disappointment—in phantom businesses, which keep them busy but don't produce an adequate income.

Instead of working themselves up from entry-level jobs (where they can refine their basic skills) to positions of greater and greater responsibility (where they can show their savvy) and then using their contacts and track records to gain a clientele as small business owners, they have short-circuited their careers.

That shoe also fits on the other foot. In my view, employers also must be on guard against hiding behind phantom reasons why they don't hire more people with disabilities.

The U.S. Census Bureau says that 73 percent of the top industries (Fortune 5,000 companies) across the country are hiring people with disabilities.

Yet, the U.S. Census Bureau's American Community Survey says that in 2006 the employment rate for people with disabilities was 37.7 percent, compared to an employment rate of 79.7 percent for people without disabilities, a difference of 42 percentage points.

Why?

According to the National Council on Disability's "Achieving Independence: The Challenge of the 21st Century," the most commonly cited reason for not hiring people with disabilities is a "lack of qualified applicants." That's closely tied to another reason we commonly hear: "the inability to locate or find qualified job applicants with disabilities."

"Lack of qualification" can include a deficiency in education, experience, "hard" skill, "soft" skill, or a specific attribute. Or, for unenlightened employers, it can signal they haven't found good sources of qualified workers with disabilities . . . just yet.

From my perspective as the executive director of the U.S. Business Leadership Network, an organization comprising more than 60 affiliates and 5,000 employers interested in advancing disability employment, disability marketing, and doing business with disability-owned enterprises, employers are simply seeking talent—genuine, bottom-line-driving talent that everyone might well possess, including workers with disabilities.

These employers are more than ready to accommodate workers with disabilities just like they accommodate all their workers (such as working parents whose children become sick during work hours, or workers who seek better task lighting, lumbar-supported desk chairs, or flexible working hours to address their religious beliefs).

President Obama's Deputy Secretary for the U.S. Department of Labor, Seth Harris, examined the accommodation issue in a research paper he wrote while a law professor at the New York Law School. In his paper, he maintains there is little truth to the overblown notion that the Americans with Disabilities Act's (ADA's) accommodation mandates "make workers with disabilities more expensive to employ than workers without disabilities and, therefore, less appealing to employers."

In fact, ADA accommodations often benefit everyone in a workplace, according to earnworks.com (http://www.earnworks.com/BusinessCase/innovation_level2.asp). For example, When A&F Wood, a small manufacturing company in Howell, Michigan, reorganized a workstation to accommodate an employee with a visual impairment, it discovered a more efficient layout for all employees to use. Similarly, Walgreens modified its distribution center's supporting technology, making it easier for its employees with disabilities to use. What Walgreens soon discovered was that the changes simplified tasks for all employees, increasing productivity.

We need a constructive dialogue between job seekers with disabilities and employers. Both are, in some ways, taking the road most easily traveled. By doing so, we're passing by each other—sometimes missing each other by miles.

This book is intended to assist all employers, enlightened or not, and all job seekers, qualified or not, to "look beyond the road most easily traveled," and find one another.

Not connecting is a loss for us all.

> John D. Kemp
> Executive Director
> U.S. Business Leadership Network

Preface

▲

An Opportunity—
Not a Responsibility

IN HIS BOOK *THE FUTURE OF SUCCESS*, Robert B. Reich (Alfred A. Knopf, 2000) identifies several outgrowths of capitalism's success. Here is an excerpt from his book that I believe is particularly applicable to hiring managers:

> In the new economy, there will be no random acts of kindness to employees, suppliers, or communities separate from their positive impact on the bottom line. If being "socially responsible" helps the bottom line by eliciting goodwill from employees, suppliers, or the public at large, then such actions make sound business sense, and the new competitive logic dictates that executives pursue them.
>
> If, however, being "socially responsible" detracts from the bottom line—handicapping the enterprise by drawing resources away from, or otherwise preventing, production that's better, faster, and cheaper than its rivals—then it creates the risk that consumers and shareholders will switch to a better deal. By the new logic, executives then pursue such actions at their peril.

In other words, businesses today are not instruments for deliberate social change. They probably never have been and probably never will be. They only reflect what's happening in society.

So, giving individuals with disabilities an opportunity to work is not your responsibility. You are off the hook. It's not your fault that the employment rate among people with disabilities has changed very little since the ADA became law in 1990.

And it may be comfortable and easy to follow your colleagues, who, like most of us, are understandably uncomfortable with disability because they may not have yet had firsthand experience with it. That's not prejudice, which is an unwillingness to change a personal attitude in the face of evidence that a certain belief is false. It's just lack of information and insight.

However, lack of information and insight usually presents an opportunity for decision makers such as yourself who are continually learning how to excel in their work. As a source for distinctive information and insight about disability within an employment context, *Perfectly Able: How to Attract and Hire Talented People with Disabilities* gives you an edge over your competitors and colleagues. It's designed to help you effectively tap the skills and energies of those with a disability who are ready to contribute to your organization's success.

Perfectly Able shows you how to:

- ⊘ Gain a better awareness of disability
- ⊘ Foster a company culture that is receptive to disability
- ⊘ Make your recruiting efforts disability inclusive
- ⊘ Identify job candidates who will thrive in your corporate culture
- ⊘ Approach people management from a disability perspective

As a business leader, here's how you'll benefit, over time, by making the most of your opportunity to attract and hire talented people with disabilities:

- ⊘ You'll build a stronger workforce by including individuals with a personal sense of dignity and self-worth. That means fewer hassles and better teamwork because you'll have employees who can stand on their own, even though they may have a disability.
- ⊘ You'll have an opportunity to choose individuals who have

learned how to interact effectively with others who are disabled or not. Those interpersonal skills will prove valuable in any employment situation you might have. Such skills will continually upgrade the teamwork, the morale, and the tone of your particular workforce.

- ⊘ You'll be able to choose from a range of job applicants who have had experience in effectively facing vulnerability, handling tough situations, and solving problems. That will give your workforce the agility it needs to do well in unexpected situations. This is especially important because businesses will continue to operate in an increasingly ambiguous environment in the twenty-first century.

- ⊘ You'll have an opportunity to cut your turnover rate, reduce time spent in filling vacant jobs, and spend more of your time managing a more effective staff. As a result, you'll be more effective in your own job, serve your customers better, and set an example for your colleagues. That will help you build your own career.

Perfectly Able helps you incorporate disability into your company's diversity program. It's a guide not only for confidently hiring people who are skilled yet considered "different" due to a disability but also for effectively approaching any hiring or retention situation without regard to disability or any other diversity issue.

It also offers you a new model for your diversity initiative: embracing differences among the individuals within your workforce because those differences add value to what you offer your customers. Such inclusion is simply good business. It enhances your bottom line. And it can help you build your own career.

Here's an example of the unexpected advantage you tap when you broaden the definitions of diversity and difference to include disabilities. By hiring individuals with a range of disabilities (learning, hearing, sight, and psychological), Phil Kosak at Carolina Fine Snacks, Greensboro, North Carolina, pulled the snack-food company out of disaster during the 1990s, according to *Fortune* magazine. Employee turnover dropped from 80 percent every six months to less than 5 percent, productivity rose from 70 percent to 95 percent, absenteeism dropped from 20 percent to less than 5 percent, and tardiness dropped

from 30 percent of staff to zero (http://www.earnworks.com/
BusinessCase/human_cap_level2.asp).

That success story reminds me of another reason why *Perfectly Able*
is unique and why I believe you'll find it most helpful as a source, a
guide, and a model for attracting and hiring talented people with disabilities. It's based on the real-world experiences of job seekers and
employees themselves.

Compiled specifically for you as a human resources professional or
hiring manager, *Perfectly Able* includes a distillation of more than 100
observations from 70 individuals with disabilities who have participated
in online discussions or personal interviews focused on disability
employment issues since 1997.

As a result, this book provides you with a real-world glimpse into the
contemporary North American scene when it comes to disability
employment issues—a glimpse that I believe you'll find informative and
inspirational.

Jim Hasse, ABC, GCDF

Acknowledgments

▲

A SPECIAL THANK-YOU TO OUR 70 CONTRIBUTORS: Peter Altschul; Ann; Art; The Rev. Daniel M. Berry III (deceased); Bonita; Brenda; Anthony R. Candela; Ollie D. Cantos VII; Carlos; Carrie; Charles; Cindy; Darrell; David; Debbee; Debra; James J. Elekes, M.Ed, MPA, CPM; Eric; Darcey Farrow; William Filber, M.A., C.R.C., L.P.C.; George; Randy Hammer; John Hargus; Jim Hasse, ABC, GCDF; Mark Hathaway; Nan Hawthorne; Senator Kerryann Ifill; Jake Joehl; John; Karen; Kate; Kathleen; Katrina; Keith; Kelly; John D. Kemp; Kim; Laine; LaRetta; Laura; Len; JD Lewis; David Lingebach; Lisa; R.M.; Marsha; Marti; Barney Mayse; Melissa McBane, MBA; Rob McInnes; Lauren Merryfield; Mike; Moses; Nancy; Natalie; Pam; Paul; Mike R.; Roger; Liz Seger; C. Fred Stout, Mike T., The Rev. Jo Taliaferro; Jeremiah Taylor; Terri; Dan TeVelde; Carolyn Tyjewski; Alicia Verlager; and Curt Woolford. Your willingness to share your insight has made this book possible.

In addition, Mark G. Ackermann, Victoria G. Axelrod, Joan Behr, Lydia J. Berry, Fernando Botelho, Herbert R. Brinberg, Theodore S. Francavilla, Mary Gargano, Tina Georgeou, Leslie Gottlieb, Pam Hasse, Natalie Jaffe, June Jee and the Verizon Foundation, Mary J. Krohn, Ana Leal, Oliver Lednicer, Peggy LeMahieu, Gloria S. Neuwirth, Nancy O'Connell, Gustav Oser, Michelle Scott, Ruth-Ellen Simmonds, Mårten Tegnestam, Fred Wertz, and Lynda A. Zakrzewski supported this project and helped it to become a reality.

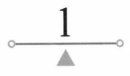

1

Gain a Better
Awareness of Disability

THIS CHAPTER GIVES YOU AN OVERVIEW of the concept of employing disabled workers. It explores the reasons why your workforce will increasingly include workers with disabilities. This will happen in the natural course of events as seniors keep working longer, but there also are solid reasons for seeking out disabled people to improve your workforce. If you leave disability awareness out of your diversity program, you truly shortchange your company and your employees. This chapter also discusses methods of incorporating disabled employees into your workforce and describes the benefits your company will derive from hiring qualified workers with disabilities.

How Inclusive Recruiting Will Help You Prepare for Coming Changes in the Employment Landscape

For most businesses today, diversity no longer means recruiting "minority" groups so the employment numbers look "representative" on paper. Instead, diversity is all about capturing and retaining individuals who are creative and talented—and doing that by fostering a workplace climate that recognizes, values, and supports ideas from every direction.

Diversity is inclusion. Diversity is embracing differences. It's the only way to compete as a business in today's marketplace.

In 2006, the overall percentage (prevalence rate) of working-age (21 to 64) people with a disability in the United States was 12.9 percent,

1

according to the U.S. Census Bureau's American Community Survey. In other words, 22,382,000 of the 172,961,000 working-age individuals reported one or more disabilities.

Are your competitors overlooking nearly 13 percent of the labor market? If they are, they are in trouble. And you can gain an edge over them. You can do this by embracing differences in both employees and customers; hiring the best talent within this pool of working-age people with disabilities; and taking advantage of two colliding, long-range population trends.

A Wake-Up Call

The Workforce 2000 Study, researched and written by the Hudson Institute for the U.S. Department of Labor, clearly demonstrates the need for employers seeking a well-qualified workforce to look beyond the prevailing white, male population, which actually makes up only one-fourth of the U.S. workforce.

The study shows that qualified workers are becoming more difficult to identify (what DuPont calls "The Great American Manpower Search") and that aggressive employers need to plan for diversity and recruit qualified people with disabilities if they are to remain competitive.

As a business executive, you track trends that may have an impact on your company's future well-being. Some of the most important trends are about your workforce.

After all, unemployment isn't just about people being out of work. It's also about businesses being able to draw on and support a productive workforce. Keeping on top of population trends gives you the preparation time you need to tap and strengthen the best potential workers available.

Any single trend in the available workforce is important to you. Sometimes more than one trend will overlap, but this isn't always starkly evident from an employment perspective. You may hear, "There will be twice as many X in the workforce," but not about some other trend affecting X (such as a population drift, the introduction of new philosophies about training those future employees, or health issues increasingly affecting that group).

Still, you may be getting only half the story if you aren't tracking these collateral trends as well. What good is it to know that your workforce will need to draw on, say, more mothers with school-age children, if those women are migrating to rural areas far from your facilities?

Two trends that do overlap and will color your decisions about human resources in the next two or three decades involve the increasingly older workforce.

Two Colliding Trends

In the United States in the 32 years between 1998 and 2030, more seniors will return to work after retirement or postpone retirement and the number of people who are blind is expected to double to at least 19.2 million, according to a 2007 Lou Harris poll conducted for Lighthouse International. Will your company be ready?

Each of the first three decades of the twenty-first century will add 25 million more Americans over age 65, according to Federal Interagency Forum on Aging-Related Statistics (see http://www.aoa.gov/agingstatsdotnet/Main_Site/Data/2008_Documents/Population.aspx). These aging baby boomers "may be headed for a financial crisis, because they have saved, on average, only 12 percent of what they believe they will need to meet basic living expenses during retirement," a crisis that will cause them to delay or interrupt their retirement to bring in an income ("Allstate Financial 'Retirement Reality Check' Reveals Financial Crisis for Baby Boomers Heading into Retirement," PR Newswire, at http://tinyurl.com/apyegq).

Many of those baby boomers may become disabled. For example, consider this collateral trend: According to the Allstate study, "Over one million Americans aged 40 and over are currently blind, and an additional 2.4 million are visually impaired. These numbers are expected to double over the next 30 years as the baby boomer generation ages."

Let's put this into a larger context. According to the U.S. Census Bureau, 51.8 percent of Americans aged 65 and older in 2005 were estimated to have a disability ("Americans with Disabilities: 2005," U.S. Census Bureau, issued December 2008, http://www.census.gov/prod/2008pubs/p70-117.pdf).

Although clearly not all of the over-65 workers you eventually retain, rehire, or add to your workforce will be disabled, it is likely you will be increasingly required to address a range of workplace accessibility issues. Workers who do not regard themselves as disabled but who do need assistance may not be familiar with the many tools that they can use to keep working productively. It will largely be up to you to prepare for this eventuality.

Trend One: Seniors Will Keep Working

Four factors will contribute to the continuously increasing number of workers who are of retirement age: economics, changes in retirement age, continuing need for personal achievement, and employers' need to keep older workers on the job.

First, many people will not be able to afford to retire. Boomers have a hard reality to face upon retiring, according to economists. In spite of all the predictions that they will redefine what it means to be retired, be more physically active, and champion consumer issues, the fact is that many, maybe even most, will simply not be able to afford not to work, especially after the severe economic downturns during the first decade of the twenty-first century slashed their retirement funds.

Those retirees who are able to work are likely to find themselves striving to keep their jobs just to make ends meet. And the likelihood is that a good many will be forced to stretch the definition of "able."

As an employer, you will be in a position to leverage this need to work by not only retaining workers but also bringing experienced workers back to fill short-term needs.

Second, the age for eligibility for Social Security retirement benefits is going up incrementally. That age will eventually climb from 62 to 67, with a substantial reduction in benefits for early retirees. During the next couple of decades, your employees won't be taking early retirement nearly at the same rate as they have in recent years.

This means that many older Americans will spend at least two to five years longer in the workforce or face a reduced lifestyle.

Third, many older people will want to keep working. While many will choose—and demand—volunteer opportunities that are substantial, others will choose to keep working or will go back to work if their need for meaningful volunteer work is not met by volunteer programs still operating on outmoded models.

You will need to recognize the value of older workers. According to the U.S. Department of Health and Human Services, Administration on Aging, the myth of failing competence in older persons is based on an anachronistic picture of the world of work based on industrial and other physically demanding labor. With technology creating a greater emphasis on brain-work over "brawn-work," employers are tapping into minds that do not necessarily fail with age.

The high-tech tools of today's workforce are extremely conducive to maintaining an older, more experienced and knowledgeable workforce. Further, the coming "senior" population represents a group more familiar and comfortable with these tools than were their predecessors.

And, fourth, despite tough economic times, you will still need these older workers. Rehiring retirees usually involves people with specific skills or specific knowledge who can fill in when work units are short-staffed.

You will find it extremely economical to rehire workers. This will especially be true of those who only recently retired from doing high-level work for you at significant salaries. Many will be willing to come back part-time or on a contract basis in what are increasingly termed "retirement jobs" for much less than they earned before retirement and with scaled-down or no benefit packages to drain your coffers.

Trend Two: The Number of Visually Impaired People Will Rise Substantially

The rise in the number of people over 65 by itself will increase the prevalence of visual impairment in the U.S. population and, by extension, among older working people.

About one in eight Americans is 65 or older according to Dr. Paul A. Sieving, director of the National Eye Institute, in his article spotlighting the institute's research on projections of an increasing rate of blindness ("Vision Problems in the U.S.: Prevalence of Adult Visual Impairment and Age-Related Eye Diseases in America," the National Eye Institute, http://www.nei.nih.gov/eyedata/). The research demonstrates that the overall increase in blindness is heavily influenced by the rising median age.

Why does an increase in visual impairment follow from the "Graying of America"? Eye diseases arising from or intensified by age become more common as the ranks of older people rise. One of the more common causes of visual impairment, macular degeneration, is primarily an age-related condition.

According to AMD Alliance International, an estimated 13 million people in the United States had some form of age-related macular degeneration (AMD) in 2009. In fact, AMD was the leading cause of blindness among Americans of European descent in 2004, says the Eye Diseases Prevalence Research Group. In addition, AMD is the leading cause of vision impairment among Americans over 65, according to Prevent Blindness America.

With the aging of the "baby boomer" generation, it is expected that the number of cases of AMD will increase significantly in the years ahead, the American Macular Degeneration Foundation points out.

There are two other eye diseases that are not limited to the aging process but increase in prevalence with age: cataracts and glaucoma. More than half the people over age 65 have some degree of cataract development, according to The Foundation of the American Academy of Ophthalmology (http://www.eyecareamerica.com/eyecare/news/August-is-National-Cataract-Awareness-Month.cfm). As for glaucoma, it affects some 3 million Americans and is a leading cause of blindness among all ages in the United States.

Retinopathy (due to diabetes) becomes more common as the incidence of diabetes itself increases—in particular the onset of adult type 2 diabetes. The National Institutes of Health has declared diabetes the epidemic of our times. "About 20 percent of type 2 patients have some eye damage when diagnosed, and blurred vision is common," adds WebMD. More than 24 million Americans have diabetes, and diabetes is the leading cause of new cases of blindness in adults 20 to 74 (American Optometric Association).

Losing vision because of age does not necessarily mean the older worker is in failing health or is losing faculties. An older person with low vision can be as sharp and fit as ever and does not need to retire from working. It just means a person needs to learn new ways to do things for which he or she previously used sight. There are a range of technologies and rehabilitation services to enable a worker to remain productive and effective on the job.

What the Collision of These Trends Will Mean for You

Referring to the increasing proportion of older persons in the United States, the National Eye Institute's Dr. Sieving cautions, "When you add declining mortality rates and population shifts, such as the 'baby boomers,' the number of older people will grow dramatically in the years ahead. Blindness and visual impairment represent not only a significant burden to those affected by sight loss but also to the national economy as well." The same statement can be made about aging and disability in general.

One way to counteract the economic impact of more workers who are older and who have a disability is to create a workplace now that is inclusive of disability. Another way is to help your colleagues become literate about the adaptations that can be made to remove the impact of disability within your workplace.

The worker who becomes disabled because of age will not be like the disabled workers you are hiring now. Younger disabled people are more likely to self-identify as individuals who happen to have a disability. These younger people are less likely to regard vulnerability as an obstacle to work. They are more likely to be aware of (and have used) adaptive technology, such as scooters, crutches, and screen readers. They are more likely to have experienced working while being disabled.

By contrast, the older adult, for instance, who starts losing vision because of age, identifies herself as an older person but not as a visually impaired individual. It is common to hear older people deny their blindness, even if they are, by definition, legally blind. They will say, "I just don't see as well as I used to." They do not know there are ways around visual impairment. They may not be aware that visual impairment does not mean an inability to keep working. And they almost certainly will not be as knowledgeable about the tools to gain access to information and to carry out on-the-job tasks.

The current emphasis is on helping older adults (at the onset of a disability) to achieve skills so they can stay independent—but not to send them back to work.

Therefore, it may very well fall to you to be the one "in the know" about what an existing or returning older employee who has a disability can do to stay on the job. Building disability awareness and developing inclusive hiring and advancement practices into your business now will allow you to be adept at such challenges before they become critical in the years ahead. This book is designed to help you prepare for that opportunity.

The Wide-Open Opportunity

In a November 2008 survey of employers conducted by the U.S. Department of Labor's Office of Disability Employment Policy, 72.6 percent of the senior executives who were interviewed cited the *nature of the work being such that it cannot be effectively performed by a person with a disability* as a hiring challenge. Attitudes of coworkers or supervisors were the least frequently cited challenges.

In the same study, only 19.1 percent of companies reported that they employ people with disabilities and only 13.6 percent reported that they actively recruit people with disabilities.

Hiring younger workers with a disability now can be your transition to and practice for being able to keep older, productive workers on the job as these two trends (older adults who are newly disabled but still working) change the employment landscape in the United States.

That means you may have to help your company reevaluate its diversity initiative.

Why Your Diversity Initiative Needs to Include Disability

"Well begun is half done." This familiar rhyme means that getting started is a major step toward a goal. But, in the case of diversity awareness programs, it can also be a caution. A diversity initiative that does not include disability is only half of a program.

Employers, schools, organizations, and government offices have reaped the rewards of creating a better understanding about race, ethnicity, religion, gender, and gender preference. But this rainbow only goes part of the way across the sky. If you leave out disability in your diversity program, the rainbow is not complete. And you will never reach the pot of gold.

Why Include Only Half?

Leaving disability awareness out of your company's diversity initiative gives you only half a program.

What You Miss with Half of a Diversity Initiative

During a time when employers in some sectors of the U.S. job market are finding it difficult to recruit and retain skilled and loyal workers, it seems strange that one group of potential job candidates goes virtually untapped. According to the President's Committee on Employment of Disabled Persons, approximately 75 percent of people with disabilities are able to work and are interested in joining the workforce but are unemployed.

Today's technology makes nearly any work situation possible for these job seekers. So, statements from employers that they can't fill empty positions are hollow. Such assertions demonstrate that employers continue to be misinformed about the opportunities they have to recruit qualified job candidates with disabilities.

People with disabilities bring unique benefits to a workplace, and those benefits outweigh the simple requirement that they receive equal opportunity to join and advance in it. As employees, people with disabilities generally have great work records. According to studies dating back to the 1950s at DuPont, "Employees with disabilities equal or exceed co-workers without disabilities in job performance, attendance and attention to safety."

In addition to considerable commitment and enthusiasm for work, individuals with a disability often have superior experience in one vital area of any job: problem solving. This is why some use the term "challenged" to describe people with disabilities. They face and overcome challenges on a daily basis. They have a lifetime of practice doing just what your best employees need to do: solve problems.

A Problem-Solving Orientation

Individuals with disabilities can be valuable employees because they bring creativity to the workplace based on what they've learned in solving—and surviving—problems that stem from their personal vulnerabilities.

At Google Research, for instance, Dr. T. V. Raman is a leading-edge expert in Web standards, auditory interfaces, and scripting languages. Blind himself, he's intrigued by how something should work when the user is not looking at the screen. He's the holder of more than twenty-five patents, has tailored Google's search service for blind users, and has developed a software program to read aloud complex mathematical formulas (see http://www.nytimes.com/2009/01/04/business/04blind.html).

So, the complete awareness training approach (one that includes disability) not only avoids overt and unintentional discrimination against minority employees; it can enhance your work unit's creativity.

And, in fact, it can enhance your bottom line by:

- ⊘ Reducing recruitment costs when you expand your access to talent
- ⊘ Avoiding productivity losses incurred from unfilled positions (when you have a larger talent pool, filling your positions can be easier and quicker)
- ⊘ Reducing turnover costs with a talent pool that tends to stay with you longer
- ⊘ Creating more efficient work processes through accommodations for your workers with disabilities that may yield an overall increase in your productivity
- ⊘ Leveraging tax incentives, when applicable, to realize tax credits ranging from $2,400 to $15,000

But, specifically what kind of record are businesses showing as a result of inclusive diversity initiatives that include disability? Let's look at some statistics cited by earnworks.com (http://www.earnworks.com/BusinessCase/roi_level2.asp).

A recent DePaul study of 314 employees across several industries indicates participants with disabilities had fewer scheduled absences than those without disabilities and that all participants had nearly identical job performance ratings.

Anecdotal and survey research indicate that employees with disabilities may be less likely to leave a company than their nondisabled counterparts. For example, HirePotential found that its placements stayed on the job an average of 50 percent longer than those without disabilities, and Marriott employees hired through its Pathways to Independence Program experienced a 6 percent turnover rate versus the 52 percent turnover rate of its overall workforce.

Remember, the costs of replacing employees, including those who acquire a disability, are high, ranging from 93 to 200 percent of an employee's annual salary; retaining them makes good business sense.

All-inclusive diversity goes beyond helping people work harmoniously in spite of different work and communication styles and experiences. It shows that an organization's leaders embrace the multitude of approaches diversity brings to each task. That encourages everyone to work as a productive team.

In fact, treating disability as part of building an awareness of diversity can help you avoid disciplining or dismissing a person because her particular behavior is mischaracterized as a performance problem.

Judy, a new employee who is visually impaired, for example, continually shows up late for your Monday 7:00 A.M. staff meetings, which you like to hold an hour before your office's regular work hours begin. You and your colleagues and her coworkers have been perplexed by such lack of promptness in Judy, who is otherwise performing well on the job. What you do not realize is that Judy is having difficulty scheduling paratransit (transportation) services for that early hour and is reluctant to tell you about the problem because she believes getting to and from work is her responsibility. Including disability awareness in your diversity initiative perhaps could have prevented that misunderstanding within your workplace.

In short, by leaving disability awareness out of your diversity program, you are shortchanging your company and your employees. Your other employees, including supervisors, will no doubt lack the knowledge and enlightenment they need not only to give opportunities to the employee with a disability but also to simply not stand in the way as he or she strives to succeed.

Demand balanced and well-informed disability awareness training from a diversity trainer. By doing so, you will be taking steps to make sure your employees have the tools to put together all the pieces of an inclusive workplace that is receptive to the concept that individuals with a disability want to control their own lives, to achieve self-defined goals, and to participate fully in society.

How to Choose the Right Disability Awareness Trainer for Your Company

You know it's important to include disability awareness in your personnel training. But how do you choose the trainer or consultant who best fits your organization?

Make sure your diversity training includes solid information about disability awareness by following your own internal policies for selecting training services plus these specific guidelines for disability awareness training:

1.   Avoid waiting until you have a disabled customer coming in or a new employee who is disabled (or a current employee who has just become disabled) about to start work. You don't want to rush it—and you may be tempted to do just that. In a rush, you'll likely prepare your staff for serving or working with just that one disability. It's more effective and efficient to get well-rounded training all at once.

2.   Decide what you need to accomplish with the training. Not every work setting is the same. Depending on your work site and business, you will likely have some specific needs. Assess how your staff will likely interact with disabled customers and coworkers. When you shop around for a trainer or consultant, be thorough in conveying your unique needs to everyone you interview.

3.   Network to find a disability awareness trainer. Contact organizations that serve people with disabilities, such as Easter Seals or your state's federally funded disability protection and advocacy agency for recommendations of trainers in your area. You can also contact the human resources departments of other companies to learn whether they have had training.

4.   Choose a trainer who is disabled or has a training team that includes at least one disabled person. Interview candidates and check references from other clients of the training firm. Just because someone is disabled does not mean he knows anything about disability issues or awareness training or a range of disabilities.

5.   Look for the same personal qualities you expect in the other trainers you choose—such as warmth and humor, which tend to put training participants at ease and communicate that no question needs to be withheld and remain unanswered.

Discovering the Difference Between Ability and Opportunity

The Pick-a-Disability exercise in the Windmills Attitudinal Training Program is a particularly powerful way to open employers' eyes to the fact that there are competent people with disabilities for all jobs.

Windmills Attitudinal Training (http://www.damonbrooks.com/

windmills.html) is a high-impact attitudinal training program developed by the California Governor's Committee on Employment of People with Disabilities. The curriculum consists of 11 sections (modules) that use participation and discovery as learning vehicles.

Early in the exercise, attendees are asked to choose the one disability that they might acquire tomorrow. Following much discussion, they are asked to raise their hand if they believe that, should they actually acquire that disability, benefit from a period of adjustment and rehabilitation, and have the appropriate job accommodations, they would be able to continue capably in their present jobs. Typically, a solid majority of hands are lifted. Attendees are then asked to leave their hands up only if they believe that, had they been born with that disability, they would have been hired into the jobs they currently hold. Preconceptions crumble in concert with the loud swoosh of dropping hands. This is the difference between *ability* and *opportunity*.
—Rob McInnes, Diversity World, January 2009

Other factors in disability awareness training need to be considered. It may be difficult to manage interaction in an auditorium full of people. And there may be a diverse array of cultural attitudes toward disability that will need to be addressed. Talk about all these issues with the trainers and consultants you interview.

The trainer or consultant you hire should be able to make a lasting impression on your staff, be well-informed, be warm, and be open. As in everything else, you want to get the most for your money. And the product you are buying here is transformation of your workplace into a truly adaptive, inclusive environment. When you invest in top-notch disability awareness training, you model for all of your internal and external associates the real diversity you want your organization to radiate.

And, to do that modeling effectively, it's helpful to understand what "self-determination" means to today's job seeker with a disability.

The Right to Self-Determination for Individuals with a Disability in Today's Workplace

You probably recall the familiar saying, "America is a place where every boy can grow up to be president." The value highlighted by this statement is self-determination. Americans like to believe we no longer pre-scribe personal life choices for our citizens based on class or economics.

"The irony is that the gender bias is so explicit in the statement, despite long battles for inclusion of those outside the 'default' gender, race, religion, sexual preference, and ability," writes Nan Hawthorne, historical novelist and author of *An Involuntary King*.

But, as a cultural belief, the statement still stands. Barack Obama and Hillary Clinton further modified the implications of the statement during the 2008 U.S. presidential election.

Opportunity is still the key. It's fundamental in self-determination.

What is self-determination? According to the Center for Self-Determination, self-determination is "broadly defined as the ability of individuals to control their lives, to achieve self-defined goals and to par-ticipate fully in society. Self-determination is used to describe a set of beliefs and behaviors adopted by people (individuals, families and com-munities) seeking to improve their own lives and by those who seek to help them" (see http://www.centerforself-determination.com).

In short, people who have a disability want the opportunity to con-trol their own lives, to achieve self-defined goals, and to participate fully in society.

What Is Self-Determination?

Self-determination is having the option to choose according to your own best interest. Using that approach, job seekers with disabilities are open-ing new opportunities for themselves. That has implications for the work-place.

Clearly, legislation—such as the Americans with Disabilities Act of 1990, the United Kingdom's 1995 People with Disabilities Discrimination Act, Australia's Disability Discrimination Act of 1992, the 1997 additions to Canada's Human Rights and Criminal Code, and Japan's Law to Promote the Employment of the Handicapped—put an emphasis on self-determination. Many such laws worldwide mandate removal of barriers to equal participation by people with disabilities in their communities. But, on the face of it, legislation usually focuses on providing access to "work"—not "choice of work."

Without choice, there is no self-determination. Remember how thir-ty years ago newspaper "help wanted" classifieds were divided into "Help

Wanted: Men" and "Help Wanted: Women"? Women had the right to work, but the division of occupations by gender was strictly limited.

The choice of work open to people with disabilities still remains limited. Here is one example. Although jobs that cannot be carried out by a person with a visual impairment of any level (airline pilot, truck driver, etc.) are few in today's job market, that person's job choice is narrow (piano tuner, transcriptionist, vendor, etc.) due to common misconceptions. That limitation is based on ingrained cultural biases and lack of knowledge—not the law.

Importance of Self-Determination at Work

Perhaps one of the most difficult self-determination issues for bright, capable, ambitious adults who happen to have disabilities is being regarded as adults. They are often perceived as and treated like children who need to be protected from the rigors of life.

Imagine how you felt at age 16. You had many of the abilities you would have ten, fifteen, and twenty years later. You certainly had the desire to make your own choices, but you could not. Legal as well as customary restrictions kept you a child—or, at least, as a nonadult. Now imagine staying at that point, no matter your age or level of maturity, your entire life. That is one of the primary barriers adults with disabilities seek to break: the misconception that they are still children.

There are unavoidable limits in life: lack of opportunity, lack of money, and lack of time. Anyone can suffer from these. But they tend to be circumstantial and can be, with effort, broken. But imagine, when for reasons that defy your own judgment and ability, others step in and establish arbitrary restrictions on your choice of occupation.

A capable person with a disability can be at a loss about how not only to overcome those hurdles but also to deal with something more fundamental: how to articulate the value of his or her own choice. Other than teenage angst, there simply aren't words in our language for what such a person feels. The person is forever trapped in a world that views him or her as a terminal adolescent.

This is where legislation stops and attitudes take over. There are laws that outline the rights of people with disabilities, but attitudes often can elude both law and reason. While evidence of that fact can be found in every walk of a disabled person's life (right to maternity, access to consumer goods and services, access to education, access to the community), it is nowhere more obvious than in employment.

Our culture equates adulthood with work. Although not long ago women who worked outside the home were looked down upon as neglectful mothers, in the twenty-first century women are more likely to be sheepish about admitting they don't have jobs.

For a person with a disability, having a job means she is that much closer to being regarded as an adult. She has responsibility; a paycheck; a reason to dress well; peers with whom to relate; and a better chance to have the other trappings of adulthood, such as a home. She doesn't have to cringe and receive odd looks when asked, "Employer?" and she has to answer, "Disabled." She is a fully functioning, contributing member of the world of grown-ups. She is not a child.

However, without self-determination, this adulthood status is on shaky ground.

Nan, for instance, who has a visual impairment, says, "I can't tell you how often it has been assumed that I could only work for—or even volunteer for—an organization for the blind. While I was training professionally, a woman commented about how nice it was that the group 'let you train.' "

This is a regular experience in the lives of most people who have disabilities. The assumption is that their options are limited. That limitation is external. While they may not actually be working in supported employment (such as a sheltered workshop), the assumption is that they need some sort of artificially erected "safety net" to work—because they are not grown-ups.

No organization or individual these days would assume that African Americans can work only in businesses operated by African Americans, or women in special employment projects for women, or Jewish people in Jewish companies. But it is commonplace to hear people consign a person with a disability, no matter how accomplished, to "special employment."

The loss is devastating to the individual with a disability whose personal dreams are shattered, whose education and training go to waste, whose potential may never be reached, and whose quality of life will be stuck in the tiny pigeonhole to which she's been assigned.

The impact stretches far beyond the individual with a disability, though. It is a loss that every one of us (and, in some ways, more so as employers) has to bear.

Importance of Self-Determination for Employers

Just as our well-being suffers from artificially limiting access to relationships, cultural life, consumption, and citizenship, business also suffers from the limits placed on the careers of those with disabilities.

What's the payoff for employers when people with disabilities have the same access to a career as anyone else? Think back to the earlier statement, "Every boy can grow up to be president," and how this contrasts with a rigidly defined class system. Victoria, no matter how suited to being a monarch, never could have ruled in her own right or likely been queen at all had she actually been a poor farmer. How many leaders were not born in the social and economic class most conducive to success? That has changed somewhat in America.

Take the example of Abraham Lincoln. The Lincoln family was dirt poor. Abe did not own a pair of shoes for most of his childhood. Yet, he grew up to be president. He's one of the three people in history (along with Napoleon and Jesus Christ) with the most books written about him. What would we have lost had his right of self-determination been denied? His intelligence. His wisdom. His way with words. His ideals. His determination.

By limiting a disabled person's self-determination in the workplace, we limit our own access to whatever makes that individual unique and wonderful. We say, "Sorry, Abe, it doesn't matter that you are destined to be a legend. You simply can't be president unless you have shoes as a kid. That's the rule."

Telling Jenny she can't teach math to teenagers because she walks with crutches means the school district has lost her ability to communicate an excitement about mathematics to bored high school juniors.

A health insurance company misses out by telling a partially sighted fellow named Juan that he can't do its legal research (due to a hiring manager's personal misconception that he can't use adaptive technology and the Internet as a research tool). That company doesn't receive the insight Juan may have had into how a new regulation affects its bottom line.

In fact, that insurance company loses more than Juan's legal insight when it throws up an artificial barrier to his pursuit of a career in legal research. The insurance company loses:

- Juan's excitement and knack for the job that led him to pursue his particular career in the first place, often against the odds

⊘ Juan's high level of commitment and loyalty to a company that gave him the chance to pursue his chosen career

⊘ Juan's impact on other employees as well as the public because he is doing work he loves with talent, commitment, and enthusiasm—not just work someone else thinks he's fit for

The key is to help your colleagues think about the best fit for each individual, based on what he can and wants to do—not what he can't do or what your colleagues simply don't realize he can do.

Supporting Self-Determination for Individuals with Disabilities

What can you and your colleagues do to support self-determination among workers with disabilities? Here are several suggestions on a number of different fronts:

⊘ **Hire them.** Hire people with disabilities to do the work they are trained for.

⊘ **Equip them.** Work with them to find and put into place the tools they need to compensate for the purely mechanical limitations their disabilities create.

⊘ **Challenge them.** Expect top-notch performance. Keep your standards high.

⊘ **Tell the world about them.** Make sure other employees and managers, the media, the community, your competitors, your clients, and everyone else knows how they have contributed to your company.

⊘ **Challenge those who limit them.** Call your mayor, write a letter to the editor, talk to your own kids, withdraw your charitable support, speak at the school board meeting and in your place of worship—and speak anywhere you see people with disabilities cast as dependent, childlike, or pitiful. Help destroy the stereotypes.

⊘ **Help the advocates.** Reinforce the emphasis organizations and individuals in your community are putting on self-determination for people with disabilities and help them.

⊘ **Demand opportunity.** Make sure the workers with disabilities you know are getting equal opportunities for an education, access to advanced training, and degrees in your field; encourage staffing services and headhunters to recruit them; and help your community be accessible and supportive of their options as much as any other worker.

Having options is simply a "good thing." It's an absolute value. The more "those" people have options, the more everyone does. The more freedom for people with disabilities the more freedom for each of us and our loved ones—whether or not disability ever becomes part of our lives.

It's your choice.

How Individuals with a Disability Define Inclusion

Self-determination, as defined by controlling your own life, having the opportunity to work toward self-defined goals, and participating fully in society, is not only based on choice; it is also based on respect, dignity, and inclusion.

Caught in Tokenism

My belief is that it is extremely difficult to determine if you are hired as the token, and if you find yourself in this situation, it may be even harder to rise above this lowly status to become a truly respected member of the team.   —JD Lewis

And inclusion for people with disabilities is the opposite of tokenism. Inclusion lies in the attitudes of those involved.

Perhaps that's what the members of eSight Careers Network are telling us. Take a look at the following discussion among seven of those members:

JD Lewis:

I worked briefly in an initial, seemingly genuine clerical position, only to later discover that I was the only blind/visually impaired employee in 200-plus locations. Despite initial treatment of equal dignity and inclusiveness, three months into the job my workload dropped off, resulting in many idle moments, and, despite my diligent efforts to be trained so I could be helpful in other departments, I was continually turned down.

Such dwindling attention made me feel as if I may have been the national token for this company. Needless to say, I ended up leaving this position. And roughly two years later, this company's particular location dissolved.

My belief is that it is extremely difficult to determine if you are hired as the "token," and, if you find yourself in this situation, it may be even harder to rise above this lowly status to become a truly respected member of the team.

Jo Taliaferro:

I still believe that many think the ADA merely involves the widening of doors (and making) the statement, "we are accessible," but with no attitudinal meat on the bones. That's another type of tokenism.

Debra:

If an employer hires someone as a token disabled person, that company may get what it doesn't want: a whiner who expects everyone to cater to him instead of being self-sufficient and productive.

Wendy:

I'm a single gal who uses a wheelchair because of my spinal cord injury. I work in accounts receivable at a large hotel.

I've worked at the hotel for seven years and have seen a lot of employees come and go. Many of them have been college students working their way through school. They can be fun. They liven up the place.

But, I sometimes don't feel as though I fit in, even though I probably have the most seniority among the clerical staff. Mind you, everyone is very nice to me, but sometimes I feel I am tolerated because it makes the hotel look good to have a "wheelchair person" on board—rather than because of the work I have done and can still do. It's kind of like being the old desk in the corner. It fits.

My supervisor calls me "Steady Wendy." I suppose she thinks that's a compliment. Yes, steady can be good and safe, but it can also be boring.

I've asked her how I could improve my work, but she always says, "You're doing just fine." It's as though she has no real expectations of me.

Molly is my one buddy at work. We always have lunch together. She works on the payroll and has been with me for five years. She's looking forward to retirement next year.

I sometimes wonder what kind of job I'd have and what kind of money I'd be making if I weren't in a wheelchair. I have an associate degree in accounting from our local college and lots of life experience. But I'm still doing the same type of work I did when I first started working for the hotel.

I do love my job, but sometimes it's frustrating and lonely being the only person who is considered "different" but "steady" and getting side glances from the new people (with no wheelchair or crutches) who always seem to be coming on board.

Pam:

For me, it is incredibly frustrating to continue to be left out at meetings where print is handed out in a job I've had for 16 years—when my employer knows very well to send me information electronically ahead of time (due to my visual impairment). I, therefore, believe inclusion is the absolute key to success for people who experience disability issues.

Liz Seger:

We don't want to be designated as special; we just want to be included and be like everyone else.

John Hargus:

Full inclusion for those of us with disabilities includes but is not limited to the right for us to live happy and productive lives. As a result of my disability, I have not only gained an interest in helping people with disabilities through activism, but I also have learned to appreciate life as a whole.

As someone who was diagnosed not only with a learning disability but also with a severe speech impairment at a very young age and with epilepsy at the age of 11, I knew early on that I was in for an uphill struggle. However, the reality of this struggle never hit home until a few months after my 18th birthday when I got denied employment due to my seizure disorder.

Since being discriminated against on that November day in 1988, I have fought the long and hard battle to obtain full inclusion for people with disabilities. My battle led me to places such as the local city council, when I heard that they were planning to eliminate the special education program in all of the city's public schools; to my U.S. Congressman's office, where I questioned a law that gives employers the right to pay disabled employees below the minimum wage; and even to President Bush when I found out that certain states were denying the learning disabled the right to an equal education despite the NCLB Act of 2001 that gives that right.

I have also set lofty goals for myself, despite my disabilities. I'm currently working on my bachelor's degree in computer/electrical engineering. Upon graduating from college, I'm not only planning to settle down but also to start my own computer consulting business.

I eventually want to go back to school and earn my master's degree in engineering. My main goal in life is to prove that the disabled can actually do more in life than learn the proper ways of scrubbing a toilet or pushing a broom/mop, because I believe that a person's disability should not be a hindrance but a tool to raise standards.

Notice the waste (scuttled talent), dishonesty (misleading appearances), and danger (infective whiners) in deliberately allowing—or lazily falling captive to—tokenism within the workplace.

Inclusion, on the other hand, focuses on recruiting and retaining individuals regardless of disability who have the talent, skills, and discernment to help an organization further extend its success. And inclusion applies to all job classifications.

You know talent and skill when you see it, but discernment can be a little more difficult to evaluate. Let's look at some potential benchmarks for discernment as it pertains to a job candidate's approach to disability.

The Role of Maturity and Self-Esteem in an Individual's Approach to Disability

A hiring manager should look for job candidates who have a mature grasp of what it means to live well with a disability. That means living, first of all, with a personal sense of self-worth.

A sense of self-worth feeds an approach to life that maintains that:

- ⊘ A person has a right to equal dignity
- ⊘ Dignity stems from mature perceptions about self and others
- ⊘ A sense of personal dignity cannot be dished out by others

In other words, a job candidate with a sense of self-worth is ready to thrive in the workplace.

In recruiting job candidates with disabilities, you want to go beyond the obvious—beyond often unasked questions such as, "Can you do the job?" and "How do you do this?" (both important questions that any candidate should voluntarily address). You want your standout applicants to get this message (perhaps in a subtle way) across to you: "My dignity is not defined by my disability. My disability does not define who I am. I am a person first. But I'm willing to talk about my challenges so I can then address your questions about my qualifications for this job."

A Mature Approach

I believe that employers are wise when they evaluate employees according to their abilities because, whether we like it or not, we all have some kind of vulnerability. Effective hiring means looking at the assets and qualifications of individuals, not their "assumed" capabilities or lack of such.   —Jo Taliaferro, ordained minister, assistive technology specialist

Thoughts about the role of disability in the lives of job candidates can provide important markers of the level of self-esteem within those individuals and how they view self-determination (namely, the sense of empowerment they feel for controlling their own lives, for achieving self-defined goals, and for participating fully in society).

Considering these benchmarks shows you've grappled with putting disability into a perspective that makes sense to you, and that makes you a more effective hiring manager.

Of course, as in any discussion within a group of individuals, your conversation can lead to a wide range of possibilities when it comes to perceptions about personal vulnerability and equal dignity.

One Variable: Born Disabled vs. Becoming Disabled

For example, let's consider just one of the variables that you could encounter during your interviewing process. There are likely to be differing perceptions about the right of equal dignity between those born disabled and those who become disabled later in life, for instance. Consider the following dialogue among five people with disabilities who are members of eSight Careers Network and who are pursuing their careers within today's so-called mainstream job market.

Mark Hathaway:

It depends on when a person develops his or her disability. I think that, if [the disability] comes on as an adult, there is a difference, since adults most likely have "established" themselves. I do not think it is right, but I believe it is so.

In my case, I was diagnosed with RP [eye disease] at a young age, but it had no great impact on me until I was an adult. By the time my "disability" became noticeable, I had a leadership position in my company. I often wonder if I would have had the same opportunity if my eye problem had manifested itself sooner.

William Filber:

As an individual with a congenital disability, I say the difference in attitude starts with those of us who have lived with a disability their whole lives. We grow up with a natural acceptance within ourselves and our disabilities. We see [our disabilities as natural] up until we enter society as an adult or a child in an educational institution that separates us from the able-bodied population.

The system itself does not encourage or promote inclusion. There's segregation from early on. That system must be changed.

But an individual with a congenital disability is usually, from early on, encouraged to achieve the American Dream. We learn to accept our disability early in life.

An individual who becomes disabled later in life, however, often has already adopted the perspective of society and employers. . . .

The attitudes will change over time, but it will take a generation and must start at an early age. The educational system is totally wrong, and this perspective [separation and exclusion] transfers into other aspects of our lives: employment, housing, transportation, etc.

Barney Mayse:

More than likely this difference in perception between born-with and acquired disabilities is just how people view things. However, the reality we should be seeking is one where it does not make a difference when one is disabled, how one is disabled, or even whether the disability is visible. A disability requires the person to work just a bit harder to do things that others take for granted.

What we can do about [a sense of dignity] is work steadfastly to achieve complete parity for all people with disabilities in all circumstances, with a focus on abilities—not disabilities. We need to focus on how to become an asset to the hiring organization.

Darcey Farrow:

Some people feel that those who have been disabled longer should be entitled to more. I do not think that should matter. Everyone should be able to have their dignity, and no one person should take away from that.

People need to realize that any one person with a disability may have low self-esteem, which I believe has everything to do with dignity. If I am disabled, so be it, but I need not be treated differently than a nondisabled person.

Carlos:

People who become disabled later in life often need time to accept it. They can become bitter. They do not believe that they are part of the disabled population. All within the disabled community have the right to equal dignity.

It will help us all if the public gets to know that being disabled is not a curse. . . . Individuals can live well despite having a disability.

Each person with a disability is on a personal journey that ultimately determines how he or she weaves the feeling of vulnerability into everyday life. That personal journey is often influenced by the individual's level of self-esteem, which, in turn, affects:

- **Acceptance:** "I need more time to accept an acquired disability."
- **Entitlement:** "I was born with this disability and am entitled to more help."
- **Competitiveness:** "I need to do better than the nondisabled to succeed."
- **Happenstance:** "I wouldn't have this job if I had been born with my disability."

In any case, a sense of self-worth in a job candidate tends to decrease the importance that disability plays in his or her personal life and work life.

How Learning to Live Well with a Disability Can Have an Upside

Of course, having or acquiring a disability is not good news. It's tangible evidence of an individual's vulnerability, which, in the United States, is commonly considered a personal liability, especially in the job market.

But many people with a disability have also learned that the implications of vulnerability are not all bad—that, in fact, there's often an amusing as well as a real upside to disability.

As the Pit Lights Faded

I was in a symphony orchestra as a first violinist. The pit lights were growing dimmer and dimmer by the minute. People could barely see the music on the page much less the conductor waving the baton. I was the one in the section keeping it all together until some lights were fixed and all was well again. I have to confess: I had a great deal of fun with those poor benighted sighted people who must have lights in order to function.

—Marsha

Consider this dialogue among nine members of eSight Careers Network about the advantages they have discovered by learning how to live well with a disability.

Marsha:

As a person who has been blind lifelong, I have been able to focus more on the sounds around me because I have never had the visual distractions that so often beset those with normal vision. For example, as a medical transcriptionist, I have been able to hear the nuances of the various doctors that just might be a key to what they are trying to say.

Another example of a bonus in being blind is the fact that one can read a book in bed without having to have a flashlight under the covers to see the print. I used to do this all the time growing up. My father would do everything he could to catch me as I was reading in bed. Because I didn't have the telltale flashlight on, it was harder for him to catch me. Unfortunately for me, catch me he did when he started just standing there listening to the soft sound of my little hands smoothly running my fingers across a line of Braille. I was most certainly caught then. Our family all got a laugh out of that one.

Nan Hawthorne:

The other day I was sitting in the quiet of my living room and work-ing on an afghan for a charity project. As I crocheted one stitch after another, it hit me that the task was easier now than it had been when my vision was just beginning to throw a monkey wrench into every-thing I did.

Yes, of course, I'm better at crocheting, although I have just taken it up again after many years. What I discovered was more sig-nificant than just practice: I'm more accustomed to doing things without my vision.

It's an example of what I write about all the time: Vision is truly not needed for many of the tasks I do (basically most of the activities of my daily life). This is normal for me now. And that's a great thing to realize.

Then I went on to ask myself: Are there benefits to having low vision? And I actually thought of several. Someone asked me, for instance, if the audio-description on CBS's *CSI* gets disgusting when they start to show the inside views of a human body. I love *CSI*, so I told her, "No, they are just descriptive. And this is one case where low vision is absolutely a bonus. I can hear what is happening with-out having to be grossed out visually!"

Anthony R. Candela:

I have learned there is more than one way to perform a task. Just when you think something can't be done, necessity spawns some new invention.

Paul:

I notice that, among my friends with disabilities, there is an abun-dance of "empathy" (not "sympathy"). Having a disability gives one a greater perspective on the difficulties others have with their respec-tive disability. It should not be necessary to have a disability to acquire understanding, but it certainly is a life-changing event for many.

The other more obvious implication is the effort it takes to do some tasks with a disability. That increased effort is the response to challenge. Without challenge, I wonder how hard I would have applied myself in the past.

Peter Altschul:

I think people with disabilities have more experience in solving problems and dealing with crises than the average nondisabled person. Also, I have discovered that people will say things to me that they wouldn't say to other professionals. Maybe it's something to do with their perception of our "semi-invisibility"—that we are sometimes ignored as if we aren't present—and, therefore, are "safe" listeners to unguarded remarks.

Curt Woolford:

Although having a visual impairment is often a considerable challenge, it does have its upside. The blessing for me has been in character development. If I compare who I was five years ago [before my vision changed] to who I am now, I have grown considerably. I am more compassionate, patient, and tolerant. I am less likely to be judgmental. I pay far more attention to what really matters. I am much stronger deep within.

Kerryann Ifill:

I've acquired this understanding: Never let people set your limitations; let situations set those limitations.

Barney Mayse:

The problem-solving capacity of people with disabilities expands everyday.

Debra:

A disability doesn't mean inability; it's more often doing things a little differently—listening, for instance, rather than looking when you hear a sound!

Examine this conversation. Notice the more concrete advantages that grow unexpectedly from learning how to live with a disability. Let's classify the insight detected in this dialogue into two categories, risk tolerance and interdependence, both of which are important qualities in the people you want on your work team.

Risk Tolerance

- ✔ Less capability does not necessarily mean less ability.
- ✔ Necessity often spawns innovation.
- ✔ Challenge can be a motivator.
- ✔ Problem solving can be learned through personal circumstances.

⊘   Limitations are only situational.

Interdependence

⊘   Personal limitation allows the luxury of focusing on nuance.

⊘   Personal vulnerability can spawn empathy.

⊘   Disability can help gain trust from others.

⊘   Personal challenge can raise tolerance for uncontrollable circumstances.

A Note from the Editor

Here's a concrete example from my own experience of Peter Altschul's comment about his experience of becoming a "safe" listener to unguarded remarks. I found the same phenomenon happened to me while I was vice president of corporate communication for a dairy processing cooperative.

I had cerebral palsy (and was visibly vulnerable because I walked and talked with difficulty), but I made it a priority to know many of the workers on the floor and at all levels of our 14 production plants. For me, that was a personal risk. But I was always amazed at what our employees would tell me. They would admit their doubts, fears, shortcomings, gripes, and frustrations—things they would not always tell their supervisors.

To gain that trust among employees, I found I needed to not only listen to individuals but also to tell their personal stories of on-the-job success. That meant I needed to write well as well as take still photographs for publication.

Photography presented a problem for me because I lacked balance due to my cerebral palsy. I needed crutches to stand on my own two feet and an extra pair of hands to work a camera. I dreaded falling and seriously hurting myself.

But, over time, I found a sound solution. I replaced one of my crutches with a folded tripod, which I topped with a 35-mm Nikon so I still had "four legs" for walking inside the manufacturing plants and two free hands for the camera work whenever I decided to stop, plant the tripod on its three legs, and do a photo shoot.

My contraption was not graceful, but, for me, it worked. It showed my vulnerability and resourcefulness (the problem-solving response to a personal challenge Barney Mayse mentions in the dialogue above) that we, as humans, all possess but don't always use. And it gave my fellow employees an excuse to occasionally help me by retrieving my second "parked" crutch when I was done for the day and putting my tripod in my car (a demonstration of interdependence).

My presence in the production plants was something like what David Frost experienced in 1977 when he interviewed Richard Nixon, who had resigned as President after the Watergate cover-up. Nixon's perception of Frost as a vulnerable individual and an underdog within the media world, according to the *Frost/Nixon* film (2008) directed by Ron Howard, gave him the freedom, in his own mind, to admit to David (on camera) that he had "let the American people down."

In my case, the perceptions I gained by being a "safe" listener gave me the opportunity to weigh the gaps in credibility I was hearing from our CEO and our employees. As a corporate communication advisor, I could then do a better job of helping our management people at all levels frame what they were saying in official company channels so they would be more credible to our employees at all levels.

What does all this mean to you as a hiring manager? Here are two recommendations:

1. Target job candidates who have learned, perhaps through some form of vulnerability, to effectively take calculated risks in developing their careers and conducting business.
2. Identify job candidates—disabled or not—who can enhance interdependence in your workplace.

In the next chapter, we'll explore each of these recommendations within the context of a corporate culture that is receptive to disability.

QUICK TIPS FROM THIS CHAPTER

⊘ The Trends

In the next thirty years, more seniors will return to work after retirement or postpone retirement, and the number of those employees who have a disability will rise substantially. Hiring younger workers with disabilities now can be your transition to and practice for being able to keep older, productive workers on the job as these two trends change the employment landscape in the United States. For more information, see "Circle of Champions: Innovators in Employing All Americans" at http://www.dol.gov/odep/newfreedom/coc2007/brochure.htm.

⊘ Full Diversity

Leaving disability awareness out of your company's diversity initiative gives you only half a program. Through balanced and well-informed disability awareness training from a diversity trainer, however, you'll provide your employees with the tools they need to make interdependency work for them and your company. For more information, see "Defining Your DDQ: Disability Diversity Quotient" at http://www.disability-marketing.com/newsletter/2006-03-article-ddq.php4.

⊘ Awareness Training

Be proactive. Avoid waiting to hire a disability awareness trainer until you have a disabled customer coming in or a new employee who is disabled (or a current employee who has just become disabled). You don't want to rush it—and you may be tempted to do just that. In a rush, you'll likely prepare your staff for serving or working with just that one disability. For more information, see "Employment of People with Disabilities: The Win-Win Scenario for Employers and Employees" at http://disabilities.suite101.com/article.cfm/employment_of_people_with_disabilities.

⊘ Self-Determination

The more freedom people with disabilities have in making career choices for themselves, the more freedom each of us has—whether or not disability ever becomes part of our lives. For more information, see "What Self-Determination Is and What It Is Not" at http://www.tash.org/mdnewdirections/factsheetsd.htm.

⊘ Inclusion

All individuals need to be treated with dignity and respect in the workplace. The key to making that happen—real inclusion instead of tokenism—lies in the attitudes of those involved. For more information, see ""Survey of Employer Perspectives on the Employment of People with Disabilities" at http://www.dol.gov/odep/documents/survey_report_jan_09.doc.

⊘ Personal Journey

Each person with a disability is on a personal journey that ultimately determines how he or she weaves the feeling of vulnerability into everyday life. That personal journey is often influenced by the individual's level of self-esteem, and self-esteem levels, in turn, can influence how employers view workers with disabilities in general. For more information, see "Restricted Access: A Survey of Employers about People with Disabilities and Lowering Barriers to Work" at http://www.heldrich.rutgers.edu/uploadedFiles/Publications/Restricted%20Access.pdf.

⊘ Disability's Upside

Concrete advantages that grow unexpectedly from learning how to live with a disability can include risk tolerance and interdependence, both of which are important qualities in the people you want on your work team. For more information, see "Disability Can Have an Upside" at http://news.bbc.co.uk/2/hi/health/7408603.stm.

Suggestion for Job Interview Topic

To allow your job candidates to explore their levels of risk tolerance and interdependence within a workplace setting, consider asking them these questions at some point during the interviewing process: "How have you successfully handled a difficult situation that really challenged you? How did that situation change your perception of what you can accomplish? Why do you feel good about the outcome?"

By doing so, you may get some insight into how they approach personal vulnerability—and you may hear some observations that will add to your own disability awareness.

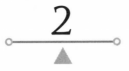

2

Foster a Company Culture That Is Receptive to Disability

RISK TOLERANCE AND INTERDEPENDENCE are both important qualities in the type of people you want to be part of your workforce. In carrying out your recruitment process, you may find individuals with disabilities who are uniquely qualified to add those attributes to your team.

But to effectively attract, hire, and keep employees with disabilities, you need to make sure your corporate culture is receptive to employees with a disability. That means you must go beyond just awareness training about disabilities. You must reinvigorate your diversity values and put those newly defined diversity values into day-to-day practice.

Put Your Diversity Values into Practice

Let's say you're in this situation: Because of the tight job market in your organization's specialty, you have decided to recruit a previously untapped resource: qualified, talented candidates who have a disability. You've worked with a disability awareness trainer to prepare people within your organization for working with employees with a variety of disabilities. Based on that training and feedback from these leaders, you sense your organization is ready to walk the talk. You're ready to start recruiting job candidates with disabilities.

But, are you really ready? Before you start hiring people with disabilities, you need to make sure that the awareness training you've all experienced translates into day-to-day practice so you can effectively integrate qualified people with disabilities into your organization. That's no small task, but as a leader there are three steps you can take to help make your diversity initiatives truly inclusive: clarify your mission and values, communicate that mission and those values throughout your organization, and align those values with daily practices.

You probably have some excellent resource people in your corporate communications and human resources departments who can assist in planning, implementing, and evaluating these three initiatives.

Clarify Your Mission and Values

The period immediately after your disability awareness training is an opportune time to review your organization's mission and values statements. You might also wish to take a second look at your statement of management philosophy.

In doing so, use your facilitation, interpersonal, and writing skills to collaborate with your fellow executives as well as a cross section of associates representing every level of your organization. Help them clarify why your organization is in business and what values guide its day-to-day activities.

The goal here is to be understandable and concrete. Help this small representative sampling of people throughout your organization develop a series of specific examples in which each of your organization's value statements about diversity come alive in on-the-job, everyday ways. Only then will your organization's values become guidelines for making organizational decisions.

Communicate That Mission and Those Values

Corporate communicators not only can help you plan and facilitate the brainstorming sessions for gaining these concrete examples of your organization's values in action; they can also summarize and distribute them to the right audiences, using the right media.

What is needed here is an umbrella communication program to show what your mission and values mean to individuals at every level of your organization. Under that umbrella, you, other members of management, and representatives from your human resources, corporate training, and corporate communication departments can personally consult with immediate supervisors/contact people throughout your organization. The discussion topic for this team of consultants: how immediate supervisors/contact people can interpret your organization's newly focused diversity values and transform them into meaningful and useful information for the people they supervise and the customers they serve on a day-to-day basis.

Align Those Values with Daily Practices

Supervisors/contact people need to know specifically how your organization's values relate to day-to-day individual, team, and organizational practices. And they need to know how, when, and where to communicate that information to the people they supervise.

Here's an outline of the questions supervisors need to answer for the employees they supervise whenever an organization is announcing a policy change, such as a revamped diversity initiative:

- Why are we changing, and why is it important to me?
- What do you want me to do differently from what I'm doing today? Why?
- How will my work now be evaluated, and what are the consequences?
- What tools and support do I get to make this change?
- What's in it for me? What's in it for all of us?

By addressing these issues upfront, your supervisors/contact people are proactively helping your organization manage change. They are also in a position to help your organization gain ongoing feedback about your diversity program. They can then review and reevaluate your diversity program initiatives, share and celebrate successes, share and solve problems, and propose and implement solutions.

The result? Your organization's diversity initiative will become more than a document. It will be alive, real, practical, and relevant. It will grow and evolve. And in this increasingly diverse world on both the employee and customer side of your business, it will contribute to your organization's bottom line.

According to a July 2005 National Survey of Consumer Attitudes toward Companies that Hire People with Disabilities, 92 percent of the American public views companies that hire people with disabilities more favorably than those that do not. And 87 percent of the public would prefer to give their business to companies that hire people with disabilities (see http://www.earnworks.com/BusinessCase/roi_level2.asp).

Nearly 30 percent of the 70 million American families have at least one family member with a disability. The disability market, which includes customers with disabilities and their extended networks (family members, friends, colleagues, support service providers, etc.), as reported by the U.S. Census Bureau, represents $1 trillion in discretionary spending.

In fact, according to MarketResearch.com, the disability market is the third largest market segment behind baby boomers and the mature market, placing them ahead of Hispanics, African Americans, Gen X, teens, and Asian Americans (see http://www.earnworks.com/BusinessCase/marketing_level2.asp).

Create a Work Environment That Values Diversity

Putting diversity values into practice is essentially a management function.

The central goal of creating a positive environment for a diverse workplace is harmony, and harmony fosters productivity.

While the normally stated goal of "doing the right thing" is all well and good (and, doing right, by the way, often results in greater harmony), your responsibility is to your company's bottom line. When people get along and act as a team, they produce more, stay longer, and have fewer gripes—all of which favor effective and efficient work.

Hire People Who Can Set the Right Tone

As a manager, human resources professional, or proprietor, you share the responsibility for fostering the acceptance of disability in your workplace.

You can do that by first selecting an employee with a disability who can help you maintain the right tone about differences in people.

When, on the other hand, staff members harbor resentments or perceive inequities, they can build an obstructionist interplay that handicaps everyone involved. No one can perform at a peak level. Time is wasted in foot dragging, absenteeism, and higher turnover. And time is money.

As a manager, supervisor, or proprietor, you are responsible for ensuring that your work environment is amicable. If your department has poor performance because of interpersonal friction or errant behavior, this performance deficit will be attributed to you. You need to set and maintain the right tone for your work unit.

There is no upside to ignoring tensions and no downside to preventing or resolving them. In fact, neglecting to give tension its due attention will most certainly result in a greater negative impact than that of any time taken to prevent that tension. Not having time to address tension is a common excuse.

Frank Acceptance of Differences Is the Key

Another underlying reason employers may not pay attention to fostering a harmoniously diverse workplace, perhaps especially in the case of disabilities, is discomfort about discussing the differences between individuals and between groups. It is natural to feel awkward about a person's disability, but, in fact, that awkward reluctance is what you must dispel in your employees.

One unique characteristic of disabilities (compared to differences in terms of race, ethnicity, or gender) is that there is an obvious mechanical difference between someone who is, say, mobile, and others who are mobile only with some kind of aid (e.g., crutches, a wheelchair, or a scooter). Glossing over this fact can only result in an uneasy atmosphere. Your staff will conclude that open discussion about disability is forbidden.

The key to fostering a friendly and, therefore, productive work environment is recognizing but not magnifying differences. Many supervisors unwittingly cast an employee with a disability in the role of child or sacred cow by communicating to him and to other staff members that he is somehow "special" or is better than others or to be more protected than others.

Being treated as someone "special" will likely foster resentment from your employee with a disability. That employee will eventually display his resentment in some form of disruptive behavior. If he tends to be a workaholic, he may try to overcome his feeling that he has not gained an equal sense of dignity by burying himself just that much deeper into his work.

An employee who has a disability is really no different from others who are not disabled. He just has to do his work with different tools or techniques. He is not more emotionally vulnerable, not unable to do quality work, not somehow more admirable or heroic because he is disabled.

You set the tone. If you coddle a disabled worker, so will other employees—and others will resent that special treatment. If you are hypersensitive about her disability, you will make everyone else uncomfortable. If you treat her as a burden, that will be the view throughout your department.

Instead, you must foster the recognition that every staff member is entitled to an equal sense of dignity, but each has his individual role, responsibility, and work style. The difference with a disabled worker falls only under work methods and refers entirely to what tools he uses to do the work he shares with his peers.

Awareness Honors All Employees

One benefit for bringing employees back quickly after they become disabled is the positive impact it has on morale. Other workers see that the individual's contribution is valued, that she is not disposable, and that they can count on being similarly valued. Ultimately, fostering harmony for a new worker or a returning worker who has recently become disabled has the same impact on those within the existing workforce.

A work environment in which each person is welcomed, valued, and respected not only benefits the employee who is "different." Companies that see all positions as necessary to the bottom line and all workers as coworkers bring out the best in people. Creating an atmosphere of collaboration rather than assertion of status encourages high performance and a sense of responsibility for results from the CEO to the mailroom clerk. An atmosphere that honors diverse (and, in particular, disabled) employees as equal contributors to the common goal allows each worker to recognize the collective talents of the group instead of a new employee's deficits.

Basically, it is your responsibility to prepare other staff members for including a worker with a disability—and it is also up to that worker to get involved. Showing her and the other staff members that you regard her as the chief educator on the subject of how she works and how to relate to her both empowers her and shows her that you expect her to take responsibility for dealing with her peers. She cannot wait for you or others to guess at what she needs. She must speak up.

By insisting on this forthright candor, you are supporting your other workers, too. They see, from your attitude, that you require equal effort from them as well as the employee with a disability.

Changing Attitudes: Top Challenge

According to a study by Susanne M. Bruyère, director of Cornell University's Program on Employment and Disability, employers who had hired a person with a disability said the most difficult change to make in order to meet that employee's needs was "changing coworker/supervisor attitudes" (32 percent of respondents).

Bruyère says that change was rated as "most difficult" by more than twice as many of those surveyed who chose the next most difficult change ("create flexibility within the performance management system," 17 percent of respondents) and at a rate of approximately sixteen times greater than those responding who selected "ensuring equal pay and benefits" for employees with disabilities (two percent of respondents).

—SOURCE: A. Brannick and S. Bruyère, *The ADA at Work: Implementation of the Employment Provisions of the Americans with Disabilities Act* (Alexandria, VA: Society for Human Resource Management, 1999), p. 10

Remember, it will ultimately be up to you, as a supervisor, to step in when miscommunication or inappropriate behavior on anyone's part has not been resolved on a peer-to-peer level. If, for example, a new visually impaired employee has asked politely and repeatedly that other staff members not change the location of important tools or supplies but they forget, you may need to emphasize to them the practical reasons for consistency. If, on the other hand, you discover that the employee has not communicated this need but expects others to "magically know" (and is becoming contentious when they genuinely don't know), you will need to make it clear that everyone, not just that employee, deserves such courtesy.

What Can You Do to Create a Welcoming Work Environment?

A worker with a disability needs no more or no less respect (a sense of dignity) than does any other employee. Neither avoid him nor heap undue praise on him. Here are some other tips for building that harmony:

- ⊘ Stress to other workers that the employee with a disability was hired because he is qualified and can do the work. His disability was not and should not be a consideration. He will have to satisfy the same performance standards as they do.
- ⊘ Encourage the new employee to be candid about his disability. Offer him a chance to discuss it at a staff meeting.
- ⊘ Discourage the employee with a disability from playing a passive or manipulative role by making sure she knows you are interested only in what she can do and how—not what she can't. Be sure her responsibilities and those of others are well defined and equal.
- ⊘ Treat everyone the same. Neither ignore nor highlight an employee with a disability.
- ⊘ Realize that employees will often have false perceptions about disability (maybe based on previous experiences with individuals who did not know how to handle their disability appropriately in a workplace situation). Be prepared to deal with those false assumptions, which often are simply due to lack of information. You must make it clear that a new employee with a disability is not to be judged until he has had time to establish himself as a member of the team.
- ⊘ Encourage a relaxed atmosphere that includes humor but does not tolerate stereotyping, bigotry, or mean humor.
- ⊘ Make sure a person taking on new duties is adequately compensated for them when you must shift a responsibility from one job description to another because of a disability. Higher pay or authority (or simply allowing for an exchange of tasks) can make the addition acceptable so it doesn't breed ill will.
- ⊘ Let the employee with a disability and her coworkers handle issues not related to work.

Finally, be vigilant about typical misunderstandings and myths.

A Note from the Editor

As a person with cerebral palsy, I have personally encountered these three common misunderstandings:

1. **I'm helpless.** This assumes that I always need help (and you, of course, can help without even asking if I need assistance).

2. **I'm heroic and courageous.** This places me on a pedestal, making it difficult for me to assimilate and function—and to live up to unrealistic expectations.

3. **I'm a totally deficient individual.** This assumption generalizes from a single disability. It assumes that I also have additional intellectual, social, and physical deficits in addition to my cerebral palsy. People often shout at me because they see that I walk and talk with difficulty (even though I have normal hearing).

You set an inclusive tone by how well you interact with an employee who has a disability. How well you welcome, value, and respect her as well as other workers will have a direct effect on how well everyone works together. Establish clear guidelines for the type of work environment (based on your corporate values) you want to foster—and then consistently follow them. The harmony (and productivity) of your staff will pay you back many times over.

Workplace Interdependence Makes Disability Irrelevant

A bumblebee, if dropped into an open tumbler, will be there until it dies. It never sees the means of escape at the top but persists in trying to find some way out through the sides near the bottom. It will seek a way where none exists until it completely destroys itself.

As a culture, the business world seems penned in, flat on the floor, buzzing around like a bumblebee in a tumbler. We continue to work toward a twenty-first-century world with workplaces where everyone can be included as members of a team trying to reach a goal. But until we understand the real and elemental nature of how people work together, differences that have nothing to do with working together will appear to be insurmountable obstacles to us. By clinging to those differences, we aren't achieving the harmony and productivity we seek.

To unburden our U.S. society of inequities and to improve business itself, it is time to change how we look at interdependency in the workplace.

The real nature of workplace relationships goes beyond teamwork. The real action is in the independence of those relationships, and interdependency makes any disability (or any other difference) you may find among the members of a team irrelevant.

Resource Trumps Function

In the complex structure of any workplace, each team member is a resource to others, and that transcends any disability. Workplace interdependence makes functional considerations immaterial.

Why Disability Is Irrelevant

Teamwork is about how our job functions interrelate. But, with cross-training, functions are not specific to the worker. There is something deeper and less tangible that makes each of us unique and can make a workplace fall apart if someone who plays a vital role leaves.

Yes, disability can have an impact on a worker's function. If a truck driver goes blind, he can't be a driver any more. But disability is irrelevant in the areas that are more vital to the health of a company—those roles that everyone else depends on.

While a person in a wheelchair may need someone to take over or assist with a job function, who does what is less important than who can best help the team achieve its objectives. That means we need to stop looking at individuals in terms of their functions and whether one individual can perform every single function in his job description without assistance from another person or a machine.

Is it true that the best candidate for a position exactly matches the description of a specific job? If, for instance, we're presented with someone who can't sit right down and use a computer without some modifications because she is totally blind and that poses an apparently irremediable problem for us, there will never be true integration.

However, integration can take place if we understand that this person, using various other tools, can share responsibilities with a sighted person and can do the work in a different way. Using any number of variations, that person, like all others, has a vital role to play in a workplace setting.

But, to learn how minor the differences are among us and what strengths a group of people have, we must get to know each other. The workplace must be integrated. And to integrate the workplace, we must understand that differences are minor and strengths are many.

At times, laws may tend to force the issue so that the integration begins.

But perhaps it can also take individual hiring managers, such as you, who can see beyond the surface issues to the profound interdependencies among us. If we are all so interdependent, why should the fact that one of us is disabled be such a problem?

Functions, Roles, and Archetypes

Most of the time, we think about our workplace relationships in terms of flowcharts and job descriptions. It can be tempting to think that the hierarchy represented in the flowchart reflects the true nature of our workplace relationships.

But the specifics of authority are not always fully reflected in flowcharts. Remember that the corporate world originally took its model from the military. Yet, instead of the chain of command, the structure of a business is based, ideally, on respective responsibilities. All employees, including the CEO and the mailroom clerk, are actually coworkers—not generals and enlisted personnel.

We need to distinguish between function and role as well as teamwork and interdependence.

Function is what you do, what your job is. Everyone has a job. Specialization is the essence of work and teams. Teamwork is people doing different jobs working together.

But role goes beyond function.

Let's examine the imaginary small team of people who operate a small print shop, Exceptional Printing. Sue believes she is the touchstone and historian, having been with the shop the longest and being in the office itself on a routine basis. Her role is to be the one you can always count on to know "how it's done." Her job title and place on the team are irrelevant. She would have this role whether she were the owner (which she is) or the delivery person.

She identifies another person at the shop, Matt, as the detail person. He can take an idea and develop it into a workable plan. Matt turns to

Sue for the long view. Sue turns to Matt to tell her if a plan is a good idea and how to pursue it. The technology expert, Lance, is a great deal more than a computer guru. He is a catalyst for everyone on the staff. He regards everyone's job as important and supports them in it. Lance is the reliable, willing team builder for everyone else.

Which of these individuals is disabled is not relevant.

We see that these three people go well beyond their interrelated job functions. Sue oversees customer service and bookkeeping. Matt presides over project management. Lance is the operations person. Clients are triaged by Sue, work on a day-to-day basis with Matt, and come to Lance to learn which process to use.

You can learn about the interdependencies in your own workplace and, as a result, uncover the genuine, underlying roles individual employees are playing. You can then see many other subtleties: how some employees manipulate others, why a certain worker seems out of place, why leaders emerge from other than leading ranks, and even how to build a team that does something better than teamwork. And you can see how little disability affects these more important workplace dynamics.

The Virtue That Transcends All

Whether the average workplace demonstrates an awareness of the interdependence of roles is a matter of debate.

A Note from the Editor

I believe qualities often seem to have more influence on a career path than skills, and that those qualities are subtly detected and rewarded with pay and influence.

How we come to rely on one another and what roles we take when the interconnections become established transcend other considerations in any grouping of people: real, fictional, family, workplace, adults, children, men, women, rich, poor, and disabled and nondisabled.

Since disability is the one "minority group" consisting of members of every single other group (anyone can be born or become disabled no matter one's race, ethnicity, gender, gender preference, religion, socioeconomic status, etc.), people with disabilities can take on any of the multitude of roles and interdependencies.

In our Exceptional Printing example above, Lance is the disabled person. He uses a wheelchair. And yet, when we discussed Lance's role as supporter and catalyst, it had nothing to do with his disability, or, for that matter, any other of the personal characteristics of that team's members. Sue's historian and Matt's strategist roles have nothing to do with the fact that neither one is disabled.

The differences and the adaptations are tiny compared to the potential that workers with disabilities offer. And while these roles cannot always be predicted, a job candidate with a disability is just as likely to fulfill a more elemental role in your company as anyone else. He is just as likely as a nondisabled worker to be the level head in a crisis or the one who always knows where to get a tool or the person who makes everyone want to work together. He is just as likely to be the person who inspires the others to work harder and reach higher standards or to break out of a rut and try something new—the person whom, when you look back on events, you simply cannot imagine having done without.

This is not an argument for hiring people with disabilities. But it is a powerful argument for analyzing your work unit and making sure it's receptive to superficial differences that have nothing to do with this important dynamic: who is going to rely on whom and what roles your team members are going to play when a new member joins your team and its interconnectedness (interdependencies) need to be reestablished.

Bridge Builders Can Be Valuable to Your Corporate Culture

Some individuals with disabilities have gained a healthy sense of self-esteem despite the negative messages they often receive from others about their perceived personal vulnerability. They know others perceive them as "different" because of their disability. These "disability survivors" tend to be bridge builders between the nondisabled and disabled communities, and their team-building skills can be valuable assets for your business.

They understand both cultures and are not taken aback by the differences between them, because they often go back and forth between each frequently. They have experience in working with individuals of different abilities, attributes, and attitudes—experience you, as a hiring manager, may find helpful in developing teamwork within your work environment.

In short, whether they are aware of it or not, disability survivors know how to use that experience in establishing interconnections (interdependency) within a work group.

Your best job candidates with disabilities may have had to develop a sense of personal dignity and self-worth without the support you would normally expect they would receive from friends and acquaintances who also have disabilities.

As a hiring manager, you want to attract and hire individuals with a disability who consider themselves "somebodies" but who also understand the subtle "rankism" that can exist between two individuals with a disability—one employed and the other not. Those "somebodies" have seen how rankism can be counterproductive in a workplace setting (because they've experienced it firsthand within the so-called disability community).

Those experiences could also make them effective bridge builders within your work team.

Dignity, Respect, and Fair and Equal Treatment

Let's look at this dialogue among seven people with disabilities who are actively building their careers in today's job market. It may tell us something about what type of corporate culture twenty-first-century companies need to build in order to be truly inclusive.

Melissa McBane:

I have to admit that, as a blind person who works full-time, I get frustrated by those who don't work when they probably could. We need to get out there and show the rest of the world that being visually impaired does not mean we cannot be productive members of society.

I think those who don't work think those of us who do work are somehow not worthy of being part of organizations for the blind. At least that is the experience I have had with others I have been associated with locally. I have been told that I am not a productive member of my local and state chapters of the American Council of the Blind (ACB). . . . I wish I could do more, but I cannot get out of work any time I want. I am also a wife, a mother, and a student, so I juggle a lot as it is. But I have many of the same concerns and problems as any other visually impaired person.

There are programs in my area that bring the visually impaired together for social outings and so forth. I can never participate because they always plan things during weekdays. Those of us who work cannot participate. I feel kind of left out and abandoned by people I thought would accept me.

Kelly:

The emotion of jealousy will rear its ugly head, and, like with siblings, it is best not to compare, even though it is unavoidable. We have to tell ourselves, instead, that we are doing the best we can with whatever God, or a higher power, gave us.

Oftentimes this is easier said than done. For example, I have a cousin who is working at a prestigious law firm and already has an apartment at age 21. Sometimes, it is hard for me to feel happy for her because I do not have this opportunity, but, at the same time, I do not want to deny her the joy a new job brings.

While this vortex of emotion is going on inside my head, I am constantly reminded of what Winston Churchill said: "Never give up, never give up, never give up."

Also, in contrast to sibling rivalry, your feelings of jealousy regarding the employed and the unemployed or the disabled and the nondisabled person can motivate you to persevere, making you stronger in your field of interest.

David Lingebach:

I've been visually challenged half my life, and I have worked with many visually challenged individuals of all types in my profession. Through personal development and professional observation and research, I have come to some basic conclusions:

- ⊘ I have heard many say over the years, "You have to earn respect." I now believe that the respect and dignity that others have for you is directly related to the respect and dignity you have for yourself.

- ⊘ Thus, if you have resentment because you are underemployed or overqualified for your job, this is a direct reflection of your own self-esteem. And it *can* be overcome!

I have observed individuals with stellar credentials and résumés who continue to be unemployed. Why?

My observation is that whether you have been [disabled] from birth or later in life is not the critical factor. The critical factor is how one perceives oneself. This is a very sensitive area, but I am convinced it is the most critical area that affects one's success or lack of success.

Barney Mayse:

Resentment or jealousy among those of us who are disabled about having better jobs may be a natural inclination. *However,* it is incumbent upon us to be bigger than that.

Resentment is based on what we do not have or want. We *can* have what we want. We may have to work harder to get it, but it *is* possible.

Each of us needs to define coherently what it is that we want. What kind of job do I want? Do I have the skills for the job, or will I need to gain training or education to be able to attain that goal? What contribution do I wish to make to the world with my work and my life? Each of us has gifts that we are here to use. What gifts do I have? How will I use them to create a better world for myself, my family, my community?

If we are happy with what we have or know clearly what we want, there will be no time for resentment because we will be busy in pursuit of our goals.

Within the disabled community, we need to stop playing games with each other and treat each other with the respect and dignity that we want the world to give us. There are no exceptions to this rule.

We need to start now and not stop until we achieve our goal of a fully integrated world. We need to discuss this openly, frankly realizing that it will not happen overnight. We need to be clear, concise and dedicated to achieving equal dignity for all people. We need to persevere regardless of the obstacles.

Dan TeVelde:

Self-respect is very important since, if you care about yourself, it will be easier for you to interact with others in any situation.

Wendy:

I don't resent the jobs others get or the achievements others obtain. I just want to be treated fairly and equally. That's all I ask.

Molly, my friend at work, says sometimes I'm a "pushover"—that

I don't stand up for myself in getting the new work and promotions she thinks I should be getting, especially because we work for a large hotel chain.

But why should I have to fight for everything I'm entitled to? Doesn't my work speak for itself?

Shouldn't my supervisor see what's right and conduct herself accordingly and give me the recognition I deserve? Why should my disability have anything to do with how I'm treated while at work?

Maybe I'm too trusting, but eventually I feel good work gets rewarded—at least when you're not in a wheelchair. And even if you're in a wheelchair, it may take a little longer, but you'll eventually win out. People with disabilities usually have to work harder to get what they want. I can accept that.

Yet Molly says I should leave the hotel and go work someplace else that offers more opportunity and more excitement. I'm twenty-six. I have my degree and quite a bit of experience. She says, "'What is there to lose?" I'm not sure. It's tough to get a new job.

My nondisabled classmates are doing very well, and I wonder when I'll get my break. But it'll come.

Charles:

Employers need to focus not on disability, but on ability (how job candidates can be assets to your organization even if they have to do it differently by means of adaptive technology).

Developing the Right Type of Corporate Culture

The previous dialogue reveals some important clues about the type of corporate culture today's companies need to develop if they are to successfully attract and hire talented people who just happen to have a disability. These seven discussion participants have personally experienced rankism, not just with people outside their social circles but also within them.

Consider these seven sentences (paraphrased and personalized) from that conversation:

1. "Being less assertive than I am in pursuing opportunities holds us all back."
2. "My feeling of not being accepted is often based on misunderstanding, not fact."

3. "Envy is seldom a positive motivator; I've found it most always is destructive."

4. "Respect that others have for me reflects the dignity I have for myself."

5. "Pursuing interesting personal goals gives me less time to resent others."

6. "I seek equal treatment."

7. "I want my abilities to count—not my disability."

Let's assume many of the individuals we have just met in this conversation would seek out employers who are:

- ⊘ Proactive in making diversity real
- ⊘ Savvy in mentoring new employees
- ⊘ Dedicated to treating all employees fairly
- ⊘ Stringent in implementing a management system based on setting, achieving, and rewarding quantifiable objectives

So, as you recruit job candidates with disabilities, look for survivors of this all too natural situation, which can yield estrangement and resentment, as well as understanding and reconciliation. In doing so, you may find an individual—a bridge builder—who is comfortable as a team player in both the nondisabled and disabled worlds and has a strong sense of identity and self-worth. That bridge builder can bring added value to your work group.

The contributors who are offering you their personal commentary in this book are "bridge builders." We all have had considerable experience in reflecting the disabled world to the nondisabled world and vice versa.

Our common goal is to help individuals in each world understand one another. And we are all particularly interested in providing you, whether a human resources professional or hiring manager, with two things:

1. A description of the type of person with a disability we believe would offer you the best opportunity to extend your personal and corporate success

2. A comprehensive "how to" process for recruiting, selecting, and managing that person

In the process of doing that, we've come up with some relevant guidelines in this chapter for making sure your corporate culture is receptive to job candidates with a disability who are bridge builders. After analyzing the feedback we received from eSight members, it's amusing to discover that what they, as bridge builders with a disability, find attractive in a company culture is indistinguishable from what any other job seekers, disabled or not, probably seek in a prospective employer. Our similarities are so much greater than our apparent differences.

The next section discusses another attribute of disability survivors: elasticity—a vital quality that you need to continually add to your corporate landscape during these rocky economic times.

Job Seekers with a Disability Can Add Elasticity to Your Workforce

Interview a survivor—someone who has beat the odds in dealing with a disability and who is competing successfully in the mainstream workplace for jobs—and more than likely you'll have a job candidate who knows how to go about resolving some tough personal problems.

Such problem-solving know-how can be transferred to a work situation and help your team develop the elasticity it needs today to compete on a global scale.

There was an illuminating discussion among eSight members on the "Swimming in the Mainstream" (SiM) blog about how to survive mainstream employment when you have a disability. Specifically, the SiM participants discussed this question: What special rules for survival have you, as a person living with a disability, created for yourself at work?

Vulnerability as a Strength

We, as human beings, are quite fragile. Unlike the penguin, we don't do well in cold weather. Unlike the elephant, we can't detect an upcoming tsunami.

We may be vulnerable, but we are adaptive and solution oriented. We wear insulated clothing. We use technology to track storms.

We also use technology to compensate for a wide range of disabilities, which in U.S. society is considered by some to be a personal vulnerability. Those of us with mobility difficulties use electric scooters and even Segways to traverse city parks and shopping malls. Using adaptive technology to compensate for our human frailty, we have found, can make personal vulnerability irrelevant.

In fact, our individual vulnerabilities are valuable—to our society as well as individual organizations and companies—because they stretch our ability to be adaptable as human beings.

In the competitive business world, that kind of reasoning is often lost. An all-able-bodied workforce, for instance, can become flabby in terms of creativity and problem solving, precisely because it lacks diversity and does not include individuals who look at opportunities just a little bit differently than the rest of us.

Individuals with disabilities can be valuable employees because they bring a creativity to the workplace based on what they've learned in solving problems that stem from their personal vulnerabilities.

And, although they may need help occasionally, they have most likely learned to be self-sufficient on a mature, adult level. They have managed to use their creativity to overcome or sidestep barriers that, at first glance, would likely block them from thriving in the mainstream.

The Spectrum

Don't be surprised if you get this reaction (or something similar to it) from your next job candidate with a disability:

> The main rule I have is not to expect coworkers to accept you in the workplace. They have "no concern" about the disabled. None. State advocates tell me, "Tell them you are visually impaired." This statement is viewed as an admission of guilt that you have a problem. Other co-workers do not have a problem. Your admission allows others to disregard your human qualities and make every attempt to disallow your right to be employed or even befriended. . . .
>
> Some workplaces have not changed from the 1950s. If you go back to this timeline and look at the difficult situations minorities had in employment, then, in the 2000 era, you'll see the disabled need to survive the same types of situations.
>
> —Anonymous

That's one individual's perception of reality. Here's another from the opposite end of the spectrum:

Choose how you're going to react to everyone and everything at work or anywhere else. You can be nasty and bitter and resentful and negative and reactionary because no one understands or you can choose not to be and help them understand while still standing your ground. . . .

My mom said to me very early on: "The unfortunate thing is you'll have to do 99 percent of the adapting to the world; they aren't going to do it especially for you." I've found that to be true. I don't go in with any preconceived expectations. I try to be friendly but also firm about my strengths and weaknesses. I know what they are.

I don't tolerate bullies or nastiness toward me or anyone else, and I'm not afraid to state my case. I do the most professional job I know how to do, but I also make sure I'm kind and empathetic to others as well. I make sure I have interests outside my work so that I am able to converse with my colleagues. I don't always talk about me, me, me. I'll ask for help if I need it, and I'll explain the accessibility issues I have—but not with a sneer or a snarky attitude.

—Liz

Workplace Survival Rules

Three SiM bloggers submitted particularly interesting, specific workplace rules for survival. They are highlighted here because you may find them helpful in selecting job candidates with disabilities who will best fit your corporate culture.

Blind since birth, Jake believes it's important for an individual to be independent but also realistic. He writes:

"There are just some circumstances where we, as individuals, cannot be as independent as we want to be. In most (if not all) cases, these circumstances are beyond our control, and unfortunately we have to rely on [others] to help us."

Melissa is between jobs and has quite an extensive list of survival tips based on her experiences:

"Don't develop a chip on your shoulder. The world did not deal you a bad hand.

"Depending on the extent of your disability, ask for accommodations that you realistically need for the job; don't ask for extras that you don't really need. This means [that you need to] do your homework about the job ahead of time and be current on the assistive technology available.

"If someone treats you in a way that is uncomfortable—like a fragile child, for instance—speak up in an assertive and polite manner. Don't be confrontational. Talk in private.

"If someone asks you a question about your disability, even if you think it shows ignorance, answer it. We can combat ignorance in small ways. Someone asked me how I ate, since it was 'obviously too dangerous for me to cook.' I explained to the person that I had enough vision to operate most kitchen appliances, but I was not above burning my homemade lasagna on occasion.

"Get a mentor at work. If you are having a problem, [a mentor] can be a good sounding board for you.

"Be assertive, not passive and not aggressive.

"[You'll probably] have to do a lot of the adapting, but employers are more receptive if you are honest about your needs and clear about them. Otherwise, do whatever you can do to make your workspace fit your needs and ask others to respect that if they use the space, too. Tell them you need them to put things back where they got them to make it easier for you to retrieve them. People will get it, if you respect them. They cannot read your mind and are not experts on the needs of the visually impaired.

"Show a positive attitude—even when you're ready to bite someone's head off. When you keep your cool and show tact, others respect you for it.

"If someone is really making your work life miserable and nothing seems to help, check to see if your company offers any resources. I had an employer that offered a hotline for all employees where they could anonymously get advice on work-related issues. I used it more than once.

"Remember, you are a viable member of the team. If someone is blatantly disrespectful or seems to be out to create problems for you, handle it as any other employee would. If you cannot work it out with the person in a civil way, follow the chain of command.

"Don't forget the human resources department. Part of its job is to provide for the needs of the employees."

Jo, trained as a minister and an assistive technology expert, is also blind. She offered this insight on the SiM blog:

"I have found that a little humor in appropriate places goes a long way toward easing tensions or fending off embarrassing moments in the workplace.

"I was a hospital chaplain and got caught trying to introduce myself to an empty bed! Nobody knew quite what to say until I quipped, 'I was just offering a little comfort to that bed; it gets pushed around a lot!'"

All three of these people sound like they would be the type of employees who could help your company or organization continue to move forward in a business climate that increasingly requires resiliency on both a corporate and personal level.

How You'll Know Your Inclusion Efforts Are Working

More than a dozen individuals on eSight's SiM blog also submitted entries about incidents in their careers that indicated to them that their coworkers were including them as full participants on the job.

The Telltale Signs of Inclusion

When do you know a work group is accepting a new employee who happens to have a disability? As an executive, a manager, or a supervisor, look for (and set the stage for) these telltale signs of inclusion.

These incidents provide the benchmarks by which you, as an employer, can measure the effectiveness of your inclusion efforts. They also show some of the savvy you can expect from employees who are living well (and working effectively) with a disability.

The six benchmarks of inclusion/acceptance are as follows:

1. Focus on customer service
2. Inclusion in social events
3. Job promotions
4. Acceptance as individuals
5. Respect for privacy
6. Learning about disabilities

Here are prime examples of each benchmark that bubbled up from the SiM blog conversation:

A Focus on Customer Service

Laura:

My experience has been that people "forget" you are blind once they know you. Not that they try to forget because it is a bad thing, but it just genuinely isn't one of the top things they think of when they think of you. They think, "Wow, she knows about computers; I can ask her my techie question."

Moses:

[Many of my colleagues] depend on my expertise and would always call me, even if they are out of the office at the time, just to check with me on how to solve sticky situations.

Darrell:

One of the ways I know I am accepted is that some of my colleagues refer to me as "The Oracle" because I have excelled in initial and ongoing job training classes and I frequently provide technical assistance to others on the various accounts we serve.

Inclusion in Social Events

Darrell:

Another illustration of how I am accepted by others in the workplace is that I am fully included in the fun activities we conduct from time to time.

Today is an excellent example. We had a sort of tailgate party to celebrate the upcoming Super Bowl game. One of the activities was a ping-pong tournament. I was able to participate, thanks to some interesting modifications to the game. When I played, I had help from a coworker to guide my hand to the ball. I also served the ball several times, mostly all on my own.

I actually won, 22 to 18! Fun was had by all! Since I had never before played ping-pong, I enjoyed this new experience.

Moses:

I very often dine with [colleagues], party with them, and even tour with them, and this is a clear sign that I have been accepted as one of the team.

Job Promotions

Moses:

Though I am visually impaired, I have received several promotions, the first job being a telephonist, and finally ended up as an Administration Manager. Receiving such promotions, just like the sighted, is a clear sign that I was accepted.

Acceptance as Individuals

Kathleen:

There are some people who will accept you for who you are. There are some people who never will. There are some people who just don't really care except [about] how it all affects them. I have been pretty well accepted on most jobs that I've held. I am blind, but that doesn't define who I am. It is only a part of who I am. If I'm willing to always do the best job I can, treat people the way I'd like to be treated, and expect to be treated in the same manner, most of the time that's the way it goes.

Respect for Privacy

Carrie:

We all need to have a bit of privacy, and I do not believe our lives need to be open books in order to gain acceptance in the workplace. If people are truly interested rather than being voyeurs, then I refer them to places where they can read more on their own. This theme in current society of "telling all" is very disturbing to me. I shall never forget when one of the managers working with me stood up in a meeting and asked everyone if they had any questions about [a person's] disability. First of all, it assumes all in the room are focused on the subject. Second, [it assumes that] if they have questions, they are going to ask them in front of everyone, and, most important, it assumes people have the language and vocabulary to talk about disability—which frequently they don't.

Nan:

> I can't say I actually draw a line between my private and public life when it comes to my disability. I am an educator of sorts and use my own experience to teach about blindness.
>
> I do draw the line, though, when it comes to appropriate behavior—whether or not related to my disability. There are off-limit topics, but they would be off-limits if I were not disabled also.

Learning About Disabilities

Lauren:

> One incident on one former job . . . did show me that upper staff in my particular area wanted to help bring about acceptance. . . . They asked me to write a memo that would be sent to all workers, explaining blindness . . . how it is for me . . . [and] ways to help others feel less frightened about me and my disabilities. The fact that they allowed me to write this memo was remarkable at the time.

Lauren capped the discussion, however, by reminding everyone that "the idea of one incident showing we've been accepted at the workplace might be somewhat simplistic, idealistic, and, though a good stepping-stone, just not the whole picture."

At its core, inclusion involves actively addressing the outdated attitudes people hold; by habit, they may be relying on what they have learned from an early age and have not taken time to update with new knowledge as adults.

As a human resources executive or hiring manager, you can be an important change agent in helping your colleagues update their knowledge about how people with disabilities can contribute to your company's success. You can lead by example—by hiring, placing, and grooming the best individuals with disabilities you can find.

In doing so, you will be helping your company develop an inclusive corporate culture—one that enables it to compete for top talent in today's job market.

And, in doing so, you will also be giving yourself the opportunity to cut your turnover rate, manage a more effective work group, and strengthen your own career.

A Note from the Editor

Back in the 1970s and 1980s, I realized there was a lag in my own development as a team player. During the 1980s, when experiential learning was the vogue in management training, my employer encouraged me to take team-building courses designed to develop my ability to trust team members through such strange exercises as rope climbing and gully jumping.

Because of my cerebral palsy, I was an active participant only as a cheerleader for my fellow team members as we endured stress and a hint of danger, but I was included and learned how gaining experience as a team member (which we, as individuals with a disability, often lack) is vital to success in today's mainstream business world.

I also now believe the experience of being included in high school sports (even though they are often emphasized too much) gives our nondisabled counterparts an edge over us as they move from school to career.

As a high school junior and senior, I was the locker room cleanup guy for the football team and ran the "riding" clock during wrestling matches. Though both occurred in 1959 and 1960 and were tangential to the public team effort, I still find those experiences valuable. I was included.

QUICK TIPS FROM THIS CHAPTER

⊘ **Putting Diversity into Practice**

Before you start hiring people with disabilities, you need to make sure that the awareness training you've all experienced translates into day-to-day practice. That's no small task, but as a leader within your organization, there are three steps you can take to help make that happen: clarify your mission and values, communicate that mission and those values, and align those values with daily practices. For more information, see ""Workplace Diversity: Leveraging the Power of Difference for Competitive Advantage" at http://www.allbusiness.com/government/
employment-regulations-u-s-equal-employment/454352-1.html.

✔ A Workplace That Values Diversity

Set the tone. If you coddle a disabled worker, so will other employees—and still others will resent that special treatment. If you are hypersensitive about the individual's disability, you will make everyone else uncomfortable. If you treat the disabled worker as a burden, that will be the view throughout your department. Instead, you must foster the recognition that every staff member is entitled to an equal sense of dignity, but each has his individual role, responsibility, and work style. The difference with a disabled worker falls only under work methods and refers entirely to what tools he uses to do the work he shares with his peers. For more information, see "Leveraging Diversity to Improve Business Performance" at http://web.mit.edu/cortiz/www/Diversity/Jayne%20and%20Dipboye%2020 04.pdf.

✔ Workplace Interdependence and Disability

In the complex structure of any workplace, how a team member serves as a resource for others transcends any disability. Workplace interdependence makes functional considerations (and thus disability) irrelevant. For more information, see "Interdependence and Role Relationships" at wagner.swlearning.com/ob5e/inet/powerpoint/ch08.ppt.

✔ The Value of Bridge Builders

Disability survivors usually have experience in working with individuals of different abilities, attributes, and attitudes—bridge-builder experience you, as a hiring manager, may find helpful in developing teamwork within your own work environment. For more information, see "How to Thrive in a Larger Corporate Environment: Effective Networking" at http://www.esight.org/view.cfm?x=1520.

✔ Disability and Elasticity

Individuals with disabilities can be valuable employees because they bring creativity to the workplace based on what they've learned in solving problems that stem from their personal vulnerabilities. Such problem-solving know-how can be transferred to a work situation and help your team develop the elasticity it needs today to compete on a global scale. For more information, see "Diversity and Problem Solving" at http://www.globalcollab.org/gps/solving/diversity-GPS.

⊘ Successful Inclusion

At its core, inclusion involves actively addressing outdated attitudes, largely because, by habit, adults rely on what they may have learned as children and have not taken time to update with new knowledge as adults. For more information, see "Business, Disability and Employment: Corporate Models of Success" at http://www.worksupport.com/research/listFormatContent.cfm/5.

Suggestions for Job Interview Topics

To allow your job candidates to explore their understanding of inclusion within a corporate culture, ask them at some point during the interviewing process to:

- ⊘ Tell a story about themselves that illustrates their ability to build effective interpersonal relationships on the job.

- ⊘ Describe how they have successfully handled a difficult work situation that really challenged them.

By doing so, you may gain some insight into how they would fit into your corporate culture—or get some ideas about how the concept of inclusion within a corporate setting is evolving during this first part of the twenty-first century.

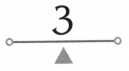

3

Make Your Recruiting Efforts Disability Inclusive

YOU'VE DONE YOUR HOMEWORK. You've raised awareness of disabilities within your workforce. You've nurtured your corporate culture into one that is inclusive. Your employees value differences in people because they realize, in doing so, they are helping to ensure continuity of your business—and their jobs.

Now you're set to recruit job candidates with disabilities. This chapter shows you how to do that. We'll start with the basics: provide answers to questions you've always wanted to ask about recruiting job candidates with disabilities and then look at the broad implications of the Americans with Disabilities Act (ADA) for you as an employer as the law stands today. Please note that the information in this chapter (as well as the rest of this book) is not presented as legal advice but as guidelines from experts and expert sources.

Frequently Asked Questions About Hiring Employees with Disabilities

Candid questions about employment of people with disabilities often go unasked and, therefore, are generally unanswered. Here is some information about how to effectively relate to a job candidate with any type of disability. The answers are based on recommendations provided by the

U.S. Department of Labor (http://www.dol.gov/odep/pubs/fact/laws.htm); the Job Accommodation Network (JAN), a service provided by the U.S. Department of Labor's Office of Disability Employment Policy (http://www.jan.wvu.edu/Erguide); and the New York Lawyers for the Public Interest, Inc. (NYLPI), 151 West 30th Street, 11th Floor, New York, NY 10001-4007 (www.nylpi.org).

Question: What's the correct term for people with disabilities?

Answer: Terminology confuses everyone. Some people with disabilities, for example, are fine with being called a "disabled person," a "blind person," etc.

Others who subscribe to the "people first" philosophy insist on "person who is disabled" terminology. They may say, "Don't refer to us as 'the disabled,' " but you will hear about a group called the National Federation of the Blind. It really is a matter of taste.

In general, the word "handicapped" is out of favor, so avoid "physically handicapped," for instance, even though "handicapped parking" seems to stay with us.

It's safe to take your cue from how the person with a disability describes himself. Without that feedback, it's best to use "person with a disability" or "person who is disabled."

Question: Do I have to give preference to a job candidate who has a disability?

Answer: No. The ADA and state and local laws protect people from employment discrimination on the basis of disability. But they do not require you to hire or promote an individual with a disability over other people.

According to the NYLPI, there are three guidelines you need to keep in mind as an employer:

1. These laws prohibit you from refusing to hire or to promote or from taking other adverse action against a person because of that person's disability if he or she can perform the essential functions of the job.

2. You can, under the ADA, choose a person without a disability with more experience over an individual with a disability even if the individual with the disability is qualified for the job.

3. You can choose a person without a disability over an individual with a disability if the two individuals are equally qualified, as long as the choice was not made because of the individual's disability.

Question: What can I ask a person with a disability during a job interview?

Answer: You can describe the essential functions of the job for which she is interviewing, and then you can ask the job candidate if she can do the work and how she would do it for your company.

You cannot phrase your questions in terms of the disability. For example, if driving an automobile is part of the job at hand, you can ask if she has a driver's license, but you cannot ask if her leg braces prevent her from driving.

The ADA says that during job interviews or on job applications you cannot ask questions about medical conditions, past hospitalizations, the nature of a disability, or the severity of a disability.

Under the ADA, it's still questionable whether asking about gaps in employment history is allowed because such a question could lead to an unlawful discussion about a job candidate's disability.

Question: Does the ADA allow affirmative action in the hiring of people with disabilities?

Answer: You may invite job candidates to voluntarily self-identify for purposes of your affirmative action program if you are undertaking affirmative action because of a federal, state, or local law that requires affirmative action for individuals with disabilities or you are voluntarily using the information to benefit individuals with disabilities.

According to the Employee Equal Opportunity Commission (EEOC), if you invite job candidates to voluntarily self-identify in connection with providing affirmative action, you must state clearly that the information requested is used solely for affirmative action purposes, that it is being requested on a voluntary basis, that it will be kept confidential in accordance with the ADA, that refusal to provide it will not subject the candidates to any adverse treatment, and that it will be used only in accordance with the ADA.

For additional information, see "ADA Enforcement Guidance:

Preemployment Disability-Related Questions and Medical Examinations" at http://www.eeoc.gov/policy/docs/preemp.html.

Question: Will we have to pay for lots of expensive equipment for an employee with a disability?

Answer: Not usually, but it depends on the individual situation. Does he need special equipment to do the work outlined in the job description? If he doesn't, there are no costs for accommodations. If he does, JAN reports, "The average cost of hiring people with disabilities is the same as hiring a person without a disability, according to three-quarters of the employers surveyed."

JAN also states that for disabilities in general the cost of reported accommodations breaks down like this:

- ✅ Thirty-one percent cost nothing.
- ✅ Fifty percent cost less than $50.
- ✅ Sixty-nine percent cost less than $500.
- ✅ Eighty-eight percent cost less than $1,000.

For more information, see http://www.jan.wvu.edu.

Question: Will hiring a person with a disability make our health insurance rates go up?

Answer: Not necessarily. Health insurance premiums are based on the health care costs (or "experience") of an entire group, not just one person. And people with disabilities don't necessarily have higher medical expenses.

Question: If I hire a job candidate with a disability, will I ever be able to lay off or fire that person for the same reasons I would let go someone without a disability?

Answer: If he is incompetent or commits any offense that calls for firing under your employment policies, you can most certainly fire him. If you have to lay off staff, you need not keep a disabled person on just because he's disabled. The point is that unless you are firing a worker because he is disabled there is no prohibition against it.

But are you actually asking, "How do I fire a person with a disability without feeling like a monster?" If so, realize that it's never easy to fire someone. A person with a disability deserves no less and no more fairness.

For more detailed information about these issues, see the next section of this chapter and Appendix A, "Comprehensive Resource List for Hiring People with Disabilities" at the end of this book. FAQs in Chapter 5 address reasonable accommodations and issues about information and confidentiality once you have hired an employee with a disability.

Now let's look at the broad implications of the ADA as it stands today.

What You as an Employer Need to Know About Current Interpretations of the ADA

The big picture of today's ADA from an employment standpoint needs to include these four components:

1. An overview of the original ADA of 1990 provisions for employers
2. A summary of some of the major Supreme Court rulings since 1990
3. A summary of some of the lower court rulings since 1990
4. A summary of what the ADA Amendments Act (ADAAA) of 2008 is all about

A Quick Overview of the Original ADA

For a picture of the ADA as it stood when it was first enacted into law in 1990, see "The Americans with Disabilities Act: A Brief Overview" on the Job Accommodation Network website at http://www.jan.wvu.edu/links/adasummary.htm.

The ADA of 1990

Title I of the ADA deals with employment. In simple language, the JAN overview describes Title I's overall provisions like this:

Business must provide reasonable accommodations to protect the rights of individuals with disabilities in all aspects of employment.

Possible changes may include restructuring jobs, altering the layout of workstations or modifying equipment.

Employment aspects may include the application process, hiring, wages, benefits and all other aspects of employment. Medical examinations are highly regulated.

The language in the original ADA left these three questions to be determined through interpretation by case law:

1. Who is disabled and, therefore, covered by employment provisions of the ADA?
2. Which employers must observe employment provisions?
3. What aspects of employment are covered and what steps will satisfy the employment provisions of the ADA?

Let's first look at how these questions have been answered by the U.S. Supreme Court in rulings on ADA-related cases during the last fifteen years. Then we'll look at lower court rulings. Finally, we'll see how the ADAAA of 2008 attempts to bring the law back to what Congress intended it to be when it passed the ADA in 1990. Of course, these are all snapshots of a fluid situation. For a current update, it's best to consult your legal counsel.

U.S. Supreme Court Decisions: Issues and Cases

The rulings in the cases discussed here are a sampling of how the U.S. Supreme Court has decided the ADA should be applied. The summaries are interpretations by the U.S. Supreme Court alone and do not include those ADA provisions that may not have been challenged yet.

Issues Involving Employment
Who is disabled?

Here's what the language of the ADA states. With respect to an individual, the term "disability" means:

a. A physical or mental impairment that substantially limits one or more of the major life activities of such individual;

b. A record of such an impairment; or

c. Being regarded as having such an impairment.

The ADA further clarifies that the person with a disability covered by its provisions must also be "qualified."

The term "qualified individual with a disability" means an individual with a disability who, with or without reasonable accommodation, can perform the essential functions of the employment position that such an individual holds or desires. That's according to the U.S. Department of Justice.

But many critics of the ADA have commented that this definition does not adequately spell out definitively what constitutes a disability. To this charge, one of the ADA's authors, Congressman Steny Hoyer, replies, "Is this what we had in mind when we passed the ADA—that lawyers for businesses and individuals should spend time and money arguing about whether people can brush their teeth and take out the garbage? Not at all. The whole tenor of the debate at that time was far broader."

Which employers must comply?

Here's what the ADA (and U.S. Department of Justice) says.
In general:

The term "employer" means a person engaged in an industry affecting commerce who has 15 or more employees for each working day in each of 20 or more calendar weeks in the current or preceding calendar year, and any agent of such person, except that, for two years following the effective date of this title, an employer means a person engaged in an industry affecting commerce who has 25 or more employees for each working day in each of 20 or more calendar weeks in the current or preceding year, and any agent of such person.

Exceptions:
The term "employer" does not include:

i. The United States, a corporation wholly owned by the government of the United States, or an Indian tribe; or

ii. A bona fide private membership club (other than a labor organization) that is exempt from taxation under section 501(c) of the Internal Revenue Code of 1986.

How must employers comply?

The ADA has always referred to a concept called "reasonable accommodation" (that is, what changes really need to be made to permit a disabled person an equal opportunity to work).

The term "reasonable accommodation" may include:

a. Making existing facilities used by employees readily accessible to and usable by individuals with disabilities; and

b. Job restructuring, part-time or modified work schedules, reassignment to a vacant position, acquisition or modification of equipment or devices, appropriate adjustment or modifications of examinations, training materials or policies, the provision of qualified readers or interpreters, and other similar accommodations for individuals with disabilities.

For example, an employer may need to provide a blind or visually impaired employee with memoranda in an accessible format, if she cannot read standard print. But the employer does not have to pay for her lunch unless he pays for everyone else's. This is because the blind person cannot read the print on her own, but nothing about her disability prevents her from bringing or buying her own lunch. She could not sue under the ADA claiming that furnishing lunch is a "reasonable accommodation" for her blindness.

Another concept introduced into the mix is "undue hardship." Here is how the ADA itself defines it:

The term "undue hardship" means an action requiring significant difficulty or expense, when considered in light of (certain) factors. Factors to be considered, in determining whether an accommodation would impose an undue hardship on a covered entity, include:

i. The nature and cost of the accommodation needed under the ADA;

ii. The overall financial resources of the facility or facilities involved in the provision of the reasonable accommodation; the number of persons employed at such facility; the effect on expenses and resources, or the impact otherwise of such accommodation upon the operation of the facility;

iii. The overall financial resources of the covered entity; the overall size of the business of a covered entity with respect to the number of its employees; the number, type and location of its facilities; and

iv. The type of operation or operations of the covered entity, including the composition, structure and functions of the workforce of such entity; the geographic separateness, administrative or fiscal relationship of the facility or facilities in question to the covered entity.

For instance, a large supermarket chain may be expected to provide expensive assistive technology for a blind or visually impaired cashier, but a tiny mom-and-pop grocery store may not, since the latter does not have the financial resources the former does.

The Cases Involving Employment Issues

Bragdon v. Abbott, 524 U.S. 624 (1998): HIV is a physical impairment covered by the ADA whether or not symptoms have appeared.

Wright v. Universal Maritime Service Corp., 525 U.S. 70 (1998): If an employer and its employees' collective bargaining organization have an agreement that arbitration must take place concerning employee grievances, the agreement cannot replace civil action when an employee invokes her rights under the ADA. In other words, she will not have to abide by the arbitration decision and may sue privately.

Albertson's, Inc. v. Kirkingburg, 527 U.S. 555 (1999): A person's natural ability to correct for a condition (in this case having monocular vision) satisfies the definition of "correction" and the employer need not accommodate "a mere difference in an individual's manner of performing an activity" unless the employee herself can prove she has a "substantial limitation."

Cleveland v. Policy Management Systems Corp., 526 U.S. 795 (1999):

A person who has applied for or is receiving disability benefits may still invoke the protection of the ADA.

Sutton v. United Airlines, 527 U.S. 471 (1999): If a person's condition can be corrected (in this case, by eyeglasses or contact lenses), she is not to be considered disabled under the ADA.

Murphy v. United Parcel Service, 527 U.S. 516 (1999): If a person's condition can be corrected by medication, she is not to be considered disabled under the ADA. Also a person who is limited in regard to only one work task may not be considered disabled under the ADA.

EEOC v. Waffle House, Inc., 122 S. Ct. 754 (2002): An employee's civil rights cannot be signed away by her, even with mutual consent.

Toyota Motor Manufacturing, Kentucky, Inc. v. Williams, 122 S. Ct. 681 (2002): In regard to manual tasks, a person may only be considered to have "substantial limitations" if these limitations are visible and functional.

Chevron v. Echazabal, 00-1406 (2002): Under regulation of the Equal Employment Opportunity Commission, an entity can refuse to hire an individual because his performance on the job would endanger his own health, owing to a disability.

U.S. Airways, Inc. v. Barnett, 122 S. Ct. 1516 (2002): When an employee with a disability seeks reassignment as an accommodation under the ADA, that employee's right to reasonable accommodation does not trump another employee's seniority rights when the employer has a seniority system.

Equal Employment Opportunity Commission v. Waffle House, Inc., 122 S. Ct. 754 (2002): An agreement between an employee and an employer to arbitrate employment-related disputes does not bar the EEOC from pursuing victim-specific judicial relief, such as back pay, reinstatement, and damages, in an enforcement action alleging that the employer has violated Title I of the ADA.

Lower Court Decisions: Issues and Cases

Lower courts in the United States have ruled on many more individual cases that have not been considered necessary for consideration by the U.S. Supreme Court.

The ADA is like a growing child, so just as no photo of a child truly reflects what he looks like at the present moment, no summary of ADA cases can be complete and up-to-date. In many cases, there may be a split between circuit courts. In other instances, the cases may no longer be law based upon subsequent decisions in that circuit or the Supreme Court. It is wise to contact an attorney who specializes in employment law to keep you current about how the ADA is being applied to specific circumstances.

However, here is a sampling of decisions so you can get a sense of the direction the lower courts are taking with the employment provisions of the ADA.

The rulings by the many lower courts have resulted in three general findings:

1. Congress had the right to create and continues to possess the right to enforce the ADA.

2. The definition of disability must be tested case by case, and there is no one definition of disability.

3. The requirement that an employer make "reasonable accommodation" so the disabled employee can perform work tasks is not unlimited and does not necessitate Herculean efforts.

Here is a little more detail about these three main decisions and some of the cases that were involved in making them.

Congress had the right to create and continues to possess the right to enforce the ADA. Numerous cases considering the status of the ADA as law may be summed up as validation of the law's constitutionality. Some questioned whether the ADA violated the Eleventh or Fourteenth Amendments to the U.S. Constitution. The Eleventh Amendment concerns whether "the judicial power of the United States shall not be construed to extend to any suit in law or equity, commenced or prosecuted against one of the United States by citizens of another state, or by citizens or subjects of any foreign state."

The rulings have determined that the states and their officials do not have immunity from suits brought under the ADA and further may be enforced by injunction. However, the Supreme Court ruled that suits for monetary damages are not allowed to be brought in federal courts (*Board of Trustees of the University of Alabama v. Garrett*, 531 U.S. 356, 121 S. Ct. 955 [2001]). The case invoking the Fourteenth Amendment challenged whether the U.S. Congress has the authority to pass and enforce a law such as the ADA. To date, rulings have affirmed this right.

The definition of disability must be tested case by case, and there is no one definition of disability. Once the ADA was enacted, it quickly became obvious that the definition of "disability" is difficult to pin down. Different courts have ruled on what constitutes a "major life activity"— with the outcome that one court deemed that procreation is a major life activity while another ruling held that if one can enjoy some major life activities, a limitation on ability to do a particular work task may not be limitation enough to make the worker "disabled."

Courts have concluded that a correctable condition is not a disability. And courts have narrowed the definition by declining to call anything but an inability to perform similar tasks across a broad spectrum a disability. For example, a man who could no longer teach but could perform another occupation was determined not to be disabled under the ADA.

Under the ADA, an individual with a disability is a person who has a physical or mental impairment that substantially limits one or more major life activities, has a record of such an impairment, or is regarded as having such an impairment.

The two bones of contention have been about what constitutes a "substantial limitation" and what is a "major life activity." Neither is precisely defined. As a result, different courts have interpreted these two concepts differently.

Is there an objective definition that covers all disabilities? No. Different rulings appear not only to be different but sometimes to be at odds.

According to The Bazelon Center for Mental Health Law:

> In *Muller v. Automobile Club of Southern California*, 897 F. Supp. 1289 (S.D. Cal. 1995), an insurance company claims adjuster who developed posttraumatic stress disorder after being threatened by a customer was found by the court to be capable of doing similar work for other employers or in other jobs. Thus, the court held, Ms. Muller was not a person with a disability as defined by the ADA.

The Bazelon Center also notes:

> In *Mustafa v. Clark County School District*, 876 F. Supp. 1177

(D. Nev. 1995), a case decided under Section 504 of the Rehabilitation Act, a teacher who developed panic disorder and anxiety contended that he was substantially limited not only in working but also in other major life activities. The court rejected Mr. Mustafa's claim, however, apparently relying in large part on the fact that Mr. Mustafa's doctors had advised him to engage in physical exercise. Also, although the court acknowledged that Mr. Mustafa's impairment was a barrier to his employment as a teacher, it held that he was not barred from employment generally.

What constitutes a "major life activity"? The original language of the ADA made reference to faculties such as seeing and hearing. But even this question has no simple answer. For example, a woman's request for time off to receive fertility treatment was turned down by her employer. The court determined, when she sued for redress under the ADA, that procreation is a "major life activity" (*Bielicki v. City of Chicago*, W.L. 260595 [N.D. Ill. 1997]).

Is a person disabled if the effect of a condition can be fully alleviated? Is a person blind if she can put on glasses and see fine? The United Transportation Union reported in *Daily News Digest*:

> The court ruled that protections under the Act (ADA) are limited to people whose conditions cannot be corrected with medication or devices, such as glasses or hearing aids.

This opinion is supported by lawsuits that were struck down: one by a truck driver who is nearly blind in one eye, *Albertson's v. Kirkingburg*, and another by nearsighted twins who applied to be commercial pilots, *Sutton v. United Airlines*.

Yet, other rulings affecting the definition of who is disabled have held that use of medication, a prosthetic device, or adaptive tools does not affect whether the person using them is disabled.

The requirement that an employer make "reasonable accommodation" so the disabled employee can perform work tasks is not unlimited and does not necessitate Herculean efforts. The ADA puts forth that business must provide reasonable accommodations to protect the rights of individuals with disabilities in all aspects of employment.

" 'Reasonable accommodations' may include restructuring jobs, altering the layout of workstations, or modifying equipment," it says.

Several lower court rulings have addressed what constitutes "reasonable accommodation." These decisions have held, among other situations, that:

- ⊘ An employer need only restructure the nonessential functions of a position in order to provide equal access for a disabled applicant.

- ⊘ The employer must address accommodations whenever a worker's disability changes significantly enough to require it.

- ⊘ Regular attendance is to be considered an "essential function," and employees may not demand an open-ended schedule as an accommodation. However, as long as personnel policy requirements for applying "unpaid leave" are followed by the employee, it can be used to meet accommodations needs.

- ⊘ Employers are only required to provide accommodations that are effective. They do not need to provide those accommodations recommended as "best" by the worker or consultants.

- ⊘ The courts are split over whether reassigning a person to a different job is sufficient for "reasonable accommodation." Further, other issues may impact this, such as collective bargaining agreements.

The lower courts have addressed other aspects of work life as well. For example, courts are split as to whether limitations to employee benefits (such as limitations on mental health treatment within health insurance coverage that may disproportionately affect employees with disabilities) are allowable.

The ADA Amendments Act of 2008

On September 25, 2008, the ADAAA was signed into law and became effective on January 1, 2009. The ADAAA was supported by more than 220 national organizations, including the U.S. Chamber of Commerce, the American Society of Employers, disability organizations, veterans' groups, church organizations, and the National Association of

Manufacturers. The bill passed the House on a vote of 402 to 17 and unanimously passed the Senate.

An Overview of the New ADAAA

For an overview of the ADAAA, which became effective January 1, 2009, see "Accommodation and Compliance Series: The ADA Amendments Act of 2008" on the JAN website at http://www.jan.wvu.edu/bulletins/adaaa1.htm.

Check out the section about practical tips you can follow right now. It will help you to be in compliance with the provisions of this new law.

To understand what the ADAAA means, though, it's important to understand why the ADA needed amending in the first place. When it was passed in 1990, the ADA had a definition of disability based on the definition used in the Rehabilitation Act of 1973: An individual with a disability has a physical or mental impairment that substantially limits one or more major life activities, a record of such an impairment, or is regarded as having such an impairment. So Congress used that definition in the ADA because it seemed to work well in the Rehabilitation Act of 1973.

However, according to Jacquie Brennan of the Independent Living Research Utilization program, a national center for information, training, research, and technical assistance in independent living, the Supreme Court in 1999 started to narrow the definition of disability in unexpected ways.

In a case called *Sutton v. United Airlines* (http://caselaw.lp.findlaw.com/scripts/getcase.pl?court=US&vol=000&invol=97-1943), for instance, the court said that when you determine whether an individual has a disability under the ADA, you have to consider the effects of mitigating measures (such as corrective lenses, medications, hearing aids, and prosthetic devices) when deciding whether an impairment is substantially limiting.

Brennan points out that the Court did one other thing in *Sutton*. It essentially overturned an old Rehabilitation Act of 1973 case, *School Board of Nassau County v. Arline* (http://caselaw.lp.findlaw.com/scripts/getcase.pl?court=US&vol=480&invol=273). *Arline* had broadly viewed the part of the definition of disability that mentions having a "record of" an impairment. The Court in *Sutton* required a more restrictive view of that part of the definition, which practically eliminated it.

In 2002, in a case called *Toyota Motor Manufacturing, Kentucky, Inc. v. Williams* (http://caselaw.lp.findlaw.com/scripts/getcase.pl?court= US&vol=000&invol=00-1089), the Supreme Court focused on the word "substantially" in the definition of disability and said that it means "considerably" or "to a large degree." The Court also narrowed the scope of "major life activity," stating that it must be something that is of central importance to most people's daily lives.

According to Brennan, between *Sutton* and *Toyota* and their progeny, the definition of disability was narrowed to such a degree that most cases became more about whether a person met the definition of disability instead of access or accommodation.

The EEOC did its part, too, Brennan explains. It had regulations that defined "substantially limits" as "significantly restricts," which was inconsistent with Congress's intent when it passed the ADA.

So that is why Congress decided that the ADA of 1990 needed to be amended.

At the beginning of every new law that Congress writes, it lists "findings," which are the reasons why the law is being written, says Brennan. In the ADAAA, there is a list of findings. They include:

- ⊘ "Congress intended the ADA to provide a clear and comprehensive national mandate for the elimination of discrimination against individuals with disabilities and provide broad coverage."

- ⊘ "While Congress expected that the definition of disability under the ADA would be interpreted consistently with how courts had applied the definition of a handicapped individual under the Rehabilitation Act of 1973, that expectation has not been fulfilled."

- ⊘ Specific statements in the Supreme Court holdings in *Sutton* and *Toyota* eliminated protection for many individuals whom Congress intended to protect.

Then it lists the purposes of the ADAAA, which include:

- ⊘ To reject the requirement, under *Sutton*, that mitigating measures be considered when determining whether a person meets the definition of disability

⊘ To reject the Supreme Court's reasoning, under *Sutton*, with regard to the "record of" prong of the definition of disability, and reinstate the *Arline* standard

⊘ To reject the *Toyota* standard that the terms "substantially" and "major" need to be interpreted strictly because that creates a demanding standard for qualifying a person with a disability

⊘ To express Congress's expectation that the EEOC will revise its definition of "substantially limits"

The ADAAA has new rules for the definition of disability. They include:

⊘ **The definition of disability is construed in favor of broad coverage to the maximum extent permitted.**

⊘ **The term "substantially limits" is to be interpreted consistently with the ADAAA.**

⊘ **An impairment that substantially limits one major life activity need not limit other major life activities to be considered a disability.**

⊘ **An impairment that is episodic or in remission is a disability if it would substantially limit a major life activity when active.**

⊘ **Mitigating measures shall not be a factor when determining whether an impairment substantially limits a major life activity. The only mitigating measures that can be considered are ordinary eyeglasses or contact lenses that fully correct visual acuity or eliminate refractive error.**

⊘ **People who are regarded as being disabled are entitled to reasonable accommodations or modifications. Previously, courts had debated whether the ADA required having to accommodate a disability that didn't actually exist.**

In short, the ADAAA is not some revolutionary new law. It simply attempts to bring the law back to what Congress intended it to be when it passed the ADA in 1990.

Walking a Wavy Line

As an employer, you may well conclude that trying to second-guess future applications of Title I of the ADA is chancy. The rulings will continue to be handed down and the ADA refined indefinitely. So what guidelines would be helpful to follow?

One response is to hire the best candidate for an open position in every single case. The mistake you may make will be to consider a disability a disqualification—a barrier to an applicant who is the most qualified person.

Disability is not inability. You should educate yourself about the realities of disability and look for the person who will perform best in the job you have open—the person who will reflect well on you and extend the success of your company.

So, let's take a look at each step of your recruiting process and suggestions on ways to make each of your recruiting efforts disability inclusive—starting with how you define "experience."

Considering Volunteer Experience May Be Essential in Fully Evaluating a Job Candidate

Volunteering not only shows that a job candidate is motivated to work in a job field of his or her choice for free to gain work experience and job skills. It also says something about the individual's values, mission, and character.

When an individual has motivation, values, a mission, and character, that person probably has been—and will continue to be—successful. That's the type of individual you will want to hire and groom for more responsibility.

Volunteering: The "After-School" Job for Applicants with Disabilities

When the typical job applicant hands you his resume or job application, you can expect to see part-time jobs and internships he's held while in college and during summer breaks. The sharp applicant will include any substantial volunteer work he's done, too. These items under "Work Experience" are what you will use, in part, to decide whether the applicant is job ready and whether he has the work experience and work habits to make him the best candidate for your open job.

But, when the applicant sitting across the interview table has a disability, his resume might be a little thin on work experience gained through part-time and limited-term jobs. This does not mean he cannot do the job—only that certain barriers to typical part-time employment may exist and may have prevented him from getting a chance to show what he can do.

A Practical Way to Develop Skills

For job candidates with disabilities, volunteer experience is one of the few avenues still open for them after college for developing on-the-job skills.

He may have had little extra time to work after studying, for instance, if his access needs (and the available tools or lack thereof) meant taking more time for his schoolwork. He may not have had transportation from home to work during breaks. And most likely he could not get hired for these typically low-paid, short-term, and part-time jobs. How many people with disabilities have you seen working at McDonald's during summer break?

The truth is that the most motivated individuals with a disability will manage to land internships during college, but upon graduation internships are generally not available. That leaves volunteering as one of the few avenues they have after college for developing their skills and proving themselves on the job.

After college, job candidates with disabilities also often endure long job searches or stretches between jobs. Some use volunteering as one of their job search strategies to widen their contacts with people who have varying experiences, backgrounds, and lifestyles. Others volunteer so they can fill in chronological gaps in their resumes.

Volunteer work can be more flexible than paid jobs in terms of schedules and other work requirements. The volunteer work you see on the resume of an applicant with a disability may be the only work he could get that most easily complemented his personal schedule.

So volunteer experience on a resume is one way a disabled applicant can show you what he can do. As Suzanne Westhaver says to disabled students in her article "Putting Your Best Foot Forward: Tips for Resume Building," on EnableLink.com:

You need to have an edge if you want an employer to hire you. Something has to make you stand out from the rest of the candidates. Affirmative action doesn't entitle you to a job. Affirmative action entitles a qualified candidate an equal opportunity for employment. In today's job market, you need to be computer savvy. You need to be educated, and you need to have experience. "How do I get experience?" a voice in the back of your mind screams. Getting experience is not as difficult as it may seem. If you are having trouble gaining experience through employment opportunities, I recommend volunteer experience.

Some Volunteering Examples

Consider the following interchange about volunteer work among four members of eSight Careers Network, all of whom have some type of disability and are actively pursuing their career goals in today's job market:

Jeremiah Taylor:

I volunteered without pay for my employer after I lost my sight so I had an opportunity to remove the fears of my colleagues and show them I could perform on the job.

Liz Seger:

I volunteer on a community editorial board with the local newspaper with people from all the municipalities in our area—young people, retired people (for some reason a lot of the board is composed of retired teachers and retired journalists), and a lot from the helping professions (a minister, social workers, etc.). Two of us are disabled.

We're a very cohesive and funny group, and we've only known each other a couple of years. We enjoy sparring because we're also all philosophical and have political backgrounds.

George Bernard Shaw wrote this about how he saw his role in the world, and I've always felt it represented my worldview well, too:

I am of the opinion that my life belongs to the whole community, and, as long as I live, it is my privilege to do for it whatever I can. I want to be thoroughly used up when I die, for the harder I work the more I live. . . . I rejoice in life for its own sake. Life is a brief candle to me. It's a sort of a splendid torch which I've got to hold up, for the moment, and I want to make it burn as brightly as possible before handing it to future generations.

When I wasn't awarded my B.Ed. degree at a large and famous Canadian university because its elementary school division felt there would never be a board of education that would hire a legally blind teacher, my mother wouldn't allow me to sit around the house and vegetate.

She had teacher friends who let me come into their classroom and volunteer. Eventually two of the principals were so pleased with my work they had me working as an educational assistant. I did that for two years while appealing my degree with not only the Ministry of Colleges and Universities in Canada but also with the then Handicapped Employment Program out of the Ministry of Labor.

The principals in the two schools where I volunteered sent a petition to both ministries, and I was finally granted my B.Ed. degree in 1980.

I also got into journalism by volunteering. My mom's friend worked on the newspaper, and she introduced me to her editor who asked me to do a few sample columns about disability issues for him. That led to a bi-weekly column in our local paper that ran from January 1981 until August 1982, when I moved to Alberta.

The paper couldn't afford to pay me, but by writing for *The Port Colborne News*, I learned how to craft a news story. I covered local events, and I had my own column at 26.

Volunteering hones your soft skills, such as learning how to be a team player. When I was out of work in the 1990s, I volunteered for our local branch of the Canadian Red Cross and worked my way up to chairman of the branch. During this experience, I not only developed new skills, but I also acquired a large and varied social network.

Melissa McBane:

Volunteer work gives people the opportunity to use the same skills needed for many paying jobs: organizational ability, teamwork, interpersonal communication—the list goes on and on. I am personally impressed by employees, disabled or not, who do volunteer work. It shows good character.

James Elekes:

I have long had a passion to observe the inner workings of government, be it on the local, state, or federal levels. As an observer, you often must take a step back, focusing on the tree rather than the entire forest.

I believe in the dignity of all humanity and expressing my opinion when unfair treatment is focused at a particular segment of the community. Professionally, I am systematic and structured when analyzing an issue.

As a result, [my] "volunteer/community service" has focused on how to improve the service delivery to the disability community—whether it be in serving on an advisory body, focusing efforts on expanding resources to bridge a gap in service funding or opening options for disabled individuals to participate in a heretofore unavailable experience.

It is ironic, but I do not look at what the activity can do for me but what I can contribute to the community to make it better. To this end, it is the life experience gained that is the reward. It is this experience that helps fill in the picture of me as a person, and, time and time again, it is this value-added, intangible benefit I bring to a prospective employer that is the difference in being the successful candidate when compared to others vying for the same employment goal.

Notice how a simple story about volunteer experience reveals much about a job candidate's orientation: She's assertive, she's resourceful, she's a leader, she's a life-long learner. . . .

As a recruiter or hiring manager, you obtain some of the same helpful information when you ask about volunteer experience as you would if you inquired only about on-the-job accomplishments.

A Note from the Editor

Let me add my own story about how volunteering helped me develop my career.

Early in my career (and over the span of ten years), I took the lead in publishing centennial books for two church congregations (one small and the other larger than average), and both times I felt I was way over my head. But both experiences taught me how to delegate, how to plan, and how to work with a volunteer group of individuals who just might have very different visions of what a centennial book should be.

Those experiences prepared me for working with senior management—and with Price Waterhouse, at the time—to plan, create, and produce annual financial reports (twenty-six in all) under strict guidelines for my employer's stockholders.

I learned how to work within an established "system" (yes, church congregations and financial auditing firms definitely have their own unique "systems") to get a job done. It's something I had not learned in college but needed in order to work with administrative people as a communicator in the secular world.

And, through volunteering in these two church congregations, I found that I enjoyed helping make the established "system" work well for everyone involved. I had found my career niche.

Not All Volunteer Work Is the Same When Evaluating a Job Candidate

There is volunteering, and then there is volunteering. Some volunteer projects can be substantive and genuinely lead toward developing necessary work habits, skills, and experience. Some may not.

You will need to find out about the candidate's volunteer work history to decide whether to take it into consideration when making a hiring decision.

What's Your Incentive to Value Volunteer Experience?

But why bother with making sure a job candidate's volunteer experience is legitimate? Why not just hire the person with the best, more traditional background? You can do that, but you will want to look at his volunteer history, too. It's in your best interest.

Most volunteers do volunteer work simply because they like to work. If they want to relax, they can do that on their own. If they want money, they have to trade labor for pay. But the incentive for those who volunteer (assuming it's not a mandatory community service program) is that they care about a cause and want to work for it.

Someone who volunteers is already a better applicant because he or she is a self-starter who values work and is self-motivated and committed.

It's a mistake to discount volunteering as not "serious work" or to believe that listing volunteer experience in a resume is an attempt to mislead you. Volunteers are the "above-and-beyond" workers you are seeking. As Peg Cheng, an academic advisor for the University of Washington, Seattle, points out, "Volunteering shows initiative and compassion."

Cheng spotlights internships in particular. "Often," she says, "interns do substantial, valuable work for an organization." She explains that they are what she calls "high-end" volunteers, whose work on boards and in grant writing and so forth requires professional-level skills— knocking down the common belief that volunteering generally involves low skills.

Characteristics of "Real" Volunteer Work

The quick answer to "How do I decide if a volunteer job really means this individual has work experience?" is the same as with a paid job. You know what sustained, substantive work looks like. Stability, reliability, responsibility, and performance all can be revealed in work of any kind.

Volunteer Work Needs to Be Relevant

It is important to know when to take volunteer experience on a job applicant's resume seriously to ensure that qualified job candidates with disabilities get an even chance at your company's openings.

Has the applicant used volunteer work to develop the skills you seek in the ideal candidate for the open job?

Some paid summer job experiences allow these characteristics to surface, but others do not. Even within the same job (e.g., summer camp counselor), you will find goof-offs and responsible kids as well as supervisors who are lax and supervisors with firm hands. You already have procedures for sorting out these applicants. Apply the same standards to those who highlight volunteer experience.

You may be tempted to dismiss volunteer experience on the basis that "there are no volunteer jobs relevant to our industry." You may be surprised at the breadth of volunteer projects available today. Not every one involves just stuffing envelopes or answering phones.

Here are two good places for getting a sense of today's volunteering opportunities: VolunteerMatch, at www.volunteermatch.org, and Idealist, at www.idealist.org. Look at the variety of fields and job responsibilities and check the complexity of many of those opportunities.

Besides, in a lot of cases, it's the work (not the industry) that counts on a resume. Does it matter to you where an applicant got his experience? Look on Idealist.org for volunteer projects that involve two volunteer opportunities far removed from stuffing envelopes: plumbing and tax accounting. One search found fourteen plumbing projects and sixty-four that were related to tax accounting (and that does not account for the hundreds of individual IRS tax help-center volunteer positions).

As with any other applicant, you can ask the person who defines her volunteer projects as experience to describe the work she did as a volunteer in terms applicable to the work she would do at your company. Volunteer work can be assessed right along with paid work when you know what went into it. For instance, if you read or hear the following, do you really care if pay was involved? "Managed four marketing events, each with up to 2,000 in attendance, which required coordinating registration, topics, and speakers with twelve committee members, including the marketing association's president and dean of business administration."

In fact, it is more likely she performed this work on her own initiative, drawing from her own talents. In a paid job, she may have been only an aide to a team performing the work and under the direction of a higher-up.

Sharp job seekers take steps to identify job titles that most closely reflect the work they did as a volunteer and to describe the work as they would for a "real" job. So look closely at the job titles under the "Volunteer Experience" heading of the resumes that come to your attention.

The University of Rhode Island community service program instructs students to document their volunteer experience well. In a study module called "Turning Your Volunteer Experience into Quality Material for Your Resume and Interview," it recommends that students compile portfolios of their volunteer work with reference letters, evaluations from supervisors, and even photos taken of them volunteering.

You certainly can ask for just this sort of evidence from your job candidate so you can evaluate for yourself his volunteer work experience and how "serious" it was.

But beware of the inclination to discount volunteer experience because the "job titles" involved don't match those used in paid jobs. Even the paid professional running the program most likely is "under-identified" as a "volunteer coordinator," when, in fact, he does a great deal more than just schedule the work.

Following are several more characteristics of a substantive volunteer project more than worth your consideration—gleaned from the professional volunteer resource managers involved in the CyberVPM online discussion network. These professional volunteer resource managers recommend looking for experience in well-organized programs with:

- A paid professional volunteer resource manager in charge of the program
- A volunteer screening and training procedure
- Position descriptions for volunteers
- Written volunteer performance evaluations
- Volunteer hours tracking
- Evidence of providing substantive work experience that uses and develops the volunteers' work skills
- Other evidence that the organization makes the most effective use of community involvement in pursuit of its mission

Look for service-learning programs and internships and other volunteer programs that are specifically dedicated to substantive work. AmeriCorps and similar programs have high standards for performance and responsibility.

But, more than anything, look for the applicant who is inspired and enlightened by her volunteer experience and is able to demonstrate this energy and commitment in an articulate and illustrative manner.

Is she taking full advantage of her volunteer opportunities to develop these less "trainable" qualities: reliability, cooperation, punctuality, focus, organization, and collaboration? Does that become apparent during your discussions with her?

With a basic understanding of how to comply with the ADA and how to consider volunteering as experience, you're now ready to go recruit job candidates with a disability on a face-to-face basis.

How to Locate Job Candidates with Disabilities on the Local Level

Steve Kendall, MR Atlanta West, cites a typical predicament for recruiters—a dilemma he has encountered many times during his 21 years in the recruiting business. Companies are continually being reviewed to see if they are hiring people fairly and often want to hire people who qualify as Equal Employment Opportunity (EEO) candidates. However, hiring managers can't ask if a job candidate qualifies for EEO without being open to a lawsuit for illegal hiring practices. They cannot ask if an individual is qualified due to being disabled, a minority, over age 40, and so on.

"My advice to [job] candidates is that they not hide their EEO status and volunteer the information," Kendall says. "It certainly cannot hurt—and could actually be an asset."

Another solution to this problem is to make sure job seekers who may qualify as EEO candidates (including those with disabilities) have access to your job announcements.

You can hope individuals with disabilities are in line with everyone else to find out about your openings through classified ads, job sites, placement services, professional networks, and job fairs. But you can't rely on it. You must make a special effort to reach qualified job candidates who happen to have a disability.

Extend the Reach of Your Job Postings

To create a more inclusive workplace, your company's job announcements must reach job seekers with disabilities.

Those with disabilities, after all, are not centralized. They are a diverse group of individuals who are dealing with specific disabilities in specific ways. Even within a specific disability (such as those restricting physical mobility), there are incredible variations in terms of type, severity, and need. And these individuals are scattered throughout every sector of society.

They come from every subset of humanity: gender, age, race, ethnicity, sexual preference, education, religion, ability, interests, politics, income, values, and so on. They often receive services from disability organizations, but they are even more likely to form relationships with groups that address other interests, such as politics, hobbies, worship, classes, professions, or sports.

Still, if you're recruiting on a local level, there are ways to make sure your job announcements are reaching qualified job candidates with disabilities. In your hometown, there are three main recruitment tools you can use to reach job candidates with disabilities: job placement/ vocational services, community social services, and consumer/affinity groups.

Job Placement/Vocational Services

- ⊘ Check your state or provincial vocational rehabilitation programs. The goal of state vocational rehabilitation agencies in the United States, for instance, is to help individuals with disabilities to become employed. To that end, these agencies (with the support of their federal partners) stand ready to provide employers with qualified job candidates with disabilities to meet the workforce needs of American business. See http://www.ed.gov/rschstat/research/pubs/vrpractices/ busdev.html to reach the vocational rehabilitation person in your state whose job it is to work with you in successfully locating, hiring, and retaining individuals with disabilities for your work group.

- ⊘ Consider veterans who have been injured or wounded. There are 2.9 million disabled vets in the United States, including 180,000 from the recent wars in the Middle East—a number that continues to rise. See http://www.cbsnews.com/stories/ 2008/05/11/national/main4086442.shtml?source=RSSattr= Health_4086442. For information about hiring an injured or wounded veteran, contact Jim Arrington, Manager, REALifelines Program, at the Military Severely Injured Center at (202) 693-4724 or e-mail him at arrington.james@dol.gov.

- ⊘ Develop contacts at local university/college student employment and placement services and job fairs—as well as disabled student services departments on college campuses.

- ⊘ Learn about local job fairs sponsored by disability organizations.

- ⊘ Check employment listings in disability publications.

- ⊘ Contact your mayor's office about municipal work programs.

Community Social Services

- Contact your local community information center or United Way to find social service organizations for various disabilities (many have programs to inform the public about the abilities and rights of people with disabilities, promote self-determination for individuals, and offer training in independent living skills).

- Ask about programs dedicated to helping people with disabilities pursue a variety of interests (including arts, recreation, and sports).

Consumer/Affinity Groups

- Get to know people who are active in state and local programs for consumer/advocacy groups, such as National Federation of the Blind, at http://www.nfb.org; American Council of the Blind, at http://www.acb.org; Blinded Veterans Association, at http://www.bva.org; and other such organizations.

- Check clubs for people with disabilities who share certain recreational or social interests, such as blind amateur radio operators or wheelchair basketball players.

Your state's Business Leadership Network (BLN) is also an invaluable source of just about anything you need to make your workplace inclusive of talented, committed employees who have disabilities. Join your state's BLN. You can start by finding out whether your state has a network. Check the U.S. Business Leadership Network (USBLN®) directory at http://www.usbln.org/affiliates.html.

State BLNs have a variety of tools designed to help businesses become more inclusive. They are useful sources of information about disability awareness trainers, adaptive technology companies, available guest speakers, state regulations, and tax incentives. They also provide great opportunities for networking and mentorships. Many offer publications, videos, or other tools to help you. Most organize training events for their members. They also provide advice and tools for job seekers with disabilities.

You can also contact your chamber of commerce to find out if your city or state has organizations similar to a BLN.

> ### How People with Disabilities Find Jobs
> The 1994 Lou Harris poll of 1000 people with disabilities reported that employed adults with disabilities were much more likely to have found their jobs through personal contacts than through structured services. Only 4 percent reported that special programs for people with disabilities had assisted them in finding employment, while 5 percent reported that generic employment services had assisted them in finding a job.
> —From National Council on Disability's
> "Achieving Independence: The Challenge for the 21st Century"

The easiest way to check up on the disability employment track records of your competitors and other businesses, by the way, is to look at your local BLN membership list or similar document. A more challenging (but, at the same time, more revealing) means is simply looking at their websites. The really challenging part is figuring out how to find the sites of those competitors whose Web addresses you don't already have. A good start would be checking online "yellow pages" sites or local online business directories.

When you find a competitor's site, check the "Careers" or "Employment Opportunities" section to read about its diversity policy and check for inclusion of disabilities in its HR initiatives.

Also pay attention to competitors who participate in job fairs. How inclusive are they in their job fair presence? How effectively do they use job fairs, which are typically local in scope, in recruiting job candidates with disabilities?

Using Job Fairs to Recruit Candidates with a Disability

Be sure to do everything you can to level the playing field at a job fair so you won't miss those top-notch candidates who may be disabled but may have just the right skills and experience to help your company (instead of one of your top competitors) continue to succeed.

A job fair is mostly for information gathering. It's not necessarily a place where actual hiring gets done. You probably attend a job fair to assess the current availability, skills, and salary expectations of job seekers in general. A job seeker may attend to see what prospects he'll have before he leaves his current job or to gather data for the salary-negotiation phase of finding a new job.

But hiring does happen. Sometimes it happens right at the fair.

When the job fair has been specifically planned for disabled job candidates, however, the veneer is somewhat thicker. It's likely some companies are there only for public relations purposes: "See how inclusive we are!" or the more sinister: "Hey, we tried to hire disabled people, but none of them were qualified."

One subscriber to the BlindJob e-mail discussion group aired her skepticism about the "reality" of job fairs for disabled job seekers. "I have some vision, so sometimes I stand to the side of the booth and listen to the vendors speak to job seekers," she says, "and I notice that they speak differently to blind people."

She adds, "I have attended the President's Committee [on Employment of People with Disabilities] job fair three times here in Washington, D.C., and I've never heard of blind people hired from the fair."

Although she knows it would violate the law, she says she almost wishes the recruiters would come right out and say they don't intend to hire her. "I have been to job fairs," she continues, "(where), for the most part, companies just talk enough to you to pacify you and to hurry you off. They always tell you they aren't looking to fill the position you're seeking, or (they) give you their information and hurry you away. I would rather hear the truth. I am not a stupid person."

The more optimistic answer is that these disability-focused job fairs are as "for real" as any other job fair. So some people will be hired. It is up to the organizations involved and their recruiters to make sure their recruiting efforts at these fairs are not a waste of time for everyone involved.

The bottom line is this: Avoid having a booth at a job fair geared toward disabled job seekers if your organization is not serious about hiring people with disabilities. But you, as a recruiter, could attend anyway. It's your opportunity to assess the pool of job candidates with disabilities.

However, with a little knowledge and forethought, a job fair (disability focused or not) can be a winner for both potential employers and employees.

How to Ensure Accessibility at Job Fairs

Effective communication, of course, is critical at any job fair, but, when you are designing your booth and developing your approach to attract any and all qualified job candidates (including those with disabilities), effective communication becomes more than just speech. It's a matter of accessibility.

Here's what you can do to make sure you are accessible at a job fair.

- ⊘ Include your organization's website and social-networking addresses in all marketing materials about your participation in the job fair. This helps people with visual, hearing, and mobility disabilities prepare for the fair beforehand, saving them time because they will be able to navigate directly to the booths that are of most interest to them. It will also save you time because you won't be discussing basic information with people who turn out not to be interested in your available jobs.

- ⊘ Make sure the organization hosting the job fair promotes the event not only to disability organizations but to the community at large. There is no "Disabled Central" where you can reach all disabled people. They are in the same work sites, stores, clubs, community meetings, places of worship, schools, movie theaters, and other community gathering places as everyone else. They don't "flock together."

- ⊘ Be prepared. Learn about disability etiquette, put your materials in accessible formats (as explained later), and talk to employees already in your company who have a disability to get their tips about accessibility. Check your personal beliefs—most often misconceptions—about what it is like to be disabled. You'll then be set to meet the candidates on a level playing field.

- ⊘ Include a person with a disability at the job fair—if that person is a member of your recruiting team. But it is not a good idea to assume that every disabled person is knowledgeable about disabilities. The person you include must know the current job market; how people with disabilities use assistive technology; and the current guidelines about discrimination, accommodation, and confidentiality.

- ⊘ Design your booth to be accessible for job candidates with a variety of disabilities. Keep the front of your booth free of obstacles for those who use crutches, wheelchairs, or scooters. An obstacle-free, table-height counter with easily movable chairs is an ideal area for completing applications for those individuals. Play a video about your organization (as long as it does not interfere with conversation) so individuals who have visual impairments can identify your booth. For those with hearing impairments, use visuals within your booth to show what types of jobs you have open.

⊘ Encourage the sponsor of the fair to recruit volunteers to act as guides. For those who read Braille, a Braille map of the fair is extremely helpful. For others, a simple large-print or audio list of companies and their booth locations may suffice. At your own booth, have staff on hand to help job seekers fill out forms and so forth.

How to Hold a Conversation with a Person Who Has a Disability

You don't need to shout, even if a job seeker is hearing impaired (she is most likely a lip-reader). You need not avoid words like "see" or "look" if the person has a visual impairment. Talk directly to the individual with a disability—not to a companion who may be accompanying her. If the individual is using a wheelchair or scooter, pull up a chair so you can sit and converse with her on the same eye level.

Avoid being sweeter and more condescending to someone just because that person is disabled. Says one woman, "I don't know which offends me more—people being rude or people being extra, extra nice."

While speaking to a visually impaired person when there are many others about, use his name. Most job fairs give participants name tags. If you turn your attention elsewhere or walk away, let him know so he doesn't end up talking to the air.

There are other guidelines that specifically apply to the job fair setting. For instance, don't start a conversation with an explanation of why the person may not be interested in specific jobs. One person with a visual impairment talking to a corporate recruiter was greeted with doubts about whether she could handle the travel involved. Although she was highly qualified and had more than twenty years of experience in the positions currently open, she was instantly told that, in her words, she "would have to travel sometimes every week, and that possibly my family wouldn't want me to be gone for long periods of time—

that maybe going to unfamiliar towns, airports, and hotels could be bothersome for me."

When her efforts to counter the recruiter's objections were met only with frustration, she says she "walked around the booth and waited for somebody to visit him. He was completely different with a sighted candidate. He told her that the travel was minimal." The recruiter's own assumptions created barriers where there were none. He could have described the travel requirements and waited for her to state any concerns she might have had.

Of course, you will not want to ask personal questions of an individual who is disabled—any more than you would of a nondisabled candidate. Avoid asking how the person became disabled or whether there's a cure for that person's disability. Treat the person like any other job seeker in this regard.

Try not to be put off by the adaptive devices some blind job seekers may use. For example, you may see individuals using a small forehead-mounted camera to read information on your whiteboards or in the back of your booth. This small camera provides a clear and focused magnified image on attached "glasses." Except in appearance, it's basically the same as corrective lenses for people with correctable sight problems.

Let other visually impaired people waiting to talk to you know you see them and will get to them as soon as you are finished talking to the person in front of them. If you can, ascertain what medium they use to read and invite them to look over your recruitment materials while they wait.

How to Make Your Printed Materials Accessible

Yes, providing materials in Braille is a good idea. But there are two very important things to know about Braille. Only a small percentage of blind and visually impaired people use Braille. Your emphasis should probably be on large-print materials, audio recordings, and CDs. The CDs will allow candidates to use their own computers to read the material however they prefer: Braille output, screen magnification, or speech output.

For the items you do provide in Braille, don't assume you can just use Braille translation software to convert your existing documents. This software is only the first step in Braille transcription. Braille does not substitute letter for letter but is far more complex (with rules that need human interpretation). If you choose to provide Braille, have your materials prepared by a certified Braille transcriptionist. Check your local library for information.

Ask each job seeker who requests your materials what medium he prefers. By demonstrating your awareness of the various accessible formats, you communicate your company's interest in hiring people with disabilities, and you put the individual at ease.

Depending on the person's amount of vision, he may reach out and take the materials you offer or need you to put them right into his hands. Tell him what the items are as you hand them over. You can also use a clock-face example to tell him where an item is: "The company brochure in large print is at two o'clock to you."

Consider Braille and large-print business cards, too, which highlight your company website—the one all-accessible vehicle you can use to deliver follow-up information to job candidates who have visual, mobility, or hearing impairments.

A Disability Job Fair's Added Benefit

Those with disabilities have always been in the workforce, but adaptive technology has been changing rapidly, opening up all but a small selection of career paths for them. A disabled-focused job fair itself is a great opportunity to learn how individuals with various physical disabilities use adaptations to perform at the same standard as nondisabled employees.

Often companies or agencies that provide training, adaptive technology, and career services for disabled people have booths alongside your own. Talk to them, try out their equipment, and ask for advice. Ask attendees who use the products to show you how they work.

And don't miss the chance to interview job seekers with various disabilities during and after a job fair. The candidates themselves are a great resource for learning about the adaptive techniques they use to live independent lives. Ask: "How do you do this?" and "How do you overcome that?" in relation to job tasks. You will learn how they have adapted to their various disabilities so they can perform well in a workplace setting.

After the Job Fair

It is up to you and your recruitment team to make sure the job fair doesn't end once the materials are gathered up and stored for the next event. Job seekers with disabilities (and their resumes) need to be put through the same process you follow for other candidates so your best prospects come to the top of your follow-up list. Such follow-up is an important key to making your investment of time and money in a job fair pay off.

Next, let's look at how you can expand your best-prospect list by extending your scope and taking your recruitment online.

Locating Job Candidates with Disabilities Online

How do you find talented job seekers with disabilities beyond your local community?

eSight Careers Network asked four job recruiters on recruitersnetwork.com and at the ACCESS job fair in Seattle, Washington, to think about the perfect tool to help them get their job opportunity information out to people with disabilities so they can reach the broadest possible pool of qualified candidates.

Recruiters need tools that give them access to information about job seekers who meet the qualifications for open positions set by their companies or clients. The individual resume is the primary tool for this task. Many mainstream job sites on the Web are, in essence, huge databases, much like a massive filing system. They have been popular with recruiters because, unlike paper files, they can be easily searched to find candidates with unique characteristics or qualifications.

The recruiters eSight interviewed expressed a strong preference for this type of tool over the more arduous and time-consuming task of simply finding places to post jobs. Since these mainstream websites allow job posting too, they offer another advantage for recruiters.

It is not surprising that this group of recruiters dreamed of a similar tool for finding job seekers with disabilities. Many referred to it as "one-stop shopping." They want websites that offer easy job posting and an easy job search for qualified candidates. And they want it to be free.

Several recruiters at the Seattle job fair mentioned state job banks (see http://www.jobbankinfo.org) as a mainstream model for any job-matching website with a disability focus. For recruiters, the most popular features of these sites allow them to:

- Search through an extensive resume database
- Post unlimited jobs

- ⊘ Get tips for creating job listings
- ⊘ Create a resume scout to search out potential employees

By itself, the fact that any job announcements would, by definition, be going specifically to disabled job seekers would solve the problem of making sure disabled people have access to the jobs you have open.

Such a tool dedicated to disabled candidates would attract even more recruiters if it had some added features. Robert, the recruiter for Washington Mutual at a job fair, dreamed of a site that would connect all the disability job sites—allowing him to submit one job announcement and have it posted on all.

Others said their ideal site would include articles about disabilities, jobs, and accommodations—written specifically for recruiters. Recruiters felt that they would be more comfortable engaging in a conversation with a disabled candidate and then presenting him as a candidate to a hiring manager if they were prepared with details about specific disabilities and what adaptations can be made to make certain jobs accessible.

For instance, one said, "I think I'd like to go somewhere where I can learn about the candidate and his disability, so I know what he can do. Maybe if I could talk to a rehab counselor or something." Her eyes widened when it was suggested that she ask the candidate himself. "Well, yeah, that would work," she admitted. "And it would be easier and faster!"

Recruiters from Safeco Insurance expressed a preference for advice that is "not sugarcoated."

One of those in the quartet said: "When disability information is too 'nice,' it doesn't help me feel comfortable. I would feel much more at ease talking to someone who has difficulty speaking if I knew not only how to do it but how not to."

Connecting Online

Employers who recognize the rewards of employing qualified people with disabilities are often puzzled about how to locate those people. The Internet provides resources that can help you gain an edge over your competitors.

Here are several existing resources that match some (if not all) of these recruiters' definitions of ideal recruiting tools—particularly the functions of learning, posting, searching, and scouting (functions you also probably value as an HR executive or hiring manager).

Job-Posting Sites

- ⊘ GettingHired is a social-networking community and job portal partner with the USBLN, a national business organization currently representing sixty BLN affiliates in thirty-six states including the District of Columbia and more than 5,000 employers using a "business-to-business" strategy to promote the business imperative of including people with disabilities in the workforce. See http://www.usbln.org.

- ⊘ The Hire DisAbility Solutions career site (http://hireds.monster.com) has teamed up with Monster.com to provide you with the most current career placement information to ensure you have fast access to the best opportunities.

- ⊘ ABILITYJobs.com (http://www.jobaccess.org) offers job and resume posting, a job search agent, a resume builder, and other career search tools. It includes a tool for applying to companies directly via the site.

- ⊘ Disaboomjobs.com (http://www.disaboomjobs.com/companies) showcases jobs for people with disabilities. It also features companies that position themselves as great places to work.

- ⊘ About.com's Resources for People with Disabilities (http://jobsearch.about.com/od/disabilities/Resources_for_People_with_Disabilities.htm) includes links to job sites for people with disabilities in the United States and elsewhere.

General Diversity Employment Sites

- ⊘ Recruiters Network (http://www.recruitersnetwork.com)
- ⊘ *Diversity/Careers* magazine (http://www.diversitycareers.com)
- ⊘ DiversityLink (http://www.diversitylink.com)

Informational Sites That Focus on Disability Employment Issues

- ⊘ eSight Careers Network (http://www.esight.org) is a cross-disability online community for addressing disability employment issues.

- ⊘ Lighthouse International (http://www.lighthouse.org/services -and-assistance/career) offers practical, real-world articles for and about employees and entrepreneurs who have visual impairments. It also includes information specifically for employers and recruiters about how to effectively tap the potential people with disabilities offer as employees.

- ⊘ HireDiversity (http://www.hirediversity.com) is a general diversity employment resources site that has news about employment of people with disabilities. It also includes job and resume postings, a job search agent, a resume builder, and other career search tools.

Staffing Services

These staffing services specialize in recruiting and placing qualified disabled and other minority and disadvantaged workers:

- ⊘ Bender Consulting Services (http://www.benderconsult.com/ index2.html) is not strictly a staffing service but, rather, a company that employs disabled individuals who provide consulting services on computer and information technology issues. BCS can place consultants throughout the United States. Its founder, Joyce Bender, received honors for her work in disabilities and employment from President Bill Clinton.

- ⊘ HirePotential (http://www.hirepotential.com) is a national consulting firm that works with corporations committed to diversity by assisting them with integrating, accommodating, retaining, and employing people with disabilities, mature workers, veterans, and individuals from other niche groups.

- ⊘ Just One Break (http://www.justonebreak.com) has been placing qualified employees with disabilities in New York City for sixty years.

- ⊘ Local Goodwill Industries (http://www.goodwill.org) and Easter Seals (http://www.easterseals.org) are programs that provide on-site employment opportunities and direct financial assistance.

- ⊘ Kelly Services (http://www.kellyservices.com) is a regular participant at job fairs for people with disabilities, so it may be a promising source of applicants. Tell your usual staffing outsource service, by the way, that you expect it to send you qualified temps and job applicants who have a disability.

Resume-Posting Sites for Qualified Disabled Job Seekers

To find sites designed specifically to help companies and qualified job seekers with disabilities find each other, visit these resume-posting sites:

- ⊘ JobAccess (http://www.jobaccess.org) offers job and resume posting, a job search agent, a resume builder, and other career search tools specifically for job seekers with disabilities. It includes a tool for applying to companies directly via the site.

- ⊘ Workforce Recruitment Program (http://www.dol.gov/odep/ programs/workforc.htm) specifically seeks to help employers target disabled students in on-campus recruiting efforts. You can search for candidates based on criteria that you select. It offers its database of "Top Talent from Top Colleges" (disabled job seekers) on a free CD as well as on its website.

- ⊘ WORKink (http://www.workink.com) offers advice about disability employment and access to resumes from disabled job seekers across Canada.

- ⊘ Diversity Staffing Group (http://www.diversity-services.com) matches qualified individuals for temporary or temporary to full-time positions, payroll services, full-time and executive-level positions, and employee leasing.

- ⊘ The National Business & Disability Council (http://www. business-disability.com) is the leading resource for employers seeking to integrate people with disabilities into the workplace and companies seeking to reach them in the consumer marketplace.

Social Media Sites

Once you have located interesting job candidates (online or in person), you can often use social media networks to find more information about them.

Commissioned by CareerBuilder.com, Harris Interactive surveyed 2,667 HR professionals in June 2009. About 45 percent of them said they were using social-networking sites (such as LinkedIn, Twitter, Facebook, and StumbleUpon) to research job candidates. An additional 11 percent said they planned to implement social media screening in the very near future.

While many recruiters now use LinkedIn as a "must use" tool for locating active and passive candidates for jobs (especially those with unusual qualifications), the real benefit of social media from a hiring standpoint is the opportunity to get to know about a prime job candidate before you even meet him in person—or, at least, before you make an offer.

As an employer, you rarely hire people for just their skills. You are looking for skills plus a well-rounded individual who fits well with your work group. A job candidate's social media presence gives you insight into his interests, communication styles, work habits, work/life balance, and so forth—information you usually didn't have at your fingertips in the twentieth century.

Essential skills in establishing online relationships include making and receiving recommendations as a networking strategy, asking and answering questions, forming and following online groups, and requesting and making introductions. You can now evaluate a job candidate's "soft skills" by watching how she handles herself online before you make a hiring decision.

And seriously consider a job candidate who has effectively used social networking (writing an effective profile, answering questions, gaining introductions, participating in groups) to specifically gain your personal attention about a job you may have open or a function you may need that is not, at first glance, readily apparent. That kind of initiative (and social-networking savvy) may be the mark of a winner.

Yet, that's only part of the story. Yes, online networking (either actively participating or passively listening) can be a real advantage for you on the hiring side of recruitment. But a recruitment environment that includes a social-networking component also further levels the playing field for job candidates with all types of disabilities.

Why? Walking, talking, seeing, or hearing (thanks to technology) is not required to participate fully in an online discussion (and perhaps to stand out due to insight, expression, camaraderie, leadership, and so on).

Effectively using targeted social networking as part of your online recruiting efforts helps you locate talented job candidates with a disability. As mentioned, GettingHired (http://www.usbln.org) is a social-networking community as well as a job portal specifically for people with disabilities. It's an excellent private-sector starting point for your disability-specific social-networking and online recruitment initiative.

Recruiting Qualified Job Candidates with Disabilities on College Campuses

If, as a college campus recruiter for a major corporation, you've had a nagging suspicion that somehow you're missing the best student candidates for positions at your company, it's very possible that you are. If you don't find and visit students who have disabilities, you have probably missed some talented, motivated people.

Why would they be "motivated"? When you live in a world that hasn't quite figured out that it's the talent you hire and not the disability, once you have a good job you tend to keep it and give it your all.

Jim Rawls, for example, has twice been named teacher of the year in his community and has had a stellar career. His potential was obvious even before he landed his first teaching job because he excelled in college and won the backing of the head of the education department.

Yet, because he is visually impaired, he says it took him 240 interviews before someone would give him a chance to prove himself. Think of all that wasted time—not just for him, his students, and his community, but for all the principals who overlooked what could have been one of their finest appointments.

By the way, nearly 2.2 million (11 percent) emerging U.S. college students have a disability. That's not an insignificant number of students to ignore. See http://www.earnworks.com/BusinessCase/human_cap_level2.asp.

Make Sure You Meet the Best Recruits

If you're recruiting on campuses without meeting students with disabilities, you may be missing the best recruits. Don't waste a recruiting trip to college campuses by missing prime applicants with disabilities.

Use the "best practices" discussed here to help you meet prime prospects.

Many major companies have successfully recruited students with disabilities on campus. For example, Katy Jo Meyer, technical recruiter for Microsoft Corporation, expresses her company's commitment to tap the potential of people with disabilities this way:

> **Our goal is to continue to create the most multicultural workplace in the high-tech industry. A diverse workplace enables us**

to attract and retain the most qualified employees and better serve the needs of a wide range of customers, including customers with disabilities. . . . We believe that people from the various disability-related communities provide us with valuable perspectives on how we develop products and services, how we market them, and how we deal with issues of customer satisfaction. In other words, we benefit greatly in terms of innovation by having these viewpoints present among our employee workforce.

In other words, Microsoft realizes that its workforce and its customer base are one and the same and that its marketing success depends on a broad and representative workforce.

Microsoft's Meyer says:

In the technology industry, people with disabilities are a large customer audience for us, so it makes strong sense to have that population represented when we're building the products. When we are out on campus, we're looking for students who are passionate about building software. We're interested in talking to anyone who fits that profile.

Meyer's statement may sound very much like your own approach. But, if you have not tried to broaden your recruitment to include students with disabilities, you may be a bit unsure about how to go about it.

In fact, the problem may not be about you or your knowledge. It is very common for a college or university to have an office called "Student Placement" or "Career Center" but send its graduating students with disabilities back to Disabled Student Services (DSS) when they seek career help.

Be sure to contact the DSS office when you plan to visit a campus. Often the career center and DSS offices on campuses do not work together very closely or at all. If you contact DSS offices in advance of campus visits, those offices can then send out bulletins or e-mails to students with disabilities to encourage them to go to meet with you.

Often, then, the message to the students, to recruiters, to hiring managers, and to other students is that people with disabilities belong in a different workforce. Part of the challenge is getting past the idea that the tools that permit accessibility belong in one place. DSS often does not have access to all the tools and expertise available at a campus career center, which serves all students. The career center's services should be accessible.

Unfortunately this "should" doesn't meet what you need when you're on campus. When a school does not provide you access to all students (including those with disabilities) in a logical place (a career center), you have to do extra work to find qualified job candidates with disabilities. You need to figure out where the disabled students are. Since they are not segregated, that may be a challenge.

You can start with programs that serve students with disabilities. Just about every campus has a DSS office. In addition, there may be specialized programs such as the University of Washington's DO-IT program. Government vocational rehabilitation programs based in each state or province can direct you to their own contacts at schools their clients attend. Further, you can check student activity programs for clubs and other associations geared to students with disabilities.

Here's how Meyer describes Microsoft's on-campus efforts:

> As far as targeting students with disabilities in particular, our team is actively working with organizations such as Career Opportunities for Students with Disabilities (http://www.cosdonline.org) to increase the number of college candidates with disabilities flowing through our recruitment process. We have also fostered relationships with colleges and universities with a high population of students with disabilities through posting job openings, attending career fairs, delivering company presentations, and [conducting] on-campus interviews.

You may want to add some initiatives of your own. Contact your best referral sources, department heads, student leaders, and so forth and tell them you want to make sure you are meeting promising students with a variety of disabilities. Arrange special on-campus recruitment efforts.

Of course, career fairs can be part of your effort. The trick is making sure that everyone hears about your presence at a career fair and that everyone knows he or she is invited. Making connections with leaders among students with disabilities can help you find the best ways to get the word out.

One such leader, for example, is Alicia Verlager, who, as a Boston student with a visual impairment, became a well-known advocate for converting books into electronic formats. She had this to say about her experiences with campus events:

> Getting news about events on campus is extremely frustrating for blind students on the campus where I attend school. The basic method of advertising is by putting up posters, which are useless to the blind (and most of the low-vision also). Since most of the bulletin boards are in high-traffic areas and people are usually standing in front of them, you don't even notice the bulletin boards. I check the news page on the campus website frequently, but I have missed many events.
>
> The only way I know there is an event is that suddenly there are lots of tables in the very narrow hall that leads to the Disabled Student Services office. This makes getting down the hall difficult with a cane and impossible with a wheelchair. Supposedly, the Disabled Student Services office has our e-mail addresses, but they only send a newsletter at the end of the semester. I mostly try to cultivate networks with professors who know me or other students with similar interests.
>
> The really disturbing aspect of this is [that] many opportunities for jobs occur before graduation, through networking, internships, etc., and waiting until graduation often puts a student at a disadvantage, aside from the fact that the student has missed many opportunities to make an impression while a possibly interested employer can see her or his work.

It's debatable whether holding two separate job fairs or other events, one for everyone and one for students with disabilities, is the best way to go. It can give the impression that students with disabilities are not meant or expected to be at the main job fair.

Terri, a campus disability specialist in Arizona, points out:

> Separate is not always equal!
>
> I am in favor of the DSS offices in universities and colleges working hand in hand with the Career Services office on their respective campuses.
>
> I have been working at the university for over eight years and my experience has been that most students with disabilities [who] land jobs in companies such as Microsoft, Motorola,

AT&T, Veterans Medical Centers, family social services agencies, etc., have done so through mainstream recruitment opportunities. That isn't to say that the DSS offices don't play a significant role in assisting these students with preparation and readiness to go out and participate in these mainstream career recruitment fairs.

Some of the issues that students who are blind or visually impaired face include: awareness of resume format(s) and layout, the most current and appropriate dress, personal grooming, body language and feedback on any mannerisms that are inappropriate. These are simply things that persons who are sighted learn by watching others, so it's a matter of a lack of access to this information for students who are blind or visually impaired.

But Microsoft's Meyer recognizes the possibilities in recruiting through mainstream as well as DSS avenues. She points out:

Separate recruiting efforts hopefully enable us to access a greater number of candidates with disabilities who possess the kinds of skill sets and experiences we seek. These kinds of job fairs may also provide candidates with some level of comfort that the companies present are ones that willingly provide inclusive environments. However, our past practices have revealed that many of our employees with disabilities have come through mainstream avenues such as college career placement centers, employee referrals, unsolicited applications, etc. Microsoft recognizes that searching for top talent requires using all available resources.

Best Practices

Meyer says Microsoft's approach to its fall recruitment efforts is to target those students graduating and looking for full-time jobs. Its spring recruitment is geared to hiring interns.

"Both full-time and intern hires are made throughout the season," she points out. "During the summer months, we are working with our interns who are at Microsoft, and we're planning for the following year."

Accessibility is the key. She adds:

When recruiting anyone, we want to make sure each person has a world-class experience. When recruiting students with disabilities, we do everything we can to ensure our entire recruiting process is accessible. Some examples of this are conducting an initial interview over Instant Messenger for a student who is deaf instead of a phone interview, providing our job descriptions in alternate formats at a career fair for students who are blind or have low vision, and providing wheelchair-accessible transportation for students who are wheelchair users.

Awareness training also plays an important role at Microsoft. Meyer states:

All of our college recruiters have gone through several training sessions about how to most effectively interact with students with disabilities. We continually strive to provide our recruiters and any other Microsoft employee involved in college recruiting with the awareness and resources they need to effectively work with students with disabilities. Some examples of the resources we provide are general etiquette tips and training videos.

Etiquette tips, for instance, include the following very basic concepts about how to work with people with disabilities:

- ⊘ Ask before offering any assistance and wait for the assistance to be accepted. Don't be offended if the offer is turned down.
- ⊘ Speak directly to the person who has a disability.

The theme in Microsoft's etiquette tips is in this core principle: When in doubt, treat a disabled person with the same respect and consideration you do anyone. For example, if you don't use first names when talking to most of your contacts at job fairs, don't do it with people with disabilities.

Peter Altschul, a consultant on the psychology of change and former diversity manager at Reuters News Service, who also is visually impaired, adds: "The bottom line is that both employers and universities have been involved with diversity efforts for a while now; those best practices that work toward including people from other under-represented populations can be adapted to include students with disabilities."

How to Make Your Screening Process Inclusive

Your application and interview processes, both of which involve screening job candidates, are prime areas for that "best practices" review toward more inclusive recruiting Peter Altschul recommended.

Both areas come under particular scrutiny as phases where mistakes can be made and lawsuits initiated. You may be in the habit of asking yourself: What questions can I ask during this interview? What concerns can I express? In what ways might my personal bias come through? After all, recruitment activities that have the effect of screening out potential applicants with disabilities may violate the ADA, according to the Job Accommodation Network (see http://www.jan.wvu.edu/Erguide/Two.htm#A).

Then, there's public perception. According to a July 2005 University of Massachusetts survey, 92 percent of the American public view companies that hire people with disabilities more favorably than those that do not; 87 percent of the public also agree that they would prefer to give their business to companies that hire people with disabilities.

And, when a company acts irresponsibly, it makes headlines, but when a company acts responsibly and ethically, it builds lasting brand trust (see http://www.earnworks.com/BusinessCase/soc_resp_level2.asp).

When those issues pop into our minds, we sometimes forget to think about the spirit of being inclusive and fair in gaining and interviewing job applicants. Fair hiring processes are intended to remove hiring barriers for the job seeker. But they also can remove barriers to achieving a company's chief objective—to find and retain the best person for the job. Why let misinformation or simply inadequate data rob your company of an employee who will contribute greatly to your organization's success?

When your screening process is stacked against someone who has difficulty completing an application, you simply don't have a way to uncover whether the person is the most highly qualified, committed, and suitable person for the work you need done.

You already have tools in place for recruiting new job candidates. But you must make sure your recruitment tools are accessible for a wide variety of disabilities. Have alternate ways to fill out applications, take tests, and interview people who may have limited vision, hearing, speech, or mobility. For example, make sure your job line has a TTY number for hearing-impaired people.

Take a Proactive Approach

It is important to make every step of your application and interview processes accessible to candidates who, together, can have a variety of hearing, speech, and sight impairments. Use "best practices" so you do not "handicap" your own search for the best person for the job!

To help you identify hidden but built-in barriers that block job candidates just because they may have a disability, consider the specific guidelines for streamlining your application and interviewing procedures discussed in the following sections.

Streamlining Your Application Process

The major disadvantage in the typical job application process for people who are blind or print impaired or have difficulty in manual dexterity is that the materials are almost always in print format. When you meet individuals who, for one reason or another, cannot sit down and fill out a neat paper application in a timely fashion, your whole relationship starts out on the wrong foot.

There are several good alternatives to applications in print format, most of which are quite easy to accomplish:

- Accept a complete resume in lieu of a completed application. You can always contact the person for additional information you need or ask the questions you may have during the interview.

- Allow the person to take the materials home so that he or she may take advantage of a sighted reader's help, use a magnifier, or even use a scanner so the application can be completed using word-processing software and then printed as a hard copy.

- Provide assistance for the applicant in your office. Make sure that the person knows exactly what to do.

- Have large-print versions of materials available at all times for those candidates with low vision. You can produce the application with a larger font. "Official large print" is 14 point, but 18 or more serves a larger group. Or you can enlarge the pages of your standard letter-size application on a photocopier so they are printed on 11- by 17-inch paper.

- ⊘ Provide a cassette-recorded, CD, or electronic version of all the application materials, including any position descriptions, applications, and peripheral information. Be sure the candidate has a means to communicate answers to the application's questions.

- ⊘ Automate your application process by setting it up as a form to submit on your website. Many print-impaired people have computers that are adapted to increase print size or to read text aloud.

Preparing for the Interview

Part of the screening process requires that an applicant demonstrate the ability to do the work, and to do the work the person must be able to get to work. So, unless you plan to have your candidate, disabled or otherwise, work from home, you don't need to do a telephone interview. A face-to-face interview with a disabled candidate who would work in your office is just as important as for any other person who is under consideration for the job.

First of all, relax. This may be one of the first individuals you've interviewed who is disabled, but you can be sure that you are not the first nondisabled person he or she has met. You already know you can't quiz your candidate about issues that may produce at least the appearance of bias on your part.

So, when you meet a visually impaired candidate, for instance, in the waiting room, behave normally. If your extended hand is not taken, just drop it. Don't be embarrassed. You can often avoid such awkwardness by simply stating, "I'm pleased to meet you; let me shake your hand," and then shaking the person's extended hand.

Offer the person a "sighted guide," which, at its heart, is just offering the person your arm. If the person refuses, accept that. Walk the person to the interview room without undue ceremony, only warning him or her of obstacles, if there is obvious need. If the person has a guide dog, you may compliment him or her on the dog but otherwise ignore it. Make sure your other staff members know this, too.

Once in the room, guide the person to a chair. Take the person's hand and put it on the back of the chair. That is all you have to do. If you offer your interviewee coffee, just be sure to put the cup and any sugar or cream where the person can easily reach them. You can say, "The cup is a couple of inches away from your right hand directly in front of you."

If you're interviewing a job candidate with a hearing impairment, you may need a sign language interpreter. For such accommodations, you can assume that savvy job candidates will request them well before the interview.

In moving from the waiting room to the interview room, job candidates who use a wheelchair, scooter, or crutches often appreciate help in opening doors and moving chairs to accommodate their particular mode of mobility.

Here are three additional ways to streamline your organization's job interviewing process for any candidate with a hearing, sight, speech, or mobility impairment:

- Ask at any point if there is anything you can provide to make the application and interview more successful for the candidate. Individuals with a disability are often the best experts regarding their own accommodations.

- Remember that the candidate most likely has had time to adjust to a disability and that you may not be aware of tools and techniques the candidate is using to build a "normal" life. Go into the interview with an open mind.

- Use accessible "surprise" materials. If you give the candidate materials that are not readily accessible to review on the spot, avoid penalizing the person for not being able to review them right then without his or her adaptive equipment.

You may give the person a copy of the job description that includes a list of the essential tasks for the job and ask the person if he or she can perform all of them with or without accommodation. And, if the person volunteers that he or she has a disability, you are free to ask about the accommodations needed, what they do, how they work, and what they cost.

The goal is to make the interview flow as any meeting with a nondisabled job candidate would, so ask the same questions and expect the same high-quality answers you would of a nondisabled applicant.

Let's take a closer look at the job interview from the point of interviewees who have a variety of disabilities.

Four Barriers Job Candidates with a Disability Encounter When They Interview for a Job

The annual professional football draft in the United States is based on uniformly collected statistics that measure on-the-field performance under a variety of conditions (weather, stadium configuration, location). Yet, one factor is constant: The playing field is always level.

Just a 2 percent grade on one end of the field or the other would skew the results and put the competitors (and the teams) involved in the draft at either a potential advantage or disadvantage.

The same holds true for evaluating and selecting job candidates. The recruiting process must be conducted on a level playing field so you end up hiring the right job candidate for the right job—and you don't overlook star performers whose potential would not be readily evident if they were continually battling that extra 2 percent grade.

More than a dozen individuals on eSight's "Swimming in the Mainstream" (SiM) blog discussed how individuals who work within your recruitment process can help make sure the recruiting field is level for job seekers with (and without) a disability.

> ## Conduct Job Interviews as Open Dialogues
>
> What can you do, as an employer, to help create a "level" recruiting field for job candidates with disabilities? Barney, one of the SiM blog participants, writes: "The hiring interview must be an open dialogue. Anything less and I can predict the outcome without too much error."

Following are some snippets from that conversation to illustrate four issues job seekers with disabilities often face in seeking employment, particularly during job interviews. Since these barriers can involve, to some degree, not-deliberate-but-false perceptions on the part of those working within your recruitment process, those barriers are not insurmountable. Resolving these four issues, eSight members say, could give them a fair shot at open jobs. The solution is just a matter of increasing awareness and gaining perspective.

Here are the four issues identified in the SiM blog discussion:

1. Assumptions about disabilities
2. Cart-before-the-horse job preparation

3. The relationship between disability and skills

4. The unresolved internal issues of an employer

So, let's set the stage for more-open job interviews with candidates who have disabilities by highlighting some of the key recommendations SiM bloggers have made for resolving each of these issues.

Assumptions About Disabilities

Mike T.:

> My experience since relocating [from the UK] to Orange County, California, has been decidedly different. At the age of 45, I think age-related discrimination as well as false, negative assumptions concerning my blindness are working against me.
>
> I have to ask the question of employers: "What do I need to do to convince you that I can do a better job than my sighted counterparts?" Come on, step up to the plate, employers, and give me the opportunity to demonstrate that my skill-set can be deployed in your company to add value for you and your customers.
>
> This is certainly not whining. I wouldn't tolerate that from anyone. I just want the opportunity to use my natural, God-given talents to benefit my local community while being responsible to my wife and stretching myself mentally. I want the chance to learn, to grow, to expand into a broader role where I can bring the greatest benefit to the greatest number. Is that too much to ask?

R.M.:

> [Let's] avoid the classic vocational rehab trap: believing that "there are a finite number of jobs that people who are disabled can hold." I have had to create every job that I've had.

Cart-Before-the-Horse Job Preparation

Roger:

> [Resolve this] Catch 22 situation: You want to work, you have skills, but, to be employable, you must have assistive technology compatible with the firms you are applying to. Yet vocational rehab can't provide this assistive technology unless you are already employed in a job that requires this particular assistive technology. Making the

workplace compatible with assistive technology commonly used by individuals who are blind [JAWS, WindowEyes, Magic] is one solution to this common problem.

Jake:

I think one way to have a very successful job interview is to tell the employer about the adaptive technology we use and possibly offer to give a demonstration of that technology. I, for one, having been a JAWS user for several years now, am very willing to demonstrate the program to anyone. One great advantage of JAWS is that a single user can install it on more than one computer at a time. I don't know if this is necessarily true with the new Internet-based authorization scheme, but it is definitely true of the disk-based authorization.

The Relationship Between Disability and Skills

Barney:

The skills to do the job do not exist despite my disability. My disability has simply created additional issues to be resolved and strengths to be tapped before my capability becomes evident.

It is about what I can do, not what I cannot do. No one is hired for what they cannot do. The focus must be on how I can contribute, which means the hiring manager must focus on the person—not the disability.

The Unresolved Internal Issues of an Employer

Barney:

There are a couple of ways to provide the hiring manager with knowledge of my competency and skills:

- ⊘ Offer to do a project for free—not a money maker, but it will demonstrate loud and clear what I am capable of.
- ⊘ Offer to work for a trial period for free—not a money maker but one that says I will put financial stability on the line to prove that I am capable.

Peter:

I think people sort of expect us (and other underrepresented groups as well) to provide advice and work for free.

I think we need to remember that finding a job in nontraditional arenas is a real challenge and that regular failures may have more to do with employer issues than with the skill-set of the applicant with a disability.

After considering these observations from individuals with disabilities who have experience in today's work world, it is apparent that creating a level playing field for your recruitment initiatives has to start with your selection process for those important first job interviews. That preparation, in terms of heightened personal awareness, will help you conduct productive interviews—dialogues in which you and your candidates can be candid and authentic.

QUICK TIPS FROM THIS CHAPTER

⦿ Questions You Always Wanted to Ask

What can you ask a person with a disability during a job interview? You can describe the essential functions of the job and then ask if the person can do the work and how he or she would do it for your company. For more information, see "ADA: Your Responsibilities as an Employer" at http://www.eeoc.gov/facts/ada17.html.

⦿ Current Interpretations of the ADA

Congress expected that the definition of disability under the ADA of 1990 would be interpreted consistently with how courts had applied the definition of disability under the Rehabilitation Act of 1973. That expectation, however, was not fulfilled. Therefore, the ADA was amended (the ADAAA), as of January 1, 2009, to bring the law back to what Congress intended it to be when it passed the ADA in 1990. For more about the ADA and ADAAA, see http://www.eeoc.gov/ada/amendments_notice.html.

⦿ Volunteering as Essential Experience

The most motivated individuals with a disability will probably manage to land internships during college, but, upon graduation, internships are generally not available. That leaves volunteering as one of the few avenues those who graduate from college without jobs still have open for developing their skills and

proving themselves in a work situation. For more
information, see "Employing People with Disabilities" at
http://www.disability.gov/employment/employing_people_with_disabilities.

⊘ When Volunteer Experience Is Real

How can you decide if a volunteer job really means a job candidate
has work experience? Use the same standards you would use for a
paid job. You know what sustained, substantive work looks like.
Stability, reliability, responsibility, and performance all can be
revealed in work of any kind. For more information, see
"Some Skills Transferable from Volunteer to Paid Work" at
http://www.nald.ca/fulltext/heritage/compartne/ExprncE.htm#Volunteer.

⊘ Locating Job Candidates on the Local Level

Employed adults with disabilities are much more likely to have found
their jobs through personal contacts than through structured services.
So, make sure job seekers with disabilities have access to your job
announcements. You can hope they are in line with everyone else to
find out about your openings through classified ads, job sites,
placement services, professional networks, and job fairs. But you
can't rely on it. You must make a special effort to reach this pocket
of qualified job candidates. For more information, see "Strategic
Connections: Recruiting Candidates with Disabilities" at
http://www.dol.gov/odep/pubs/fact/connect.htm.

⊘ Recruiting at a Job Fair

Effective communication, of course, is critical at any job fair, but,
when you are designing your booth and developing your approach
to attract any and all qualified job candidates (including those with
disabilities), effective communication becomes more than just speech.
Ask yourself: Am I and my materials accessible to all job candidates?
For dates and locations of Diversity Recruitment Career Fairs by Equal
Opportunity Publications, see http://www.eop.com/careerfair.html.

⊘ Locating Job Candidates Online

The USBLN is an invaluable source of just about anything you need to
make your workplace inclusive of talented, committed employees who
have disabilities. For more information, see http://www.usbln.org.

⊘ Recruiting on College Campuses

It is very common for a college or university to have an office called "Student Placement" or "Career Center," but to send its graduating students with disabilities back to DSS when they seek career help. Be sure to contact DSS offices in advance of your campus visits so those offices can send out bulletins or e-mails to students with disabilities to encourage them to meet with you. For more information, see "Recruitment of Students with Disabilities" at http://www.neads.ca/en/about/projects/student_leadership/access_to_success/access_aguayo.php.

⊘ Inclusive Screening Processes

When your screening process is stacked against someone who has a disability, you simply don't have a way to uncover whether the person you ultimately hire is the most highly qualified, committed, and suitable person for the work you need done. Why let misinformation or simply inadequate data rob your company of an employee who will contribute greatly to your organization's success? For more information, see "Opening Doors to All Candidates: Tips for Ensuring Access for Applicants with Disabilities" at http://www.dol.gov/odep/pubs/fact/opening.htm.

⊘ Barrier-Free Job Interviews

Creating a level playing field for your recruitment initiatives has to start with your selection process for those important first job interviews. That preparation, in terms of heightened awareness, will help you conduct productive interviews—dialogues in which you and your candidates can be candid and authentic. For more information, see "Focus on Ability: Interviewing Applicants with Disabilities" at http://www.dol.gov/odep/pubs/fact/focus.htm.

Suggestion for Job Interview Topic

Here's your opportunity to turn the table on your job candidates at the end of their interviews to see how they handle an unexpected question. You may ask: "What have you learned during your current search for meaningful work that could help me make my recruitment efforts more effective?"

By doing so, you will show you're open to suggestions. You may get some insight into how to further improve your own recruitment methods. It'll also give you an opportunity to compare how well your top candidates handle ambiguity and risk. You'll be giving them an opportunity to show how they'll fit with your work team.

4

Identify Job Candidates Who Will Thrive in Your Corporate Culture

YOU'VE NOW PUT IN PLACE RECRUITMENT techniques that will enable you to locate and appeal to individuals with disabilities. If all goes well, you should start having job candidates with disabilities responding to your recruitment efforts. Now you must determine who the best job candidates with disabilities are for your company, those who will do well in your corporate culture. How will you identify the right candidates with disabilities? Are there certain traits you should look for? This chapter provides guidelines to help you recognize the best job candidates with disabilities.

Job Candidates Who Approach Employment from an Entrepreneurial Perspective

One of your best bets is to look for a job candidate with a disability who may have been looking for the right job for some time, has the right focus, but is carrying out her job-marketing plan and hasn't given up hope that she'll eventually find her dream job.

That type of individual is approaching employment from an entrepreneurial perspective. From her vantage point, a meaningful job is not an automatic right. It's something she knows she must earn by proactively accumulating the knowledge and skills required by that job. And she also realizes that she then has to go out and convince others that she's right for that job.

In on-the-job terms, she is passionate about her work, thinks in terms of possibilities instead of pitfalls, is adaptable in difficult circumstances, is a motivator for those who are around her, and is determined to succeed in what counts. That's the entrepreneurial spirit you want in a job candidate.

> ### "Sell Me."
>
> Relax. Don't be put off by the disability. It's not your job to tiptoe around or to compensate for it. It's your job to find the best person for the job and to tell a candidate what the job involves. It is the candidate's job to tell you whether he can perform the tasks. And he has to sell you on his being the best choice. If a disabled person does that, I'll hire him.
>
> —Terry Besenyody, human resources manager,
> Pitney Bowes—Spokane, Washington, office

This entrepreneurial approach is something she may have developed by learning how to put on her shoes in her own unique, sequential way with hands that don't always obey her command or using adaptive software in a certain way to compensate for her lack of manual dexterity.

As a result, she has developed the tenacity, based on a sense of personal dignity, to achieve personal goals. The key question is this: Has she learned to transfer that personal tenacity to a business setting for achieving bottom-line results? If she has, that's an added value other job candidates (new college graduates without a disability, for instance) may not yet be able to offer you as a hiring manager. Her competitors for your job opening may have experience, but have they truly been tested?

Of course, all of us have experienced difficult situations and a perceived loss of dignity at one time or another—particularly during times of workplace transition: Plants close; jobs go overseas; a particular job sector is flooded with job applicants; new jobs require a whole new skill set; and so on.

But not individuals with a disability who approach life's challenges with persistence. They may have learned how to focus on achieving a goal that was difficult to reach. They may have learned to do it by pacing themselves and savoring what is going well with their lives while also plugging away at the drudge work needed to accomplish a specific personal feat—such as landing a meaningful job.

Achieving such a focused yet balanced life in today's world is not easy for anyone. But focusing on one or more special needs with a steadfastness that is not normally required of nondisabled folks and still achieving that balance can give someone who is disabled the sense of entrepreneurial confidence you need in an employee at your workplace.

How can a job candidate's apparent personal resolve be transferred to achieving bottom-line results in your business? Look for revealing personal stories from those you interview that show those job candidates have made that leap (or have the potential for doing so).

Entrepreneurial spirit and business success, however, sometimes don't follow each other. Keep that in mind as you assess a job candidate who may tout her small-business experience.

Job Seekers Who Are Successfully Operating Small Businesses

U.S. society emphasizes work as part of individual meaning and value. It can be tempting to avoid criticism for not working by inventing a fictitious business. Here's how to tell if your job candidate is operating a bona fide business.

Not too long ago, few people expected individuals with a disability to work. In fact, people generally could not imagine how those with disabilities *could* possibly work. At worst, they were dependent on families or on begging. At best, they might have some sort of half-ersatz job, such as stuffing envelopes, stringing beads, or selling pencils outside the subway station. A very small number of people with disabilities had meaningful work.

But expectations have changed. For several decades, rehabilitation has included vocational training. Now there are laws not only allowing people with disabilities to work but requiring employers to consider them equally in filling jobs for which those without disabilities are qualified. The implication is quickly becoming that not only can they work, they *should* work.

The dilemma for many people with disabilities today is that the world of work is still largely off limits. They are probably decades away from full enfranchisement. Yet, they are starting to face judgment from others around them if they don't work. The pressure to satisfy these others is powerful. How does a person handle the pressure to prove his worth through work in an environment where access to work is limited?

Faking It as a Small-Business Owner

One "coping strategy," as social workers refer to it, is simply to "fake it." This strategy is not peculiar to people with disabilities, by any means. The character who has lots of plans but rarely follows up on them is commonplace in American popular culture.

You may be familiar with McGill, the character actor George Clooney plays in the film *O Brother, Where Art Thou?* McGill is a talented and intelligent good-for-nothing who loses his family, his friends, his home, and his freedom—and yet persists in developing, pursuing, and even roping others into grandiose schemes. In true life, our society is replete with get-rich-quick schemes and bogus businesses (and plenty of people who fall for them).

Fertile Field for Recruitment

The National Institute on Disability and Rehabilitation Research's Research & Training Center on Rural Rehabilitation Services, connected with the Montana University–affiliated Rural Institute on Disabilities, conducted the first-ever national study of people with disabilities who are self-employed. Four of ten respondents said they chose the entrepreneurial route because they "needed to create their own job."

Rural Institute research director Tom Seekins says, "Research has shown that there are nearly as many people with disabilities who own their own business as those who work for federal, state, and local governments combined."

Does networking with the small-business owners in your geographic area or business sector make sense as a recruitment strategy for your company? By doing so, you could identify potential job candidates with a disability who are ready to apply their solid small-business experience to your corporate effort.

People with disabilities in the United States have a bit of an edge over those in lesser-developed countries because they generally have access to a steady, if not overgenerous, means of living from disability income through the Social Security Administration. Such a "safety net" makes it easier to get away with inventing a phantom business. With the pressure to prove worth not only to others but to themselves, it is relatively easy for them to fall back on a fictitious business to avoid unkind scrutiny and criticism.

This doesn't mean, however, that those people who do hide behind insubstantial work are doing it to be deliberately deceptive. It is far more likely that an individual really wants to develop a viable small business but doesn't know how to go about it or is not successful in launching it.

A Note from the Editor

I would be the last person to condemn those caught in this situation because I, myself, have fallen into this temptation to hide behind a phantom business, particularly when it's counseling or consulting. I have had a few real businesses, but I have also had a few that might best be described as "optimistic." I wanted to turn the latter into real work, but for various reasons, failed. I continued to use them to save face when I had to answer the question, "What do you do for a living?"

The two "businesses" that seem to be the most common "covers" for not really doing anything these days are "writer" and "Web designer." "Consultant" is right in there, too. What do these three have in common?

- ✓ They involve work in highly competitive fields with a limited number of opportunities and lots and lots of practitioners.
- ✓ The work itself is easy to do but not easy to do well.
- ✓ They elicit respect from others without needing to prove anything.
- ✓ The "product" is intangible, compared to building or making something, and it's easy to get away with not actually providing evidence of success.

I have been a writer and a consultant. What's more, I have both pretended to do and really have done these tasks. But I have never noticed a difference in how others respond to those business reports—even though they were at times real and, at other times, just pipe dreams.

I did notice my own response, though—especially now that I'm no longer "faking" it. It bothers my sense of pride that I don't get any more (or less) affirmation for the work I am doing now. I now know I can get away with a falsehood.

Most of those who have questionable businesses are sincere in their desire to have meaningful and gainful work. Those with a disability who really want to have jobs or businesses but simply cannot achieve them would perhaps be wise to look into simply doing work they love—via volunteering or as a hobby. In fact, if we, as a society, really valued work as work and did not, in fact, require the validation of pay, we'd probably all be happier and healthier.

However, a large number of people, nondisabled and disabled, just don't know what a real "going" business constitutes. Perhaps they don't have the knowledge, the tools, the discipline, or the work habits to create something substantial.

How to Tell if a Job Candidate's Small-Business Experience Is "For Real"

There are both tangible and intangible indicators of whether a business is "for real." Here are questions to ask yourself as you consider job candidates who cite their small business as a source of relevant experience:

- ⊘ Can they explain, in a more or less succinct matter, what product they sell or what service they provide? A lot of people, when asked what they do for a living, give a kind of vague "I'm self-employed." Self-employed at what?

- ⊘ How did they start their business? Did they spend time planning, doing research, growing start-up capital, and obtaining the tools of their trade? Do they have a business plan? Do they have a business license? Did they register a trade name, or are they at least familiar with trademark law?

- ⊘ Do they have specific business goals? What steps are they taking to achieve them? What measurements are they using to assess their achievements?

- ⊘ Where is their place of business? A business has to be somewhere. It can be a storefront, a home office, a workshop—or even a closet or file cabinet where they keep inventory, records, tools, and so forth.

- ⊘ Are they actively keeping records on their work and their finances as well as the administrative and legal side of their business? Or are they at least making sure those records are kept?

- If they consider themselves in a full-time business, are they actually spending at least thirty-five hours a week directly involved in some aspect of it?

- Are they making contacts with others in their line of business? Are they networking or actively inviting scrutiny from others who know the signs of a serious business?

- Do they have customers or clients? Having customers or clients is a sure sign that they are actually producing and are serious.

- Are they making money? Do they report their income and pay taxes on it? Could they sell their business for money? These financial indicators are probably the most important proof that they indeed are in business.

Think unconventionally. Gear your recruitment efforts to tap talented individuals who have a disability and relevant experience as a successful small-business owner. But make sure that experience stems from a legitimate enterprise in the "mainstream" marketplace where they've functioned as fully engaged members of society.

People Who Have Moved Beyond Self-Absorption to Become Fully Engaged Members of Society

An ideal job candidate has learned how to go beyond self-absorption and can interact effectively with others—disabled or not. Those interpersonal skills will prove valuable in any employment situation and will affect the teamwork, the morale, and the tone of your work unit.

The key considerations in selecting such a job candidate are the answers to these two questions:

1. Has the person learned to manage his disability so that it's no longer the center of his life?

2. Does he have the time, inclination, and skill to effectively reach out to others and be a productive member of a corporate effort?

Many times job candidates with disabilities have devoted a considerable amount of personal time to:

- ⊘ Developing daily living skills
- ⊘ Obtaining an education
- ⊘ Getting accessible living arrangements
- ⊘ Forming primary relationships
- ⊘ Gaining accessible transportation options

Prime job candidates (disabled or not) have addressed these issues and are ready to contribute to your company's further success.

Moving Beyond Disability

Your prime job candidates need to know how to use their interpersonal skills to effectively interact with others despite their disabilities.

Finding such individuals among those with disabilities may not be as challenging as you may first think. Such balance may be found, for instance, in job candidates who have a big-picture perspective. They realize that relating well to other people and dealing with issues outside of their immediate concerns are paths to independent living.

They garden. They cook. They raise kids. They enjoy pets.

They let their coworkers know that they can count on them to get tasks done on the job.

This doesn't mean they pretend that systematic discrimination doesn't exist in some segments of our society. It does, and, at one time or another, it affects their lives. They advocate for themselves.

In *Somebodies and Nobodies: Overcoming the Abuse of Rank* (New Society Publishers, 2004), Robert W. Fuller expresses the need for self-advocacy this way:

> Social justice is never handed to those who lack it. Only when the victims of unfairness are aroused and demand dignity and equity (dignity being a central tenet in most religions) for themselves does the status quo change. . . . What primarily marks people for mistreatment today is not race or gender, but low rank and the powerlessness it signifies. In plain language, what matters is: Are you a "Somebody" or a "Nobody"?
>
> These attitudes affect the kinds of jobs people get, where

they live, and their social experiences. **The Civil Rights move-ment taught us that laws alone don't change attitudes. Awareness must be raised and assumptions challenged.**

Your prime job candidates know how to use their interpersonal skills to effectively raise awareness and challenge assumptions as fully engaged members of society. For example, consider the six attributes that emerge in the following discussion among members of eSight Careers Network:

1. Holding your own in fair competition
2. Integrating with the nondisabled population
3. Taking charge of confusing situations
4. Responding appropriately
5. Networking with others
6. Foreshadowing what to expect from those who follow you

Holding Your Own

Daniel M. Berry III:

To build effective interpersonal relationships with the sighted world, people who are blind must stop acting victimized or inferior. We have to stop creating the impression that we believe the rest of the world is out to get us, and we have to stop assuming that we can't hold our own in a fair competition.

We've got to spend time with sighted people and not just with-draw into our own little world.

Integrating

Anthony R. Candela:

If we aspire to effective interpersonal relationships with all people (disabled and nondisabled), perhaps the psychological divide that sometimes separates us from nondisabled people will not be so wide. I have found that spending as much time as possible with nondisabled people helps "normalize" me in their minds and they in mine.

Taking Charge

Jeremiah Taylor:

If a person is uncomfortable around a disabled person, there is little the disabled person can do but be friendly, personal, outgoing, and reassure the other that the disability is "just the way it is." Now please pass the salt.

Since losing my sight years ago, I've made several new friends, changed jobs, got promoted, and never found it difficult when dealing with new acquaintances or situations.

The more "take charge" the disabled person appears, the more at ease the other person will become. I think problems arise when a person feels he is supposed to act or do something different when dealing with a disabled person.

The disabled person needs to take charge so the other person learns that, if something special is needed, the disabled person will tell them. It is the unknown that causes the problem.

Responding

Liz Seger:

Each of us chooses how we will respond to a remark or a given situation or even a feeling.

Today, while shopping, I was packing my groceries a little too slow for the people behind me, and one man said, "Can't you move any faster; what are you blind or something?"

The checker, who only knows me from shopping at that particular store, gave him and another old lady "hell" for being nasty.

I just said, "I'm sorry. I shop for a month, and I'm working as fast as I can. And I'm sorry, too, that you woke up in such an ugly mood. I hope your day goes better."

There was dead silence with the rest of the line. No one said a word, except, "Oh, excuse me, please" and "May I get the door for you?"

I could have stormed out and made an ugly scene, but what for? Those two people looked more foolish than I ever could. And everyone in that line knew it.

Networking

Barney Mayse:

I concentrate on working well with whomever I am assigned to work with. I try to be inclusive when I have the opportunity. I network with coworkers and others with whom I interface. It is a process and requires constant diligence, perseverance, and patience.

Foreshadowing

Mike:

I feel strongly that folks who have a disability can make excellent workers, and, if they do their best, then they help other disabled workers who might want a chance to work in that field. We are judged by our abilities, but, often, we are also judged because of those who preceded us. The experiences employers have had with disabled folks have a direct bearing on how they perceive other disabled people, rightly or wrongly.

Notice how these people have moved beyond themselves—and their disabilities. They'll advocate for themselves and others when appropriate, but their focus is on integrating with the nondisabled population.

Let's further explore how an employee with a disability can use effective interpersonal communication to enhance the teamwork, morale, and tone of your particular work unit.

Individuals Who Take Personal Responsibility When They Become "Easy Marks" While at Work

In the film *North Country*, crusty Glory (played by Frances McDormand) is shown as the first woman to be hired by a mining company in northern Minnesota.

She has learned how to survive in the corporate environment, which is hobbled by blatant sexual harassment—partly because the male employees generally believe the women are taking away much-needed jobs from the men in the community.

Glory survives by being assertive, expressing her wishes in terms understood by her fellow employees, using her sense of humor when appropriate, and becoming part of the union leadership. She personally stands her ground.

Still, the job of exposing and combating sexual harassment within the company falls on newcomer Josey Aimes (played by Charlize Theron), who eventually realizes that accommodating to the charged atmosphere, working through channels, and even going to the CEO does not resolve the situation.

Josey seeks a solution (a class-action suit) that the other women employees, such as Big Betty (Rusty Schwimmer), do not wish to pursue because they are afraid they will lose their jobs by raising the sexual harassment issue with management.

In work environments (and in situations) much less charged than the one in *North Country*, managers often find themselves leading teams that have a Glory, a Josey, and a Big Betty and are locked in conflict over a vulnerability issue.

That vulnerability could involve sexual harassment, but it could just as well stem from another difficulty: One team member recognizes another as an "easy mark" because that employee has a disability—and it's disrupting the team's performance.

Here's an example from an anonymous member (let's call her Lisa) of eSight Careers Network:

Lisa:

> I have had jobs where I cashiered. It's not hard for people to tell that I can't see well, so it made me a target. When it first happened to me, I almost lost the job. I was so angry at myself and angry at the man who short-changed me. I could have chewed nails! I swore I would never let it happen again, but no matter how careful you are, there is always some slick person out there with no morals who can pull one over on you.

Value Assertiveness

Recruit job candidates who know how to take responsibility when they become "easy marks" while at work. They should have the inclination to resolve these issues for themselves. Having such proactive individuals on your staff can boost your work unit's morale.

Members of eSight Careers Network generated some insight about taking personal responsibility to nip the problem in the bud before it becomes a teamwide issue. On the "Swimming in the Mainstream" (SiM) blog, the SiM participants discussed this question: "What's the best way to handle a work situation in which a person is taking advantage of you due to your apparent vulnerability?"

The SiM participants generated four tips about how to live well in a rough-and-tumble world with a sense of personal integrity, how to fashion a life beyond being an "easy mark," and how to take personal responsibility when an "easy mark" situation comes into play at work.

Why are these tips important to you? By hiring people with disabilities who have this kind of insight and experience, you, as a manager, can save time, money, and effort because you won't be handling issues that employees with a disability can often personally resolve themselves. And that expertise comes in handy in resolving issues that have nothing to do with disability as well.

The four tips eSight members (all with disabilities) generated among themselves for handling "easy mark" situations are question, prepare, communicate, and act.

Question

Melissa:

First, make sure you are being taken advantage of before you go any further. You have to take responsibility for your own actions.

Take a look at the situation from the other person's perspective. What has made you vulnerable besides your disability? Make sure you are not doing anything careless. Be on your P's and Q's, as they say. Are you doing or not doing something that leaves the door open for this other person to walk right through?

The temptation can be strong to assume the other person's attitude has to do with your disability. That is a mistake. If I've learned anything in my life as a visually impaired person, it's that the other person (probably) isn't even thinking about me at all—and my disability is not a consideration!

Nan:

As a group, people with disabilities are far too sensitive to what others are thinking about us. We assume any slight, or any perceived slight, is against us personally and caused by the other person's bias. This really is giving others too much credit for awareness. It is virtually always safer to assume disability has nothing to do with the bad behavior until something concrete is said or done to convince an observer. . . .

More often than not, the difficult person is acting out of some type of fear: fear of losing her job, fear of the unknown, or fear of a perceived threat.

We often think of the person as difficult because of a simple misunderstanding or a bit of poor communication. And, yes, sometimes people can be just plain perverse out of selfishness, ambition, immaturity, meanness, or stupidity.

Prepare

Jake:

Do whatever it takes to be less vulnerable. For instance, in addition to folding my bills differently, a former skills tutor (for people with visual impairments) labeled all the sections of my wallet in Braille, using my Braille label maker. So I can now either fold or keep every bill straight and in the appropriate compartments.

Nan:

In general, the best strategy you can take is to tap into your own self-esteem and assertiveness. If you are clear about your own role and rights in a situation, you will be far more likely to understand where the conflict is coming from—and what is (and is not) your responsibility.

You are only responsible for your own behavior. You are not there to "fix" difficult coworkers. Part of your behavior must display respect and courtesy. This can be difficult, but it is the one area you control absolutely in interpersonal situations. You may not like the way the other person is acting toward you or others, but keeping a consistently civil tongue keeps you from simply becoming part of the problem.

Liz:

Documenting everything is a great idea (dates, times, places, incidents). If you can, make copies and give them to a superior.

Communicate

Len:

Address the person straight on who is taking advantage of your vulnerability and ask that person to please stop. Express to him or her that you wish to be treated with dignity and understanding.

Melissa:

When you have your facts in order, you may need to confront the person. That depends on the situation. When I say confront, I do not mean get confrontational because that will be counterproductive.

Talk to the person in private, and do not use a bunch of "you" sentences. Tell him what you have observed happening and your role. Tell him your perspective and what you believe the facts to be. Maybe you can work out the problem between the two of you.

Document your conversation. Take mental notes and write them down later. It might make the person defensive if he sees you writing during your exchange.

If you are uncomfortable with the idea of addressing the issue on your own, or if the problem threatens your employment, then go to your immediate supervisor or human resources with your documentation.

Act

Melissa:

If it is feasible, make every effort to actively work out the problem. Be assertive and stand up for yourself. If you do not, the problem will continue and likely get worse. You deserve just as much respect as anyone else, disabled or not.

It is obvious that the coworker is not team-oriented and is inconsiderate and disrespectful if he is intentionally taking advantage of you. If he is doing it unknowingly, he may appreciate the fact that you want to address the problem in a civil way privately.

If he happens to be an uncooperative jerk, then someone in authority definitely needs to know what is going on and what kind of person is working for the company.

If I had an employee who was taking advantage of another

employee, I would like to see them work it out like adults (if it is a relatively minor infraction). If the person did not change his behavior or was not willing to listen, then I would want to take formal disciplinary action against that employee. His behavior is not only unacceptable and inappropriate; it is also likely to lead to bigger problems.

Do any of these people sound like they would be the type of employee who could help bring the morale within your work group to a little higher level? They show they have "emotional intelligence." As you interview your job candidates, look for individuals who have the emotional intelligence to hold their own in "easy mark" situations.

A Note from the Editor

I'm no recruiter, but during my career in business, I've helped make decisions—as a senior executive, middle manager, and executive board member—about who should be hired. I've interviewed people for HR positions, project coordinators, field managers, customer service reps, writers, and internships.

When I interview a job candidate with a disability, I want our conversation to reveal something about how well that person has adjusted to living with a disability and how that applies to the job tasks at hand. I should not have to ask that question directly (and indeed cannot under the ADA). A candidate's disability perspective should naturally flow from a conversation in which two people are leveling with each other.

Remember, during job interviews the ADA prohibits you from directly asking questions about an individual's approach to disability. You can describe the essential functions of the job for which she is interviewing, and then you can ask if she can do the work and how she would do it for your company.

Your most savvy job candidates will volunteer to speak openly with you about how they intend to perform the job in spite of their obvious disabilities. Within that opening, you may then ask for follow-up examples of what they have achieved in the past under similar circumstances.

How to Identify Individuals with Emotional Intelligence

There are a handful of vulnerability issues that, taken together, can be windows to what is now commonly called a job candidate's "emotional intelligence." Following are some of those issues, distilled into hypothetical questions that cannot be asked of job candidates but that you can ask yourself as you evaluate your conversations with job candidates, whether they're disabled or not. Once a job candidate has first brought up the topic of her disability, it is hoped that she will voluntarily provide enough insight during your conversations—through either formal interviews or follow-up chats—so you can have a good hunch about what she would say in such a hypothetical dialogue.

Unasked Questions

Consider job candidates who take the initiative to address unasked questions about how they've learned to handle their disabilities. They could help you set the right tone for your work unit.

In highlighting these questions, we introduce you to a few of the people who are dealing effectively with their personal vulnerabilities and who provide the type of anecdotes you might voluntarily receive during your own interviews.

Does she accept who she is?

This is the central question you need to answer in your own mind for each job candidate you interview. All of the others we discuss flow from it.

Katrina, another eSight blogger, recalls that as a child and as an adolescent she always felt inferior to sighted people. "I thought that acting sighted as much as possible was what I should aspire to because I thought sighted people were so much better, even personality-wise, than myself."

But, at about age 17, Katrina started feeling a lot better about herself as a person and realized the biggest compliment someone could give her was *not* this statement: "Oh, I didn't know you were blind; you can't tell."

Katrina writes, "Now I feel that my blindness is just part of my identity. And I am happy to be able to say that, at the age of 31, I fully accept this and love myself for what I am."

Here's another example. In learning how to scuba dive, David discovered something unexpected: "I learned I don't need to try to pretend any more to be a sighted person living in a blind person's body."

And then there's Kim, a teacher who writes about his hesitancy to use a wheelchair at an elementary school where he taught: "I learned from [my students] what no book could have taught me: that my disabilities don't make me less of a man—no matter what anyone might say. I don't need fixin'. I'm OK just the way I am."

Has she gone beyond condescension and overcompensation?

Here you're looking for discernment and assertiveness (not aggression) with the ability to project oneself as an adult.

A Note from the Editor

As a person with cerebral palsy, I noticed well-meaning people would tend to call me "Jimmy" instead of "Jim," even though I was no five-year-old anymore. In fact, I was 49 and vice president of a Fortune 500 company. I finally gained the insight into this unintentional condescension and started reaffirming that "My name is Jim" to those "Jimmy" people who were automatically falling back on a common but incorrect perception that individuals with disabilities, even as adults, are really children to be protected.

"At one time," Carolyn Tyjewski writes, "accepting responsibility for this societal psychosis made sense. It made sense to accept responsibility for not fitting in, for not playing the game right. It made sense in the same way that taking the comment, 'I forgot you're blind' as a compliment seemed appropriate. I'd flinch or suddenly become queasy from the comment but shake it off as nothing, an apparition, my imagination. After all, there was no harm intended. . . ."

Carolyn has grown since then: "I don't accept responsibility for other people's psychoses anymore."

Can she join others in laughing about herself?

You're not looking for belly laughs. And we're not talking about humor that devalues anyone. What you're looking for is the ability to not take oneself too seriously and to let others know that it's okay to enjoy the amusing things that often happen because of disability.

When Brenda reentered the workforce in 1996, she worked as a volunteer for a congressional candidate. She folded, stuffed, and labeled envelopes for mailings and answered the phones.

"I had been around the campaign for several weeks before the candidate realized I did not see just like everyone else," Brenda writes. "He won his race hands down and asked if I would consider working for him in the Congressional District Office. I was delighted! I started out answering the switchboard (what a hoot!), but I mastered that and moved on to data entry with the help of a Magnisight 60X, receiving enlargement through the computer system."

Has she been able to put personal pride in perspective?

Putting pride in perspective is closely tied to the ability to laugh at oneself.

Marti operates her own business and is visually impaired. "I wear glasses sometimes," she writes. "They help a little, but I think they've become a habit."

Marti tells about purchasing several new pairs of glasses as spares because she sits or steps on them a lot. She remembers that one time at a meeting where she was presenting a proposal to a prospective client she slipped on a pair of her new glasses to study a passage in the proposal he was questioning. "I didn't notice the odd looks I got," she says, "but my partner later pointed out that the left lens of the glasses still had the factory sticker in the middle."

Does she know how to get beyond feelings of inferiority?

This probably all leads back to self-esteem and self-confidence. Does your job candidate establish eye contact, project confidence, and make people feel comfortable?

Ann Dyer projects that self-confidence. Ann was a practicing nurse. Then she suddenly had surgery to remove large tumors from her brain. After being on Social Security for twenty-five years because of her disability, she now has her master's degree in vocational rehabilitation and has been working in a meaningful job with benefits.

Does she disavow being a victim?

Look for a job candidate who does not identify with "being the victim"— no matter how severe the disability or how unfair life has been.

Listen to Liz Seger: "I am a person first, who has low vision, wears an ostomy, wears glasses, is blond, middle aged, has blue eyes, a wicked wit, a curious nature, is educated and becoming a wise woman as she matures. I'm nobody's victim of anything!"

Does she swim in the "mainstream"?

The ideal job candidate with a disability has experience working in the so-called mainstream workplace, despite setbacks and difficulties.

Check this story. Nancy was 31, an aerospace engineer working on a very exciting defense contract. One morning on her way to work, a van struck the vehicle in which she was riding. She instantaneously became a quadriplegic.

Nancy's advice: "Let time carry you to a new place, a new reality."

At the time Nancy wrote her posting, she was back working full-time—for another aerospace company.

Does she understand the truths as well as the falsehoods within the nondisabled and disabled worlds?

A Note from the Editor

In 1993, I didn't have the awareness to compile the recommendations in this book. I was too tied into the "mainstream" workplace. Born with cerebral palsy, I had very little contact with people who had disabilities. I worked for a Fortune 500 company and eventually became a vice president.

I then retired from the company to start my own business. That's when I started to reconnect with people who have disabilities—something I had not done since grade school.

I now have a somewhat better understanding of the legitimate concerns and uninformed understandings within both nondisabled and disabled worlds when it comes to employment. I cringe when I hear job seekers with a disability ask that employers give them "a chance to prove themselves" when I believe that is the job seeker's responsibility (not the employer's). I also wonder why employers have for so long ignored disability in their diversity initiatives.

But my understanding is a journey. I'm still learning.

Similarly, each candidate with a disability you interview may have not yet addressed, on a personal level, all of the vulnerability issues we have discussed. And that's okay. Even those that a person has considered may not be fully resolved in that individual's mind. And that's okay. We're all in the process of "becoming"—especially in terms of emotional intelligence.

According to Steven J. Stein and Howard E. Book in *The EQ Edge: Emotional Intelligence and Your Success* (Jossey-Bass, 2006), emotional intelligence is an individual's ability to form optimal relationships with other people through the attributes of hope, empathy, trust, integrity, honesty, creativity, resiliency, consequence-thinking, and optimism so he can build stronger social networks and manage difficult situations.

Emotional intelligence is the ability to "unlearn" helplessness and hopelessness when faced with adversity—an attribute every one of us (nondisabled and disabled) has acquired since birth through personal struggle and discovery.

The main skill in emotional intelligence is delaying gratification in pursuit of long-range goals. Learning how to live well with vulnerability can reinforce that skill in anyone, regardless of one's intelligence quotient (which cannot be changed through study and practice).

Emotional intelligence has a surprising relationship to success in a business setting. MetLife, for instance, has found that its sales associates who score high in one aspect of emotional intelligence, specifically "learned optimism," outsell those with low emotional intelligence by an average of 37 percent during their first two years of work (see http://www.centerforappliedei.com/#benefitsofEI).

How important is a person's level of emotional intelligence about disability to you? It depends on several factors. Are you interviewing for a high-profile position, which will involve dealing with customers or suppliers? Does it require refined teamwork skills? Is it a supervisory or management position? If so, how you think a candidate addresses personal vulnerability can be critical.

For inclusive recruiting, one thing is clear: To accurately assess a job candidate's emotional intelligence about personal vulnerability, you need to have a basic understanding of both worlds: the prevailing attitudes about disability in the "mainstream" workplace as well as the current snapshot of the evolving disability rights movement. By doing so, you too can become a bridge builder—for your organization and society at large—between those two worlds.

That's no small task. But it's not time-intensive. It's a matter of gradually cultivating your discernment about disability over time. That will yield benefits for your organization because you'll be in a better position to hire the people with disabilities who also tend to be bridge builders between our mainstream culture and the disability rights movement. You'll attract individuals who have found a way to develop emotional intelligence about their own personal vulnerabilities and about personal differences in others. And you'll build a team at work that consists of effective networkers.

Those networkers will help set the tone for your work group and your company. And that will help your company prepare for an older yet still involved workforce in which disability is more prevalent—and make your job as an executive, a manager, or a team leader easier and more rewarding.

Job Candidates Who Can Gracefully Accept and Decline Help

A job candidate's level of emotional intelligence is sometimes difficult to access. But check how he or she has learned to live with ambiguity and risk (essentially "uncertainty") every day because of his or her vulnerabilities. Reactions to ambiguity and risk are sometimes more evident for candidates with disabilities.

For instance, one way to measure how people (disabled or not) deal with uncertainty is to watch how and when they ask for help. The key question is: Have they learned how to gracefully interact with others when they truly need help—or when it appears that they do but really don't?

Another Attribute of Leadership

Has your job candidate with a disability developed a sense of when and how to ask for help from coworkers?

Ernest Hemingway may have thought "grace under pressure" was courage, but perhaps personal courage has more to do with a sense of dignity and self-worth because it denotes self-control and a sense of how to deal calmly with unexpected situations. If that's the case, then handling vulnerability, asking for help, and declining unsolicited assistance in a graceful manner are not only marks of courage but also attributes of a leader.

Questions You Might Ask a Job Candidate

To identify job candidates who can gracefully handle vulnerability, you might ask all of them (disabled or not) these questions (with no reference to disability) during a job interview:

- When have you needed to ask for help on a work project from one of your coworkers?
- How did you go about obtaining that help?
- What was the outcome?

Let's look for traces of gracefully handling vulnerability in this discussion among eSight Careers Network members (who happen to have a disability):

Liz Seger:

At some point in our lives, we usually realize that we're going to need help from someone and that it's not awful or weak to ask for someone's help. In fact, it's knowing that you can ask for help and usually receive it that makes us psychologically and emotionally mature adults.

C. Fred Stout:

Everyone requires help—some more than others.

The brightest and most capable of blind people must have continuous help.

At times, one can be offered unsolicited assistance when none is really required. The manner in how such offers are managed is important. Demonstrating and expressing appreciation holds double value. It's often an emotional and sensitive matter. Should the person offering help feel rudely treated, unappreciated, and rejected, that individual will likely never offer such assistance again.

In my 52 years of blindness, I have enjoyed many such wonderful personal interactions, and I don't think that I ever hurt anyone's feelings.

Lauren Merryfield:

I usually say, "No thanks, I'm okay." But, if I'm in trouble, I usually say, "Thanks, I guess I do need help this time, but it's not because I can't see—it's because _____ (I'm having trouble with . . . ; I need to get somewhere in a big hurry; I'm not feeling very well right now; this is above my lifting limit; I've done this lots of times, but today I'm just worn out; I'll understand where it is if you go with me this one time; it's windy out and I can't hear the cars very well; etc.)."

Curt Woolford:

Sometimes I need to ask for help, and I choose to tough it out instead.

Debra:

What works best in an ongoing relationship is to set boundaries first about what you can and cannot do, what you would like to do yourself, and what you cannot do yourself.

Kerryann Ifill:

I smile and say, "Thank you, but I can manage." Or I make a slight joke of it, and I assure them that I'll do fine. Otherwise, I invite them to watch and be assured.

In this brief conversation, notice the opportunities these individuals have discovered in situations in which they apparently (or really) need help. Those opportunities include:

- Demonstrating emotional maturity to friends, colleagues, and strangers
- Managing ongoing relationships at work, home, and play
- Making use of "teachable" moments about disability, especially when unsolicited assistance is offered

These are opportunities everyone (especially if one has a disability) has for proactively showing friends, colleagues, and strangers how one person can support another in times of uncertainty.

Those who take advantage of such opportunities show leadership. As guides, they use authenticity to help another person feel more comfortable about her apparent vulnerabilities. That builds community in families, neighborhoods, workplaces, and society.

Let's further explore how such leaders have made the transition from feeling vulnerable to being able to carry their load as members of a team, from feeling weak to being authentic in on-the-job matters with their coworkers, and from feeling uncertain to being practical risk-takers and workplace entrepreneurs.

That process will help you discover the attributes you need to find in job candidates (disabled or not) who will perform well within your work team.

Individuals Who Can Carry Their Load as Members of Your Team

Not long ago the term "teamwork" primarily applied to sports teams. As business recognized that a work team and a baseball team interact in a similar way, the term has been more frequently applied to staff relationships. The comparison is useful: As with baseball, football, hockey, rowing, or any other team sport, the success of a work team depends on each member playing well in a unique and necessary role.

The team can succeed only when each player shares his part of the common load—just as a baseball team can expect to win a game only when the pitcher, first baseman, center fielder, lead-off man, and all the other players do their particular tasks well.

Teamwork involves:

1. Listening to each other's ideas
2. Asking each other questions both to clarify and to challenge ideas
3. Encouraging team members to share their ideas
4. Showing respect
5. Helping each team member understand ideas
6. Sharing one's insights and information
7. Participating fully and equally in the task at hand

An environment that does not build and foster all these skills in team members will not fully succeed. The individual who cannot (or will not) participate fully and equally in all seven behaviors can slow, block, or even sabotage a joint project.

Often, disability does not make a team member "the weakest link." Instead, being "the weakest link" is the sum total of how an individual participates in a team. Disability, however, can be a factor in that sum total.

When an Employee with a Disability Is the Weakest Link

To examine how an employee with a disability might allow her disability (and how she, herself, views it) to weaken her connection on a team, let's look at a few fictional cases. Please meet Bob, Carol, Ted, and Alice.

Bob

Bob, a teacher with low vision, cannot even get past "listening" in his participation in the local Parent-Teacher Association (PTA). He somehow manages to bring the focus back onto him and his disability no matter what point another team member is making. He uses his disability not only to get attention but to bludgeon others into spending time on his agenda without giving them the respect to hear what issues concern them.

As a result, the PTA is wholly ineffective. Other members avoid Bob because he has set up a wall between him and them. Bob is intelligent and has a lot of insight into what matters to the community. He could be a vital part of the team, implementing not only programs related to disability but addressing many other issues in the schools.

Carol

On the other hand, Carol never says a word. She uses a wheelchair for mobility because of a spinal cord injury while on her high school's swim team. Even though she is a marketing associate in a food company, somehow she has internalized her family's cultural belief that people with disabilities, and women in general, should not assert themselves. In fact, in one-on-one conversations, Carol is a bright star, beaming with enthusiasm for projects that could keep the most demoralized team going.

But that skill is wasted. She simply pulls back and lets her "betters" talk in a meeting. Energy for the task, as a result, often flags. Carol's ability to invigorate every member of the team is lost, and the team's projects tend to bog down.

Ted

Ted is—well—needy. He has multiple sclerosis, but his disability has not in the least prevented him from being a crack salesman. He works in his father-in-law's tire store and easily has the highest sales record.

But, although he contributes to the team's success by identifying prospects, making an effective pitch, and closing a sale, he does not work on a par with his coworkers. Worse, he wheedles personal favors from them, such as getting them to go get coffee or give him a ride after work. He turns each and every team member into a personal assistant.

He will do the sales pitch, but he won't follow up with the paperwork or with customers. He uses his disability to get out of work he simply does not want to do or learn to do.

Therefore, other members of the sales staff and the clerical staff have to do more than their share. Even though Ted's sales would be merit-worthy, his coworkers resent him and believe he is actively sabotaging them, something they won't bring up because he is, after all, the boss's son-in-law. He blames their reluctance on their having a bad attitude toward people with disabilities. Total sales would be way up if everyone cooperated, but Ted drains cooperative spirit from the whole group.

Now let's examine a case where a person who happens to be disabled is fully integrated into a successful team.

Alice

Hard of hearing, Alice is a reporter on a small, rural weekly newspaper. A coworker in the business office, Amy, who has cerebral palsy, has developed a whiny tone and appears to believe that no one will ever give her the tools and information she needs to do her work.

Alice had to deal with the fallout from Amy's behavior when she first got her job. Others at the paper assumed Alice would be just as difficult to be around as Amy.

But Alice is nothing like Amy. She is a resourceful self-starter who likes her independence. She cheerfully reminds people when she needs help in hearing at a meeting and mentions her hearing condition only as a fact of her life—like anyone else might mention having kids or grow-ing up on a farm.

She is proud of being a contributing team member. She readily offers to help the others in the office who have extra work. Her deafness is not irrelevant, but it might as well be when it comes to teamwork on the editorial staff.

These four examples show that simply carrying out job tasks is not enough to be a valuable team member. Whatever the source of Bob's, Carol's, and Ted's failure to be effective team members, they handicap both themselves and the team. Each needs a more productive attitude to gain the respect Alice has earned (in spite of initially landing in a difficult situation).

> ### Ask Yourself This Question
> Is this job candidate willing—and able—to work within my team?

Questions You Might Ask a Job Candidate

To identify job candidates who will work well in a team environment, you might ask one of these questions during a job interview:

- ⊘ When have you felt like you've been a productive member of a team?
- ⊘ What personal attributes do you believe you possess that make you an effective team member?
- ⊘ What work situation can you cite to show you've learned how to work well with your coworkers?

The Right Balance

The essence here is that effective team members balance opportunities for helping and for receiving help. Knowing when to ask for help (but not overdoing it) is a common dilemma for individuals with a disability. In some cases, for instance, Alice can manage on her own. In others, she cannot, and she tries to consider which other team member might be most appropriate to ask for help.

Other eSight members agree. Keith, Eric, Debra, and Liz, for instance, recommend candor in dealing with other team members.

"I am very honest with coworkers. When I need assistance, I simply state this need, and it appears to be well received," says Keith, the director of student development at a small university.

Eric, who does telephone support for cable modem subscribers, also deals with problems directly. "When I run into a technical issue at work," he says, "I present to my coworkers what the problem is and what needs to be improved. In return, they help me come up with suggestions to resolve the issue so I can work more independently."

He has also drawn on a useful tool to deal with workload and equity issues: his mentors through the DO-IT Careers Program (http://www.washington.edu/doit/) at the University of Washington.

"I work with the mentors on helping to resolve customers' issues," Eric says. "When I tell the mentors what is going on, they present me with a potential resolution to the problem. My duty is to follow through on the resolution that they present to me."

What if an employee does his best and others still resent him?

Debra, a switchboard operator who is blind, observes that being honest and forthright can help others avoid misinterpreting both her words and her actions. She recounts, "I have tried to help coworkers with things that I can do that they can't get to. I've been available for them as much as possible. In spite of this, there is a lot of written material and sight-dependent material that needs to be adapted for me."

However, no matter what she does, she believes some coworkers think, "[I am] lazy, too 'special' to do the work, or don't care. Those things are the furthest from the truth."

Liz admits, "Not everyone is going to be thrilled to have you there [in the workplace] or like you. You're not going to like everybody there either, but that's life: Deal with it. But deal with it in a mature, responsible manner that shows your integrity, responsibility and accountability. [If conflict arises], report it, advocate for it—but do so in a way that makes it a win-win situation for everyone."

Liz points out, "I think . . . that goes without saying in any type of job. Your work habits, your accountability, and your integrity demonstrate how committed you are to your work."

Sharing the load equally—at different times and in different ways—is the key to the success of any team. Each team member shares his own skills and abilities in different ways.

Disability need not be a detriment to that sharing. In fact, it can create an even more diverse and richer source of sharing when a person with a disability who knows how to interact effectively with others is involved.

That brings us to another attribute to consider in a job candidate: authenticity.

Job Seekers Who Possess the Authenticity Valued in the Business World

Comments among members of eSight Careers Network at several different levels often converge in a way that may be valuable for you as an employer.

That has happened with this discussion topic: the apparent vulnerability of individuals, often evident as a "disability," and its relationship to working with authenticity in the business world.

> ## What to Look For
>
> As a hiring manager, you should look for employees who will level with you, who are problem solvers, and who build valuable networks inside and outside your company.

To illustrate this relationship between vulnerability and authenticity, let's draw from comments submitted by eSight members within the following five eSight venues.

From Curt Woolford's "Thriving in a Larger Corporate Environment"

"I have found that visual impairment is often accompanied by humility, and I am no exception. Although I feel that humility is an admirable trait, it is not a prevalent corporate attribute," observes Curt Woolford, who has written a series of articles for eSight Careers Network's Career Management Resources section about thriving as an employee with a disability in larger corporate environments.

"As a visually impaired worker," Woolford counsels his counterparts, "you must bear in mind that you are competing with colleagues who have not benefited from the character development that can accompany the rigors of living with a disability. You may be more familiar than others in your work group with the physical, emotional, and psychological vulnerability of human beings."

Vulnerability can bring with it a healthy sense of humility and an ability to empathize with others.

From Dale Carnegie

"Dale Carnegie may seem 'old fashioned' today," says Jim Hasse, "but taking Carnegie courses over the years has helped me to break out of my shell as a person with cerebral palsy. I still think his guideline to 'express genuine appreciation to everyone you meet' is relevant. The post-Enron buzz words for the same concept: being authentic.

"Being authentic in business relationships means an employee needs to first be comfortable with herself and be ready to build a future on positive memories," Hasse points out.

Here's what Carnegie in *How to Stop Worrying and Start Living* (Simon & Schuster, 1984, p. 49) says about self-acceptance: "Be yourself! Don't imitate others! You are an original. Be glad of it. Never before, since the dawn of time, has anybody been exactly like you; and never again, throughout all the ages to come, will there be anybody exactly like you. So make the most of your individuality."

Through that kind of self-acceptance, people with disabilities are breaking into mainstream employment every day. Those who do make that breakthrough usually have the quiet creditability that matters in today's business.

Those who are comfortable with themselves know, from firsthand experience, that vulnerability is a part of life that stimulates problem solving. And that skill, combined with recognition of the universality of vulnerability in people, can produce individuals who know how to reach out and create valuable business-generating networks for your company.

They are also the individuals who recognize they need to earn and create a niche for themselves in today's competitive workplace. They don't seek a "free lunch."

From "Ollie" D. Cantos VII

Olegario "Ollie" D. Cantos VII has served as special assistant and then special counsel to the assistant attorney general for civil rights at the U.S. Department of Justice as well as associate director for domestic policy at the White House. As guest speaker for an eSight Careers Network phone conference, Cantos provided eSight members with an excellent blueprint for avoiding isolation and changing attitudes—and being authentic.

"Add value to your networking contacts through displays of genuine appreciation of another's strengths," Cantos, who has been blind since birth, advises. "That builds people up," he says.

And then he adds, "Help develop partnerships by matching the strengths you discover in others with needs among the people you meet."

But Cantos goes one step further. In an e-mail follow-up to a question from Annette, one of the participants in the eSight phone conference, he wrote: "I ask that you please do whatever you can to help others in the way that I have taken the time to help you. 'Pay it forward' by being of assistance to at least three people, and in return for what you do for them, ask each of them to help still three others and to make your assistance conditional upon their promise to help at least that number."

From eSight's "Blindstorming" Forum

Participants in an eSight Career Network Blindstorming discussion also reaffirmed Cantos's "add value" guideline for networking.

For instance, Blindstormer John writes:

"Networking allows for the discovery of mutual interests and concerns that are important in a work setting. It is more than just making friends. It has to do with wanting to work together in a certain direction or toward a common goal."

Roger, another Blindstormer, tells this story:

"I learned to consciously focus on ways I can be a valuable contact for those I network with. We need to control the urge to concentrate on our needs and, instead, to also be of value to the contact.

"Here's what I learned from the past governor of Florida about securing the contact through follow-up.

"I met this Florida governor on a flight from New York to Georgia. We talked for some 15 or so minutes; then he excused himself and took a tape recorder out of his briefcase and recorded my information. Later I received a letter about how he enjoyed our conversation on the flight. I, while on the flight, had no idea that he was the governor of Florida, and it was quite an experience to receive the letter from his office.

"This happened about 20 years ago, yet I will never forget it. Such is a great lesson for networking: Extend the connection through later contact."

Blindstormer Mike offers this example about how to use networking to resolve a problem:

"Networking with your management people will help them better understand what you need to better perform your job. One way in which this helped me was the problem of getting written communication to visually impaired [workers] in a timely manner.

"After networking with a sighted coworker who read memos to the visually impaired workers, we came up with the idea of adding voice-mail boxes to the existing voice-mail system in which supervisors and other individuals could leave all important items that were normally distributed in written form.

"This has worked well and is much more cost effective than producing the information in Braille."

Another Blindstormer, Karen, writes:

"I stopped leading with my challenge and networked based on the career interest. . . . [It turned out] I was the best expert on how my visual challenge might or might not impact my job choices."

From eSight's "Swimming in the Mainstream" Forum

Contributors to eSight Career Network's SiM forum had a chance to tell how they surprised others by rising above the low expectations others had for them. They shared stories about not only feeling vulnerable but also being authentic in workplace situations.

Their discussion question was this: When have you surprised others in the workplace by rising above the low expectations they had for you?

Says Jake:

"My work and social involvement in Natural Ties was a very positive and rewarding experience for me. From the moment I received that call from my friend, Dan, who invited me out to lunch, I knew the experience was bound to be a good one—and it was."

Natalie writes:

"I remember when I was 17 and a junior in high school and had the opportunity to attend a language camp in Bemidji, Minnesota, because my study emphasis was Spanish. My grades were very good in this subject, and attending this camp was an opportunity to further my education in this area and get college credit. I was the first person with a visual impairment to attend this camp and the only one at that time.

"All the campers and counselors were sighted, and they wondered in astonished silence how I could keep up with the curriculum and how I could take care of my personal needs. . . . I was assertive in my communication skills, practicing Spanish and demonstrating my manual typewriter, tape recorder and talking watch.

"It didn't take but a couple days before everyone started looking at me as Natalie, not that poor, little, blind girl just being there for nothing better to do. I still keep up my Spanish practice and am quite fluent.

"I'm looking for employment in human services and [a job] in which I can use my Spanish. I like to help people, especially those with visual impairments and other disabilities."

"Upstate," on the other hand, admits:

"Many people have very little interest in [disabled] people. Able-bodied are having a tough time of it themselves, and this trend may continue for many years.

"This is not the same nation of 15 years ago. To 'create opportunity' will perhaps mean many us of with disabilities will need to establish careers as entrepreneurs outside of the business organization as [it] exists today."

And Roger asks these probing questions for society in general:

"If we encourage people with disabilities to gain an education and apply for any job they are capable of performing because it helps them achieve their full potential, what modifications does society have to make for that kind of accessibility?

"Do we jail potential employers who refuse to hire [those with disabilities]? Do we restrict access to transportation, access to information/the Internet, and isolate them into enclaves of 'disabled' who survive but are considered second-class citizens with limited rights?

"Do we allow [people with disabilities] to actively participate in deciding their careers, educational pathways, lifestyles, quality of life, or do we allow government-based 'experts' to design their programs for the 'poor' disabled?

"We need, as a society, to begin to address these questions before those [with disabilities] can assume their rightful place in society as a whole."

Attributes of Authenticity to Identify in Job Candidates

In your recruiting efforts, search for individuals with disabilities who know how to establish authentic relationships with you, their coworkers, and your customers. Perhaps that means you need to look for these attributes in a job candidate:

- ✐ Honesty in assessing and working with one's personal strengths and weaknesses

- ✐ Ability to accept and work with the personal strengths and weaknesses of others

- Skill in candidly and effectively expressing personal needs and wants
- Ability to accept and work with the personal needs and wants of others
- Ability to make decisions based on well-thought-out personal values

You'll likely have an opportunity to identify these attributes in a job candidate you're considering as you discuss what (if any) accommodations may be needed for the job at hand (see Chapter 5).

Terry Besenyody, human resources manager at Pitney Bowes' Spokane office, cites this example: One of her call center workers (let's call him John) is partially sighted as a result of diabetic retinopathy. He's been with Pitney Bowes for more than ten years.

"At the beginning," Besenyody points out, "he brought his own access tool, a glasses-mounted monocular." (A monocular is like a small telescope but for close viewing.) For some time, John was able to see the text on his monitor with just the monocular. But, when John's eyesight worsened, he needed to go to software that magnified what was on his monitor.

"He was still very easy to work with," says Besenyody. "He knew exactly what he needed, where and how to obtain it, who would install it, and how long it would take. He even found a way for us to share the expense with Services for the Blind."

Knowing when to gracefully accept help? Carrying his share of the load? Leveling with his supervisor? Recognizing a risk worth taking? Approaching the job as if it were his own business? You bet. Working from apparently vulnerable circumstances, John demonstrated his entrepreneurship, his authenticity, and his independence.

Targeting Candidates Who Are Willing to Take Reasonable Risks

As an employer, one of your most economical solutions to a high turnover rate is to hire and retain qualified employees with disabilities.

But, as an employer of individuals who have a disability, you'll probably gain that advantage of lower turnover only if you heed one pitfall.

Here's how eSight Careers Network member Bonita describes that pitfall:

"The attitude is sometimes very subtly conveyed that we must stay at one job and maintain a tight grip with gratitude on what we have because someone gave us a chance. That is wrong. We should be hired because we can do the work. If it is not workable, then changes must be made. I know of cases where [disabled] employees have been taken advantage of because the employers thought they would not or could not quit. Always seek to better yourself—your whole self."

In other words, you'll gain the advantage of perhaps less turnover with an employee who has a disability only if you provide the same opportunities for development and advancement that you provide employees who are not disabled.

Another Sign of Independence

Members of eSight identify an interesting twist in the traits to seek in job candidates with a disability. Even though they may give you less turnover, they can also be among your best leaders because they know how to take appropriate risks in building their personal lives and their own careers—skills they can apply on the job.

Participants in eSight's SiM forum shared their personal experiences about when they realized they were functioning as an adult by taking a calculated risk in a career-building situation.

Specifically, the SiM participants discussed this question: When is it time to ignore advice to "play it safe" and take a risk by changing jobs?

This discussion yielded three traits you, as a potential employer, might want to consider as you seek job candidates with a disability who are right for your organization. Those traits are a sense of self, a feel for reality, and a taste of success.

Why are these traits important to hiring managers? Job candidates with disabilities who possess these three characteristics can become some of your best leaders because they know how to take appropriate risks.

Here is how the SiM bloggers revealed those traits during the discussion about their own risk-taking experiences.

A Sense of Self

Cindy:

I was a case manager—was placed with [an assistant] who had no computer skills and was going to school full-time (which left me with no help to accomplish my job tasks). I resigned my position after five months because I was set up for failure.

Debbee:

The time to ignore advice is when the voices you hear in your head and in your heart become louder than those on the outside.

Laine:

Funny, every time I "play it safe," I find the safe way was much more trouble than I expected. Avoiding risk has kept me in relationships and on jobs far longer than was personally healthy. On the other hand, taking a risk often has unforeseen consequences.

I arrived on this planet with no material things and will leave the same way. So, I have decided that the collection of stuff isn't anywhere near as important as my growth as a human being. I have discovered that risk aversion is another term for fear of the unknown, and, frankly, no one really knows what is around the corner, anyway.

A Feel for Reality

Paul:

Good jobs are not easy to find for those with visual impairments. I say have your ducks in a row before you even think of quitting.

Fred:

Sometimes you have to learn how to be nonconfrontational, and, at the same time, you can't take "no" for an answer.

So, balance and persist at whatever you are doing. If the job is too much trouble, find another one before you leap into the unemployment percentages.

People may expect you to jump through flaming hoops, but you can put the heat on if you need to when it comes right down to it. I wouldn't give up the security of my job unless it was intolerable—and, before I gave up, I'd fight.

Most jobs that I left I was adept enough to have secured another job equal or better prior to resigning. Proper notice and effective resignation are very important.

No matter how well you have prepared for an occupation, overcoming the disability barrier is a major event. Once the job has been secured, be observant, plan, strategize, know if you are fitting in, and either plan to advance in that environment or begin laying the groundwork for the next job. Every job should be the platform for a higher level.

Peter:

I have made a career of changing jobs when the costs of a given job significantly exceeded the benefits. By and large, I am happy with all of these decisions, but it is worth remembering that it is harder for us [with disabilities] to find work than it is for those who are [not] impaired.

Kate:

Countering inappropriate workplace practices is not easy. If you are prepared to risk putting out a call for help, then you may find you don't have to do it alone. This has been my personal experience.

A Taste of Success

LuRetta:

The day when I stood up and defended my personal, strength-based career goals [refusing to simply take the first job that came along] was the day I embarked on my adult career journey. The result was a very beneficial and largely satisfying two decades in information technology and management.

Liz:

I moved 2,000 miles away from my friends and family to a small town in Alberta that wasn't exactly welcoming in 1982 for someone who was from Ontario and who had a disability. I lived independently, ran a household, shopped, cooked, cleaned, and taught.

I did the best job as a special education teacher that I could. I did it so well that I taught myself out of a job the next year, but I learned that I could live on my own and function as a mature individual when a lot of the "professionals" around me didn't. I built my self-confidence and self-worth.

The students' parents said I was the first of twelve previous special education teachers in that school who actually gave a damn about the kids and worked on their behalf, rather than sucking up to the administration.

I knew I had done a good job placing them in schools and classes where they would get the best teachers and education—which is what they deserved. My kids knew they were capable, wonderful human beings and not "space cadets" (the label the administration used to describe them).

This to me is a fully functioning adult: looking out toward the community and doing the best you can with what you have to make a difference.

Natalie:

I've been lucky to have good family support and good friends. They have encouraged me to do the best I can and then some. I really started to believe it this last semester, when I finally realized the truth in what they are saying—that I can do a lot better and need to believe in myself.

I am now in a much better position to reach out to the community and use what I have to make a difference. I know I'm a lot better than I give myself credit for.

In another comment on the SiM blog, Liz gave her fellow participants a new context for an individual's willingness to take risks on the job and within a career. She wrote:

All life is a risk to those of us with disabilities, be they physical, emotional, or cognitive. We take risks from the time we acquire our disabilities or are born with them, and we get so used to it that we don't even realize it. We've been risking things all our lives; we just may not have recognized it.

A Note from the Editor

Here's one more example of using a sense of self, a feel for reality, and a taste of success to "jump ship" and build another career. Even though I 'm considered "severely disabled" in a medical sense due to cerebral palsy, I decided to take what, in retrospect, was a sizable risk: quit my job as vice president of communication for a major firm in the dairy business at the age of 51 and start a small business as a consultant. Why? I found I was repeating myself in a comfortable work routine after nearly twenty-eight years of work in the same company. I was bored. I wanted to prove to myself that I could succeed outside of my comfort zone.

Even though I took a year to prepare for my jump into the field of career coaching for individuals with a disability and had a relatively soft landing once I made the leap, my wife, Pam, and I lived through some lean years as I tried to set up my consulting business during the economic boom of the 1990s. But, I did eventually find my niche in a slightly different venue (thanks to the Internet): helping to develop eSight Careers Network, a ten-year collaborative effort of online interactivity, research, writing, and editing—the result of which is this book.

Look for job candidates with disabilities who know how to take appropriate career risks, who are entrepreneurs at heart, and who know how to function effectively in the nondisabled world.

QUICK TIPS FROM THIS CHAPTER

⊘ Identify Those Who Approach Employment as Entrepreneurs

Achieving a balanced life in today's world is not easy for anyone. But focusing on one or more special needs not normally required of nondisabled folks and still achieving that balance can give someone who is disabled the entrepreneurial spirit you need in an employee at your workplace. For more information, see "Guest Post: What Gen Y Wants from Work" at http://webworkerdaily.com/2007/07/16/guest-post-what-gen-y-wants-from-work/.

⊘ Identify Those with Successful Small-Business Experience

Look for both tangible and intangible indicators of whether a job candidate's small business is "for real" and is a source of relevant experience. For more information, see "Small Business Startups: Statistics Show Realities" at http://www.esight.org/view.cfm?x=215.

⊘ Identify Those Who Have Moved Beyond Self-Absorption

Prime job candidates with a disability know how to use their interpersonal skills to effectively raise awareness and challenge assumptions about personal vulnerabilities as fully engaged members of society. They know the difference between being aggressive and assertive. They are not self-absorbed. For more information, see "Strategies for Dealing with Self-Absorbed People" at http://www.lib.sk.ca/booksinfo/DailyHerald/Dh2003/dh030112.html.

⊘ Identify Those Who Assume Personal Responsibility

Recruit job candidates who know how to take responsibility when they become "easy marks" at work. They'll probably have the inclination to resolve these issues for themselves. Having such proactive individuals on your staff can boost your work unit's morale. For more information, see "Work Bullies: Bad for the Victim and the Bottom Line" at http://abcnews.go.com/print?id=4546375.

⊘ Identify Those Who Have Well-Developed Emotional Intelligence

Consider job candidates who take the initiative to address the unasked questions about how they've learned to handle their disabilities. They could help you set the right tone for your work unit. For more information, see "We Make All Our Decision Based on Feelings" at http://www.emotionalintelligenceatwork.com/cms.php?show=decisions.

⊘ Identify Those Who Can Gracefully Accept and Decline Help

The ability to handle vulnerability gracefully is an attribute of leadership. For more information, see "How to Accept Help and Generosity in Your Life" at http://ezinearticles.com/?How-to-Accept-Help-and-Generosity-in-Your-Life&id=2082106&opt=print.

⊘ Identify Those Who Can Carry Their Own Load

Effective team members balance opportunities for helping and for receiving help. Disability need not be a detriment to that sharing. In fact, it can create an even more diverse and richer source of sharing when a person with a disability who knows how to interact effectively with others is involved. For more information, see "Examples of Good and Bad Interpersonal Skills at Work" at http://courts.michigan.gov/mji/curricula_guide/Examples_of_Good_and_Bad_Interpersonal_Skills.pdf.

⊘ Identify Those Who Are Authentic

Effective employees know how to build authentic relationships with you, their coworkers, and your customers. To detect authenticity, look for these attributes in a job candidate: honesty in assessing and working with one's personal strengths and weaknesses, ability to accept and work with the personal strengths and weaknesses of others, skill in candidly and effectively expressing personal needs and wants, ability to accept and work with the personal needs and wants of others, and ability to make decisions based on well-thought-out personal values. For more information, see "Authenticity at Work" at http://www.allbusiness.com/management/ change-management/3875604-1.html.

⊘ Identify Those Who Are Willing to Take Reasonable Risks

As an employer, you'll gain the advantage of perhaps less turnover with employees who have a disability only if you provide the same opportunities for development and advancement that you provide employees who are not disabled. Here's why: You want individuals on your team who will take risks in building their careers. For more information, see "Disability Confidence" at http://www.realising-potential.org/disability-confidence/.

Suggestion for Job Interview Topic

Each of this chapter's nine tips for identifying the job candidate who will best fit your work situation describes some aspect of emotional intelligence. So this could be one of your interview topics: "Cite an example of when you felt you were illustrating your 'emotional intelligence' in a work setting."

As a result, you may learn how that individual would handle unexpected problems and opportunities while on the job within your organization or company.

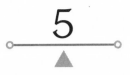

5

Approach People Management from a Disability Perspective

ONCE YOU HAVE HIRED ONE OR MORE people with disabilities to work for your company, you must work to incorporate your new employees into the workforce. What can you do to help the worker with a disability grow in his job and become a productive member of your work team? How can you work to remove barriers (both intentional and unintentional) to achievement that can hold back the employee with a disability? What are reasonable accommodations? Do you have to pay for adaptive technology? How can you prevent a disability discrimination lawsuit?

This chapter answers all these questions and many more. It ends with the example of how manager Curtis Bryan and employee Randy Hammer made blindness irrelevant in serving customers. Their story sums up what this chapter—and this book—are all about.

How Self-Esteem Affects Workplace Performance and Behavior

Nathaniel Branden, in his book *The Six Pillars of Self-Esteem* (Bantam, 1995), says, "Self-esteem is like calcium in our diet—lacking it we do not die (like when we don't have food or shelter), but it impairs our ability to function well."

Self-esteem is life supporting and life enhancing. It builds us up so we can function in a healthy manner toward ourselves, our loved ones, our coworkers, our supervisors, and our society at large.

Why Self-Esteem Is Important

As one of the pillars in emotional intelligence, self-esteem provides a capacity for regeneration—an attribute that gives top-notch job candidates with disabilities the resiliency to effectively cope with personal vulnerability.

That resiliency can be invaluable in job candidates because that resiliency can help your work group continue to succeed.

Job candidates with disabilities are probably in a good position to help you recognize their strengths. The best of them will show you why they're the best choice for your job opening. Look for a short but compelling story of one of their key successes.

"To trust one's mind and to know one is worthy of happiness is the essence of self-esteem," writes Branden. "It is a motivator, more so than a feeling or a judgment; it inspires behavior." In other words, how we act in the world and our level of self-esteem influence each other profoundly.

So what are the traits of high self-esteem and low self-esteem?

A General Profile of Self-Esteem

Our levels of self-esteem fluctuate every day, based on our individual actions, emotions, and experiences. But generally we all have a baseline of self-esteem in terms of how we feel about ourselves and our actions and our behavior in the world.

Put very simply, we could say that those with high self-esteem love themselves, their families, their friends, their work, their coworkers, their bosses—and society at large. They think that they are doing well at whatever they choose to do or say or think.

Those with lower self-esteem generally live in fear. They fear they don't measure up to other people. They fear that they are incapable in the eyes of others (and in their own). They don't trust themselves to make effective decisions. No one has ever given a whit about them, and no one ever will, they believe. They are alone and lonely in the universe, and they know why—because they don't deserve any better.

However, that's too generalized and too simplistic, according to

Branden. So, think of the previous two paragraphs as a self-esteem pro-file. Not everyone's self-esteem is so black and white; most of us have a little of each kind of self-esteem in our actions, thoughts, and beliefs.

Liz Seger, an educator and a journalist who has written extensively about self-esteem, points out that people with higher or more positive self-esteem seem to demonstrate a majority of similar positive traits compared to persons with lower or negative self-esteem.

Self-Esteem in the Workplace

Let's examine higher and lower self-esteem in the workplace.

Have you ever heard of someone who appears to the world as having it all (a good job, lots of money, power, and influence)? The person has all the outward trappings of what we call "success." Yet, the person does something stupid and totally self-sabotages a career or a legacy.

This is typical of people with low self-esteem. They fear they are imposters. They fear that eventually someone will find out that they are not as good at their jobs or as smart as they've been told they are. So they do something to show the world that its judgment of them is absolutely right. They self-sabotage. They fear their own success, so they do some-thing to prove to themselves that they are not capable or talented or deserving. It's kind of like the old Groucho Marx line: "I wouldn't join any club that had me as a member."

On the other hand, people with high self-esteem recognize their achievements and know that they have worked hard to produce them and, as a result, deserve whatever prestige or accolades come their way. They've done the work, either as individuals or within a team, and they've achieved what they expected to achieve.

People with lower self-esteem, however, fear being different, so they scapegoat or pick on someone whom they perceive as having lesser sta-tus. That's how bullying starts. It's in the workplace as well as in the schoolyard.

Name-calling, nit-picking, making inappropriate remarks, using intimidation, and having a gang to surround the person they are target-ing are all tactics bullies use. And generally they do it because they fear anyone else getting ahead or finding out they're not as good at their jobs. They will do, think, and say anything to preserve their status and to prove that they are valued and valuable on their jobs.

People with higher self-esteem, however, aren't intimidated by others and their achievements, Branden explains. If anything, they are supportive. They have no need to feel superior to anyone else because they are confident in their abilities to do their jobs, take criticism, and not necessarily have to be one of the members of the "in group" to be effective.

They can assert themselves appropriately without throwing a "hissy fit" and calling attention to their abilities. People with high self-esteem stand up for themselves and their achievements as well as take criticism gracefully. They don't need to prove their worth or value to themselves or to their employer. They know they do well in their jobs because their work gives them happiness. They enjoy doing well. They accept the accolades and the promotions, but their feeling of confidence is not dependent upon them.

People with lower self-esteem often fail to make good choices. They fear anything new or different in their personal and working lives because it is different and might upset their beliefs about who they are and why they are there.

They often fear innovation and creativity because it may shine the light on them, and they prefer to be invisible. But they try to get all the "goods" on others to reinforce their viability and value within the company.

By contrast, people with higher self-esteem do not fear others, are not judgmental, and think that what they have or do or are is enough to be happy in the world. Joy is their motivator—not fear. They wish to experience happiness and believe they are worthy of it. They do not wish to always be suffering. They are not continually judging themselves or avoiding themselves. They tend to attract people into their lives who have similar levels of self-esteem.

Bragging about what one has or does is not high self-esteem. Being arrogant and making others feel inferior has nothing to do with high self-esteem. Rather, it is the mark of low self-esteem. It's an effort by a person to prove to himself that he is worthy and valuable.

Branden writes:

> A well developed sense of self-esteem is a necessary condition to our well being. Its presence doesn't guarantee fulfillment, but its lack guarantees some measure of anxiety, frustration and despair. Positive self-esteem is the immune system of consciousness, providing resilience, strength and a capacity to regenerate.

That is not to say positive self-esteem doesn't fluctuate, but it helps one be more resilient and overcome life's difficulties.

A Story About Resiliency

Resiliency, based on a healthy sense of self-esteem, can turn a bad situation into a good one. Liz Seger writes that she has had to be resilient in her life, and many times, was positive she was "down for the count."

Here's her story:

"The first really horrible event was when, at two weeks before graduation, the Dean of the Faculty of Education called me in and said, 'We're not granting you a degree, despite the fact that you passed all your courses; no school board will hire a blind person.'

"I came out of his office in shock and angry. I mean, sure, take my money, educate me, and then yank it all away! Why? You know, I was disabled when I came in. It's like teasing a dog or cat with a treat, and, as soon as they are about to take it, you yank it away. Well, you know what happens in the animal world—someone gets bitten or scratched.

"In the human world, you can either fight back (high, positive self-esteem) or slink away and beat yourself up (low, negative self-esteem). For a time, because I was young, I did just that—I stood back and beat myself up. I must be stupid or something. Who takes a degree away just before graduation?

"My mother let me grieve for about two months. Then, she said to me, 'You're not sitting home doing nothing. What are you going to do about this?' My parents had gone up to the university to investigate this and came home saying our poodle had more intelligence and empathy than the dean—and Natasha was not the brightest poodle on the planet.

"My dad just kind of wanted me to go do something else—go back to school and take secretarial stuff. We both looked at him and said, 'Oh, yeah, that'll work.'

"However, my mom got her cronies involved. A friend who was a teacher said to me, 'Come and work in my classroom. I can use the help and it will keep your teaching skills sharp. I can't pay you, but the experience will look good on your resume.'

"Another principal heard about it and called me and asked, 'On the days you're not at St. John Bosco, can you come volunteer in our itinerant special education classes? I can't pay you; you're not certified. But the experience could be valuable for you.'

"I also acquired a lot of personal references for when I did pick up the fight, and it wasn't long before I got feisty.

"Being with those kids those years convinced me I was indeed a good teacher. I filled in at story time when the librarians were busy. I went far further than an educational aide could in a class. I taught special education kids, and the kids were 'inventing behaviors' to get into my classes.

"All the while my mom was writing letters to the ministry and getting her friends to write letters to the ministry in my support. But, the best of all, my mom found an old friend who was the local radio talk-show lady.

"Joan had a fairly controversial talk show for two hours each day, and she tackled some very difficult subjects. I had a mad crush on her nephew all through high school, and so he and I were friends as well. I think the word made it to Tommy that Lizzy-tish was having some problems, and he talked to his aunt Joan who, in turn, had been talking to my mom.

"Joan interviewed me on the radio with a woman from the Handicapped Employment Program, now known as the Council on Disability and Work, part of the Ministry of Labor. The case worker, Dorothy Dacy, and I hit it off like popcorn and butter and her executive director, Barb Earle, formed the final part of the triumvirate. Together we were going to take this very prestigious Canadian university down.

"Using the emerging disability rights movement and Independent Living movement in Canada, we found out that this university had been given government grants specifically to train teachers with physical disabilities but, in the five years of grants, had never graduated a teacher with a physical disability. We found the mother-lode when we came upon that piece of information.

"I don't know what happened, but I heard via the grapevine from a few of the profs I had that the you-know-what hit the fan when Mrs. Earle marched into the Dean's office with that piece of information and an implicit threat that, if my degree wasn't granted and my Ontario teacher's certificate wasn't decreed, all hell was going to break loose. The anchorman from our national broadcasting agency had been chasing me for six months, wanting to do a story on this. The great-granddaughter of one of our chief justices of the Supreme Court was after me to sue and make sure the case got up to the Supreme Court.

"The university caved in. Since two-and-a-half years had gone by at this point, I had to do my practice teaching over. I went, and I got 'A's from my profs at my undergraduate school.

"The principals and most of the teachers at both of the schools where I was volunteering signed petitions to get my degree and certification reinstated.

"In 1980, my B.Ed. degree and Ontario Teacher Certificate were granted—two years late (but at least they got granted).

"I went from being in the depths of despair almost three years earlier to thanking God for giving me this experience so I could go out into teaching and give that faculty of education the middle-finger salute. And the best part: I got a teaching job with a board of education that next year.

"I subbed on and off with that board for 10 more years. I taught in a school in Alberta for a year, ran my own tutoring service, and wrote for a newspaper, covering education and disabilities.

"So, from a totally negative experience that could have left me crying into my pillow, I not only made some incredible friends and colleagues along the way but also taught kids who I loved and came to inspire (so I'm told)."

And that is Seger's story of strength, resiliency, and regeneration—sparked by a healthy dose of self-esteem. That self-esteem helped her to surround herself with supportive friends and acquaintances; to happily volunteer in order to gain experience; and to build an independent, vibrant life for herself despite her visual and other physical disabilities.

Accomplishment outside of work can foreshadow what to expect from a high-functioning job candidate with a disability who joins your team—someone who has experienced:

- ⊘ A taste of success
- ⊘ A proof of his or her abilities
- ⊘ A thirst for independence
- ⊘ A hesitancy to be judgmental of others

Being a people manager comes a little bit easier for you when you have more people (disabled or not) within your work group with that kind of experience. And recognizing that each of those experiences has extended meaning for those you manage who do have disabilities adds a new dimension to your management style.

Avoiding Paternalism in the Workplace

Paternalism can sap your company's productivity and competitiveness because it chokes off the potential that employees with disabilities have for helping you effectively and efficiently serve customers. It's a damper to self-esteem.

Participants on eSight Career Network's "Swimming in the Mainstream" (SiM) blog talked about how individuals with a disability can best deal with paternalism on the job. In the process, they came up with some insight about what employees as well as employers can do to both prevent and combat it.

The Payoff in Stamping Out Paternalism

By eliminating paternalism, you'll tap the full potential employees with disabilities have for helping your company compete successfully in today's marketplace.

Through this blog's dialogue, we discover that paternalism typically flourishes under these two conditions: a new employee's lack of work experience and society's misguided approach to disability.

A New Employee's Lack of Work Experience

It may be tempting to see yourself as a father or mother figure toward someone who joins your company and has no corporate or teamwork experience (a situation that can be fairly common with individuals who have a disability).

Take a look at what Mike writes:

"I hold a master's degree in Public Administration from the University of North Carolina at Pembroke. The topic for my thesis, required for completing my master's, was about 'Employing People with Disabilities, with Emphasis on the Blind.' In my thesis (see http://employtheblind.blogspot.com), I discuss relevant issues and statistics that contribute to the 70 percent unemployment rate of legally blind and visually impaired people in the United States of working ages between 18 and 65.

"Let me add further that I have had trouble not becoming yet another statistic. Trying to acquire a decent job when you are visually impaired is extremely difficult if not almost impossible. Though I possess the formal education, I still lack much-needed experience in my field of study and expertise where I can get my foot in the door.

"However, I will not give up, but I am afraid I may not be headed in the right direction in order for me to get where I believe I need to be at this point in my life."

Mike is maybe someone who could flourish "under the wing" of a supervisor who is willing to "give him a chance" despite his lack of work experience. The common inclination is to help him adjust to work life.

But, as a leader, you might be more effective in pairing an individual such as Mike with a mentor assuming the role you normally take as a manager or supervisor and letting that mentor/mentee pairing work out any lack of experience he may have.

Society's Misguided Approach to Disability

In job candidates or individuals newly hired with a disability, look for the ability to project themselves as adults, despite society's tendency to treat them as children.

For example, as a radio personality in Canada who is blind, Alyzza finds condescending pats on the back for doing what everyone else does particularly aggravating. "It's almost like social expectations [for people with disabilities] are so low that even the most mediocre activity warrants praise with abandon," she writes.

Liz Seger, a teacher and writer, puts such paternalism into perspective:

"I think most of the time the people who treat those of us with disabilities as children or marginalize us do it out of ignorance. They've not been exposed to disability, they've believed all the myths or they're just plain frightened and may suffer from their own handicap of foot-in-mouth disease. . . .

"You want to be treated like an adult? Do the best job you know how to, act professionally but with humor and empathy, and then show how it's done."

Barney concurs with Liz. He actually sees the tendency to treat adults with disabilities in a childlike manner as an opportunity: "Acting like an adult should bring adult responses. . . . We have the opportunity to teach them who we are and what we are capable of. We are looking for allies and supporters. Everyone will not fit this bill but do not dally. Try to convert people. Know who you are and act accordingly."

But, consider the following two before-and-after examples of how pervasive paternalism can be in a variety of circumstances.

"I have been a PWD [person with a disability] since I was almost 40," blogger Art says. "Among my greatest surprises was that . . . most [people] will underestimate my age by at least five years."

He adds: "Most suggestions that a PWD's age is lower reflect a failure to see the PWD as an equal. Unless the deed as well as the intent are eventually recognized, there is an open invitation to further demeaning treatment."

Jeremy also notices a gap in credibility:

"For many years, I did my best to hide my disability (very poor sight). But, with a little sight I had and a lot more confidence than I felt inside (and no small amount of smoke and mirrors), I could fool the casual observer into not knowing I had a disability—this way enjoying equal respect.

"Obviously closer observers were aware, and, now that I think about it, I had to spend more time than necessary convincing those people that my ideas or opinions were valid and relevant.

"But I must admit that after 'coming out' and using a cane (which incidentally changed my life), I have also noticed a tendency of people to doubt my maturity. . . .

"I co-run Disability Solutions, a consultancy focused on disability integration issues, and I have definitely noticed this tendency to regard [me] as not quite an adult. I know my business partner, Guy, who is a paraplegic, can relate to this, too. . . .

"I have noticed a tendency in clients to be more cautious when making a decision about using our services. They are simply awed at having to deal with PWDs on the same level as they, particularly since they have little or no experience with PWDs at their level in the organization. . . .

"I was most annoyed recently when I was told that my training on disability awareness was too expensive. This was from a client who had spent more on a diversity program that had left disability out. As far as I can ascertain, most diversity programs over here (New Zealand) leave disability out or deal with it very sketchily. Yet, diversity sells well."

Maturity, respect, credibility—all three are in jeopardy for both the individual with a disability and your corporate culture when paternalism is allowed to grow, largely due to lack of awareness and misinformation.

Here are four benchmarks of productive organizational behavior—

behavior that can prevent paternalism from sprouting and spreading in your workplace.

1. **Recognize true commitment.** George combated being late to work (due to paratransit) by buffering his start time by an hour and telling the transit personnel that he had to be to work at 7:00 A.M. instead of 8:00 A.M. So, he often shows up too early. Other employees and bosses see this as an extra commitment on his part.

2. **Acknowledge the person's experience in the right way.** Says Liz, "I do think, though, when someone calls us 'inspiring' or 'special,' it sometimes comes out of a place where they want to acknowledge our experience but can't find the right words so, because our culture is so 'hero'-oriented anyway, they call us 'heroes' or 'heroines' or 'inspirational.' Maybe one day none of us will have to endure being 'special,' as Dana Carvey's 'Church Lady' would say."

3. **Treat employees as individuals.** Recognize both strengths and weaknesses in an employee with a disability. Sara may be able to pay attention to detail and have the ability to accurately and precisely communicate and process information far better than her coworkers, but, at the same time, she may not be able to see the big picture and plan for the future like George, her coworker, can.

4. **Recruit people with disabilities who have interpersonal skills.** As one eSight member, let's call her Barb, tells her fellow bloggers: "You need to be an adaptable, social, and likeable individual before you can ever expect to become an employable professional at any level. Learn to golf, laugh, and make friends."

Remember, from a corporate as well as an individual vantage point, the opposite of paternalism is validation.

A Note from the Editor

Validating an Employee with a Disability as an Equal Member of Your Team

Since 1965, I've collected tips for validating an employee with a disability within a corporate setting. Now that I review them, I realize they boil down to just plain effective management.

But, when we hire an employee with a disability, we sometimes tend to stumble over ourselves, forget the basics of supervision and leadership, and try to accommodate that person in inappropriate ways. That sets up unrealistic expectations for the organization, for the person with the disability, and for that person's colleagues.

As a person with cerebral palsy who walks and talks with difficulty, I've worked as a newsletter assistant, middle manager, corporate communications vice president, and organizational development officer. I've dealt with acceptance and validation from both an employee and employer perspective—and as a person with a significant disability. Validation is an issue for any employee who is presumed different because she doesn't quite fit accepted norms.

Seven Guidelines from the Editor for Fair Treatment

Follow Jim Hasse's seven guidelines for helping an employee who has a disability feel like a full member of your team. They'll put you on the path toward fair treatment for that employee as well as your other team members.

Here are Hasse's seven recommendations for effectively supervising an employee with a disability.

1. Avoid Parent-Like Behavior

Resist the temptation to run interference for an employee who has a disability. That's not your job and it wastes time.

"I once took a one-day business trip to interview a new manager for an employee publication," says Hasse. "When I arrived for the interview, I discovered that one of my colleagues had called ahead to point out to my interviewee that I had a disability. I felt about three feet tall because someone else was shadowing me. I had a father figure back in the home office."

Paternalism has no place in a corporate setting, but we tend to transfer to the office what we know and do at home when we see someone we think is vulnerable and needs help and protection.

2. Allow Ownership of Mistakes

Paternalism can go further than calling ahead to forewarn an interviewee. It can lead to burying mistakes that the employee with a disability makes and not allowing him to fail—or succeed.

Hasse says: "I once made an end-run call without consulting with my boss or field staff director. My decision created all kinds of questions in the field. Customer service reps were getting telephone calls without knowing why. I should have 'caught hell' for making such a stupid mistake. But I didn't. I later found out about the ramifications of what I did only after I took the initiative and asked the people in the field."

It is best to confront mistakes and failure with the person who has a disability so that person can learn and grow from it. And avoid lowering your established expectations for results just because the work involved is being performed by someone with a disability.

3. Assign Responsibility

The tendency to hide mistakes and failure from an employee with a disability can lead to the more serious issue of reassigning her shoddy work to others. That's unfair to her because you are not giving her the opportunity to improve her work. It's also unfair to other members of your team, who may be expected to pick up the slack because of her poor performance. And that breeds resentment.

Like others on your team, the employee who has a disability needs clear assignments and well-defined areas of responsibility. When those responsibilities are not met, deal directly with her about correcting those work problems.

4. Follow Promotion Policies

If you choose to reassign or promote an employee with a disability, do it in an evenhanded way according to your organization's established assignment and promotion policies. If it's a promotion, make it clear that it's a promotion—just as you would with any other employee.

"In my own experience of climbing the corporate ladder," Hasse says, "I've noticed a tendency to discount promotions that involve people with disabilities as not as significant as those involving nondisabled people. Perhaps those promotions are done quietly—almost apologetically— with the realization that latent resentment among nondisabled colleagues could be a problem for the organization."

5. Keep Job Functions Intact

Another temptation is to dilute job functions to meet your preconceived notions of a disabled employee's ability or inability. It's true that productivity is enhanced when jobs can be tailored to a particular person's skills and interests, but levels of responsibility and authority must also be kept intact for specific jobs.

Hasse says: "I've found that I always needed to ask specifically for secretarial services—even when I was a vice president and corporate officer. Somehow it was assumed that, since I had keyboard skills, I did not really need that kind of support, when, in reality, the lack of it hampered my productivity."

6. Praise Real Accomplishment

Putting your employee with a disability on a pedestal is just as harmful as downplaying his skills or diluting his job function. Completing a routine research project using a screen reader doesn't warrant lavish praise just because it may take extra effort. That kind of overcompensation shows you really have not accepted him as a fully contributing member of your team, and it gets old fast. It becomes silly in his eyes as well as from the perspective of your other team members.

Instead, compliment your employee with a disability just as you would other members of your team—for outstanding, beyond routine results, for instance. Use your own pattern for recognition and reward. Just make it consistent for every member of your team.

7. Avoid the "Inspiration" Label

Here's another easy habit to form and a difficult one to break once you've fallen into it. One of the last comments an employee with a disability probably wants to hear from her colleagues and her boss is that she's an "inspiration" for them. It's bad enough when you say it privately to her. But if that type of sentimentality is expressed publicly—especially in a large forum by a corporate officer—it can be deadly, for it can really damage her credibility among her associates as well as those above and below her in the chain of command.

When your associates repeat the "inspiration" label often enough for that employee, it becomes a part of the accepted corporate culture for your organization and brands her with an identity she will find difficult to change. It could become a burden for her because she'll continually feel the need to perform and inspire others instead of becoming just another one of your team members working toward a common goal. And becoming that is usually all she wants.

It's trite, but it's probably true—and it best sums up these seven guidelines for validating an employee with a disability: Most employees with a disability want to be treated like everyone else.

Assigning a Mentor for Your Newly Hired Employee with a Disability

When the legendary adventurer Odysseus set out for the Trojan War, he left his son, Telemachus, in the capable hands of a trusted friend named Mentor. Since then, the word "mentor" has been used to refer to any adult who guides the development of another person, whether a child, a student, or a person new to an environment.

Studies of Big Brothers/Big Sisters of America have revealed remarkable success in its efforts to prevent young people from detouring into drugs, pregnancy, and crime. No wonder, since a synonym for mentor is "coach," and the impact coaches have had in the success of individual players and entire teams in sports has been understood for decades.

Many people can credit at least some of their success to the support and advice of a mentor. For most of us, that mentor either sculpted our growth into adulthood or provided the feedback and encouragement we needed in choosing and pursuing a career.

For decades, the corporate world has recognized the value of mentors. In many organizations, mentoring programs for new employees have been a long-standing practice.

Mentors can assist workers within an organization in a variety of ways. Just as mentors can help young people make good life decisions, mentors can help business owners make good business decisions and employees make good career decisions. Within a company, experienced workers, in their mentoring roles, extend initial training and provide individualized feedback and guidance, with the new employee's specific tasks and adjustment issues in mind.

Assigning mentors to new workers is, in fact, a cost-effective and value-added way to make the probationary employment period a success. The employee makes good decisions and develops well. The mentor gains a sense of his importance in the company and recognizes his own influence on its future. And the employer gains new workers who are more effective and satisfied. Mentoring is truly a win-win-win situation.

Specifically, what are the benefits of a mentoring program for new workers? Let's take a look:

⊘ New employee training often ignores adult learning theory and presents too much information in too short a time and in a way that adults have trouble retaining. The mentor, in an informal way, helps reinforce and extend that "traditional" training for the new employee.

⊘ The mentor is available to guide the new worker, answer questions, and offer constructive advice when a supervisor may not be readily available.

⊘ The mentor can assist the new worker in adjusting to the climate of the company, both in terms of overt expectations and in the less tangible aspects of organizational culture.

⊘ The mentor often intervenes before a worker's poor work habits get to the point where they are noticed by the supervisor. This encourages the worker to improve and head off problems before their impact is damaging or simply a drain on time.

⊘ The mentor's consistent relationship with the new worker gives him a more accurate impression of the worker's strengths and weaknesses and a greater understanding of the source of any problems, making evaluation easier and more realistic.

⊘ Simply having someone "on the new worker's side" increases the chance that this new worker will feel comfortable seeking out and making use of constructive criticism. The inevitable but invisible wall between an authority and the follower (the supervisor and the new employee) is not present in the mentor/mentee relationship and does not act as a barrier to development.

⊘ Mentors show new workers that a job is more than just a job. It is a career or even a profession. The mentor models the pride and sense of accomplishment that will and should be expected from the worker as he grows in the company. The mentor, chosen for his exemplary qualities of teamwork and collaboration, instills these qualities in the person he's coaching.

Three Key Mentoring Attributes

Pair a new employee who has a disability with a trusted, capable, and supportive coworker in your company's mentoring program.

Some businesses may be concerned that hiring individuals with disabilities is a drain on company time and resources when the new employee has real or perceived limitations. Assigning mentors to these newly hired people directly addresses that concern. Here are specific examples:

- ⊘ If the relationship begins immediately, the mentor can provide the individual assistance a worker with a disability may need while in training.

- ⊘ The mentor can continue this one-on-one attention during the probationary period to ensure that the employee can handle the double challenge of learning a new job and learning how to use the adaptive tools to do it.

- ⊘ The mentor models acceptance of and cooperation with the employee who has a disability; that helps other staff, including managers, learn how to work with the employee.

- ⊘ The mentor, if properly trained, can reflect back to management which problems arising from the new employee's assimilation into the organization are due to the disability and which are simply performance deficits. The mentor is likely to have a more accurate idea of what the worker is like.

- ⊘ Since a new employee is bound to worry about others' attitudes toward his disability, the mentor can act as a trusted and accepting ally as well as an interpreter of which coworker perceptions are real and which are not.

- ⊘ With trained mentors, the section supervisors do not all have to become specialists in helping employees with disabilities adjust to a workplace setting. The mentor, through training and experience, can take his specialized role and free the supervisor so she can concentrate on real work issues and other people-management priorities.

A mentor does not necessarily just teach an individual how to reach a goal. He teaches that individual how to be the person who can and will achieve it. A mentor for an employee with a disability, for instance, needs to go beyond the "how to do the task" to "how to be a skillful and reliable performer of a task."

Choosing Mentors

Mentors in business settings must first of all be experienced employees, both in terms of knowing the business and the job and in knowing the nuances of how the company operates on a day-to-day basis. In addition to an ability to understand and interpret the corporate culture, effective mentors must possess strong interpersonal skills.

Mentors paired with individuals with a disability need not be highly trained in issues about disability and employment. A good mentoring candidate will be someone who is open and enthusiastic about learning. It is no more of a benefit to have a mentor who holds the employee with a disability to lower standards than it is to have someone who is biased against him.

The mentor must be open-minded but not so far open that, as the saying goes, his brains fall out. He is doing the person with a disability a disservice if he gives him so much rope he gets tangled up in it. The mentor must be able to distinguish between the purely mechanical challenges of a disability and the psychological habits that can come with "getting away with murder" because of it.

Ensuring Mentor Success

The first step in developing a mentoring program is to be very clear what you want it to accomplish. Every aspect must be designed to support the company's interests by enabling the best level of work any new employee can do. When you know why you are assigning mentors and the potential value of those relationships, then you can confidently communicate to others in your organization the importance of those mentors and gain support for them.

It is essential that you choose people who can succeed at mentoring. It is very difficult to teach someone without the combination of empathy and good sense that make up a great mentor. As all great chefs say, "You must start with the best-quality ingredients."

Be sure the tools the mentors need are in place. They will need effective training in the techniques of mentoring and a thorough understanding of policies and procedures as well as your management's vision for mentoring new employees. They will need access to ongoing advice for themselves: They need mentors, too! And they need the trust and confidence not only of you and their assigned mentee but also of coworkers and supervisors.

In addition to providing opportunities for feedback and support, you need to make known your intention to hold the mentor responsible for the development of an assignee. You must demonstrate that you value good mentoring and will evaluate the mentor's performance.

Give mentors opportunities, venues, and other tools as well as support in time assigned away from their usual duties. The Internet is a perfect tool to use in supporting your mentors with the least impact on everyone's time and workload. The International Society of Automation (http://www.isa.org), for instance, has developed a thorough understanding of how online support can help achieve the goals of a mentoring program in the most efficient way.

For the mentor assigned to help an employee who is disabled, there are a few additional supports you need to supply. You must clearly articulate that you want to see the individual who is disabled succeed right alongside those who are not disabled. The employee with a disability earned her position; it was not given as a gift. Tie the value of an employee with a disability to your company's success, and make it known that you expect her skills and qualities to be evaluated and developed.

Provide "reeducation" about disabilities for mentors. Avoid calling it "sensitivity training," since that generally focuses on courtesy instead of the basic cold facts of a disability's real impact on an individual from a mechanical perspective. You don't have to be extra polite to individuals with a disability. But you and the mentors should know something about how they carry out activities that others not familiar with their situation may believe cannot be done.

Mentors must be made aware that the disability experience is nothing like what they may think it is. In fact, it is not always all that bad. One adjusts, and, for some people, it truly is all they know.

Provide both mentors and new associates with opportunities to mingle with other employees and the staff in other departments. The education your workforce will receive through the modeling of a positive and mutually enjoyed relationship will go far to boost the effectiveness of your mentor program in the future.

Finally, take pains to check back with everyone involved to see how effective the mentoring has been and how satisfying and rewarding it turned out to be for the new employee, the mentor, the worker's supervisor, and the company workforce in general. Be prepared to make changes, to retrain mentors, to better articulate expectations, and to learn. Only then will inclusion of an individual with a disability in your workforce become a reality and a source of pride.

Using Your Leadership to Help an Employee with a Disability Grow in His Job

When there is no leadership in a company, people stop listening to each other, people stop doing good work, teamwork disintegrates, the work-place gets nasty, and people start picking on each other—particularly those who are considered "different."

But people picking on each other is just the beginning. The situation continues to go downhill from there, according to John Baldoni in his handbook *180 Ways to Walk the Leadership Talk* (Walk the Talk Company, 2000). Product and service quality take a nosedive, some employees quit, customers start leaving, and business dries up, he points out.

It's a real danger signal when you see people picking on each other. It could be that you're already halfway down the slippery slope; you're at a point where you're going to lose your best employees and best customers.

How can you tell for sure?

An Employee Who Is "Different" Can Be a Bellwether

In one sense, your employee with a disability, as a minority and as an employee who is "different," is a bellwether. If other employees are pick-ing on him, either he doesn't know how to handle his unique situation within a work setting (in which case he may not be the right person for you in that job or he may need your counseling in correcting the situa-tion) or the atmosphere has deteriorated in your group because of your leadership.

18 "Grooming" Suggestions

As a manager or supervisor, your leadership can pave the way for notable, on-the-job performance from a person with a disability. Consider Jim Hasse's eighteen tips for taking the lead to groom that per-son for added responsibility.

Assuming you've done the background work so the job and the per-son with a disability are a pretty good fit, there are some things you can do as a leader to encourage notable performance on the job from that individual. The next section examines these tips.

Leadership Tips from a Disability Perspective

As a business leader with a disability for more than four decades, Jim Hasse has been collecting ideas about how to effectively lead from a disability perspective. Following are eighteen of them that he finds particularly helpful. Baldoni also cites some of these tactics in his handbook.

1. Set up a place on your company's intranet in which each of your employees (not just the person with a disability) can privately post compliments, suggestions, and complaints in a nonthreatening way to facilitate your in-person communications with each individual.

2. Build relationships with leaders in other companies to learn from their successes and setbacks in employing people with disabilities. Such networking, particularly with others from diverse backgrounds and functional areas unlike your own, will provide you with lots of new ideas.

3. Pave the way so your employee with a disability can make good things happen for himself. You can do that by listening—finding out, on a continuing basis, what your employee truly needs to do his job better.

4. Live by your words and set an example. Treat your employee with a disability according to patterns that you would like his coworkers and your colleagues to follow.

5. Be proactive and look for potential problems before they become real issues for your employee who is disabled or his coworkers. Approach your leadership role with the concept that problems are really solutions waiting to happen.

6. Use appropriate discipline to protect individuals within your group from infringing on each other's individual rights or the rights of the group. Remember that your employee with a disability can be the one who is hurting others as well as the one who is being hurt. However, know when your employee needs to solve a problem himself—and when you need to intervene.

7. Be forgiving. Most people deserve a second chance if they

demonstrate that they are willing to learn from their mistakes. But also make sure that your employees, disabled or not, realize what you expect of them. Forgiving is not lowering your standards for performance. That's particularly important when your employee with a disability is involved.

8. Tell stories, particularly those that illustrate behavior that applies to issues your employee who is disabled is currently facing. Let him draw his own conclusions about how the story applies to him.

9. Develop a story folder of anecdotes that you can draw upon to make your points with your employees. Your employee with a disability, by the way, needs "nondisability" stories as well as those that address his personal issues about disability.

10. Give your employee with a disability the same orientation and basic training you give others within your group so that he will be prepared to succeed.

11. Make it a habit to make regular contact with each of the members of your group—not just your employee with a disability. They should not have to come to you.

12. Talk to your employee about his disability. Get to know his situation. Empathize.

13. Use that empathy to reinforce your awareness that you are ultimately responsible and accountable for the actions of each of the others in your work group as well as your own.

14. Be patient while your employee with a disability is learning a new task. Remember, those who learn the fastest are not always the best performers or those with the most "staying power." Your patience shows that you respect others—and that others can trust you.

15. Respect and encourage as well as console your employee with a disability when he has experienced failure. Show concern—but also show your appreciation that he tried and encourage him to take another (maybe lesser) step forward.

16. Include your employee with a disability in cross training—just as you would other members of your team. He will become more enthused about putting his new skills to good use, and you'll gain a better qualified, more well-rounded team.

17. Check for teamwork experience when you interview a person with a disability for a job. If the candidate responds to your query about such experience enthusiastically with concrete examples of collaboration, you may have a team player. But remember that not everyone is a team player. Some individuals work best alone. Let them "do their thing" if they're good performers.

18. Learn how to manage a diverse team of individuals, including those with a disability. Show that, under your leadership, a team can produce exceptional results precisely because members have learned to tap each other's strengths and compensate for another's weaknesses. Create opportunities for each team member to show what he can do on a team or with a special assignment.

A Mutual Interest

In one sense, you and your employee with a disability may have a mutual interest. As someone who is "different," he has a larger than usual stake in how well you perform as a leader. And he can be your bellwether. The extra time you may be required to spend in helping him perform well in his job and as a member of your team may actually provide you with an opportunity to showcase your skills—and grow—as a leader.

Removing Intentional and Unintentional Barriers to Achievement for Employees with a Disability

You've done the smart thing. You hired the best candidate for your job opening, and you didn't let the fact that she has a disability deter you. You are confident both in her abilities and in your capacity to put her to work with the accommodations she needs. You anticipate a bottom-line benefit from your decision.

If you want to realize that benefit, however, your work doesn't end there. You also must empower your employee so she can work toward achievements beyond her entry position.

Empowered Instead of Restrained

Employees with disabilities are empowered instead of restrained in an inclusive workplace, and that has a positive impact on the bottom line.

Some barriers that impede the development of a worker with a disability are "sins of commission," and some are "sins of omission." There are, in some cases, intentional barriers. Intentional barriers usually have their roots in the hiring decision. You hire a person with a disability for the wrong reason: to fulfill a quota, to show what a good guy or company you are, or to fill a job with someone who comes cheap. You may develop "set aside" positions with little responsibility or challenge because you figure that's all a person with a disability can handle.

Most obstacles to achievement among employees with disabilities, however, occur unintentionally—even in companies with genuinely inclusive philosophies. Many times the barrier is simply an oversight, a situation of "Gee, I never thought of that!" Training materials are not accessible. Because of local transit deficits, the worker cannot get to work on weekends to put in overtime. It may be that you simply don't realize you are using different language when talking to a disabled worker—just as studies in the 1980s found that teachers were unaware that they called on and expressed confidence in female students less frequently than their male counterparts. Or you may not have realized a key player in personnel development either has an overt bias against people with disabilities or simply needs more education.

Whatever the cause of unintentionally overlooking the potential in an employee with a disability, you squander possibilities for you and your company as well as the individual.

If You Don't Do It for Them, Do It for You

Obviously most employees (and certainly the most valuable to you) want to succeed and advance in their careers. Providing clear and open paths for personal development and leadership within a group is a well-known strategy for boosting employee morale. In fact, this strategy can be even more effective in terms of turnover and morale than the short-term benefit employers often realize when they reward employees with across-the-board pay raises. Fulfilled workers don't leave, and that can mean less work for you.

But achieving a lower turnover rate among employees and avoiding the expense of replacing workers who leave are not the only bottom-line benefits of helping workers reach their full potential. Well-trained, motivated employees simply are more productive and do better work. If employees with a disability start out willing to give their proverbial 110 percent, imagine what they'd accomplish in positions of higher responsibility. And that's a reflection on you as a mentor, a supervisor, a manager, or an administrator.

So it simply does not suffice to hire a person with a disability, give her the accommodations she needs to work, and then walk away. Like a garden, you must fertilize and cultivate your employee's efforts to harvest her true potential. If you do walk away, you may never see the heights she could reach on your company's behalf.

Yes, she wants to advance, but more important, you want her in a position where she can have the most impact. Chances are she'll best contribute to your company's success and most effectively reflect your leadership skills if she is allowed (and empowered) to find her place on the corporate ladder.

Reaffirm Your Initial Good Judgment

Be sure to make continuing education accessible for the individual with a disability who you have hired (just as you do with those you have hired who are not disabled). Doing so will show everyone within your company beyond a shadow of a doubt that you hired that person because you believed in the contributions he or she would make to the overall success of your company.

—Jo Taliaferro, ordained minister, assistive technology specialist

The key is to look at those areas where a superior employee shines and how she is making her best contributions so that you can make sure no artificial barriers exist in those areas where she is likely to excel.

The Four T's: Tools, Training, Teamwork, and Travel

There are four basic areas where employees gain the skills and contacts to access positions with more challenge and responsibility: tools, training, teamwork, and travel. Each of these areas can be problematic for employees with a disability. Although otherwise quite capable of excellence, they can be held back because of a lack of accessibility. Lack of accessibility can lead to lower expectations. That stymies perceived potential, and as a result, they lose opportunities to learn. Without training and development, they miss out on being able to show what they can accomplish. Their work, then, is often judged with a lower standard.

Let's look at each of these four areas and how, with nurturing on your part, they can become springboards to achievement for your employee with a disability.

Tools

The first area is simply a matter of having the tools to do a job. You don't send a plumber out without a pipe wrench. And you wouldn't expect a receptionist to take calls without a telephone. The assistive technology and other adaptive tools people with disabilities use are no different.

For instance, seating someone with a visual impairment in front of a monitor without screen magnification and speech output is tantamount to seating her in a corner facing blank walls. She couldn't produce there without her adaptive software—not because of any lack in her abilities but because, just like the phoneless receptionist, she would lack the tools to use the equipment. Providing the access tools is simply part of your investment in a promising worker.

Some tools are less tangible. A software development company wired its coffeemaker into its computer network. Developers saw a coffee cup icon on their monitors when a new pot was brewed. They would all drop what they were doing and head to the break room. What was the benefit to the company? It was in the exchange of ideas and the problem solving that occurred when every developer stopped midstream and brought challenges and breakthroughs to the table, literally.

Your workforce is not only a platoon of hands but of minds. Your employee with a disability is most likely a practiced problem solver. If you unwittingly deny or diminish his involvement in "group-think" activities through lack of access to the right tools, you hamper his development and you lose out on his contribution.

Training

Do you provide skill improvement opportunities beyond the employee's initial orientation? It is likely you do. Whether in-house or outsourced, such training probably includes skill upgrades, new-system training, certification readiness, tuition reimbursement programs, professional symposia, or even just opportunities for professional betterment through seminars and conferences. Training adds to employee knowledge, skills, and productivity and brings new information and ideas to your company. It is widely regarded as an employee benefit. Those employees who seek training opportunities are also most likely your high achievers.

But is the training you provide accessible to your employees who have a disability? If not, it's a mistake. You are squandering a resource. You don't provide the training to be nice; you provide it to produce better results for your company through better informed, better equipped, and more motivated personnel.

The individual with a disability who cannot access your intranet's training modules, cannot get transportation to off-site seminars, or cannot gain access to a professional development conference (or simply is not told about it or not expected to obtain further training because of low expectations) is being handicapped more seriously than by any disability. In such cases, you're not doing what's best for the company because you're not empowering someone who would probably use the training to its fullest.

Teamwork

Bluntly put, if your worker with a disability isn't drawn into teamwork situations and allowed to contribute within a group, you are losing on several fronts. You are not getting her input and her ideas. You aren't seeing her in action or getting feedback from other team members about how she can most effectively contribute to their efforts in solving problems. You are enforcing her isolation and just making her struggle to reach her full potential more difficult.

You are also sending a far from constructive message to other staff members that the worker's contribution is not valuable. Further, you may be contributing to tension and distrust among your workers, if they perceive you as a leader who is not fair but uses circumstances as an excuse for treating individuals differently.

By your example, on the other hand, you can demonstrate true inclusive practices and create a "norm" of mutual assistance as well as mutual benefit.

Many companies have special committees or events specifically designed to help build cross-department teamwork and relationships. Whether it's a community service committee, a safety committee, aerobics classes, or a company picnic, your disabled worker can and should strive to become an involved and contributing member. Avoid "ghettoizing" her into your company's diversity council or disability awareness committee (which, taken by itself, may be carrying out a constructive role) if her greater strength is elsewhere. Encourage and support her in that effort to be fully engaged in whatever special committees or events your company offers.

Travel

Let's break down travel into two types: local and business. You may not have a lot of control over the transportation options available to your employee for getting to and from work. Local transportation is not your responsibility; it's the worker's. If he can't take the initiative to ensure that he can get to work, he shouldn't have applied for the job.

Local travel presents a barrier to achievement, however, when an employee cannot equally contribute to overtime efforts. In your estimation, a worker may be falling behind because he doesn't want to put in after-hours or weekend time, but it may be just a transportation problem. It's your responsibility to brainstorm with your employee to find alternatives for maximizing extra work time, such as sharing rides or working at home.

Then there is business travel. At a job fair geared to job seekers with disabilities, David was rejected out of hand by a recruiter because his openings involved travel—and David is blind. People who are blind travel all the time. There is absolutely no reason to assume that a person with a disability cannot travel on business.

If a worker's disability is the only reason he isn't given assignments that involve travel, then he misses an opportunity to grow and (even more important) to demonstrate to you what he can do. Often business travel involves sales or persuasion in some way, and such success on the road can tangibly impact the company's bottom line. Networking done during business travel can bring an influx of new ideas; new tools; new intelligence; and, potentially, new employees and customers.

Your business traveler is a goodwill ambassador as well as a scout. An achieving worker with a disability may miss out on such an important contribution. The company itself is risking an opportunity by not sending its best persuader. Don't let that happen because of false assumptions.

Clear Their Way to the Top

Having "a retarded guy in the mail room" is not inclusion. It's tokenism. And it does little good for the individual or the company.

Inclusion is about hiring the very best people without regard to the artificial differences among us. Let's say Jane is a wheelchair user, and Joan is not. If hiring Jane would have turned out to be the best decision you ever made but you go with Joan because it's easier or because you can't imagine how Jane could do the work or you expect she might be an underachiever, you have chosen the second-best candidate for the job.

Realizing that sometimes the best may be a person with a disability should also remind us that the best are often ambitious achievers with high commitment and a desire for ever-increasing responsibility and challenge. Why would you hire a hot prospect and then stick him in a corner to waste away?

Affirming the career goals of capable employees with a disability means keeping an eye on their promotability. Give them all the same opportunities to grow and to achieve as well as to show off what they can do.

Remember that a person with a disability, Franklin D. Roosevelt, was President of the United States. Since we now know John F. Kennedy was dealing with Addison's disease throughout his presidency, we can probably say the United States has had two presidents with disabilities. A blind person, by the way, was recently the British Home Secretary. Another blind individual, David Paterson, has served as governor of New York. Yes, people with disabilities can be very strong leaders.

Make it clear as well to your employee with a disability that just because he got the job his own responsibility for his career advancement has not ended. Make sure he knows that he is expected to work hard and to look for ways to contribute beyond his job description. Don't accept "I can't." Expect him to find a way. And problem solve with him to make it both possible and his duty. By doing so, you will have empowered him for his best effort.

An inclusive workplace offers employees with a disability the same chance to achieve and advance in their careers as nondisabled workers. Instead of "walking away" and dusting off your hands once a disabled person is hired, stay with him, pay attention to him, and never let your assumptions or lack of access get in his way.

That also means understanding his specific disability and working with him to put in place any "reasonable accommodation" he may need to do his job effectively.

Adaptive Technology Is Making Major Forms of Disability Irrelevant in the Workplace

Disabilities are usually a result of accidents, an illness, or a congenital physical or mental condition. A disability can be a condition (such as a brain or spinal cord injury) that is not progressive in how it affects an individual, or it can be progressive (get worse over time) if not treated properly. A disability can be acquired later in life through accident or disease or be a lifelong condition.

Let's take a look at some general types of disabilities and the adaptive technology that is available today for making each condition largely an irrelevant factor in how a person can perform in the workplace.

The Job Accommodation Network (JAN) is a service of the U.S. Department of Labor's Office of Disability Employment Policy. It offers a Searchable Online Accommodation Resource (SOAR) system (http://www.jan.wvu.edu/soar/) to let users explore various accommodation options for people with disabilities in work and educational settings.

SOAR divides potential accommodations into four broad disability categories: cognitive/neurological impairments, deaf/hard-of-hearing impairments, motor impairments, and visual impairments.

Cognitive/Neurological Impairments

Cognitive disabilities impair, since birth, an individual's learning process in a particular way. Cognitive disabilities, many of them nonapparent, can affect many different functions, including the ability to pay attention, learn and retain information, solve problems, and use language to express thought. Examples of such disabilities are dyslexia (typically a reading impairment) and dysgraphia (typically a writing impairment due to lack of fine-motor muscle control of the hands and/or processing difficulties). Note that a cognitive (learning) disability is not the same as an intellectual disability.

For information about twelve nonapparent disabilities and suggestions for hiring and interviewing job candidates with those disabilities, see Muhlenberg College's "Employer's Guide to Hidden Disabilities" at http://www.muhlenberg.edu/careercenter/emplguide/cognitive.html.

Here's a partial list of frequently requested adaptive technology products that SOAR includes on its website for people with cognitive disabilities:

Deficits in Math
- Calculators
- Mathematic Software
- Talking Calculators

⊘ Talking Tape Measures

Deficits in Reading

⊘ Color Contrast Overlays

⊘ Color-Coded Manuals, Outlines, and Maps

⊘ Portable Handheld Reader

⊘ Reading and Language Development

⊘ Reading and Writing Software

⊘ Reading Pen

⊘ Text Reader

⊘ Word Processing Software

Deficits in Writing

⊘ Electronic Dictionary

⊘ Form Generating Software

⊘ Reading and Writing Software

⊘ Word Prediction/Completion and Macro Software

Difficulty with Time Management and Organization

⊘ Color-Coded Manuals, Outlines, and Maps

⊘ Electronic Organizers

⊘ Job Coaches

⊘ Locator Dots

⊘ Organization Software

⊘ Professional Organizers

⊘ Timers and Watches

⊘ Word Processing Software

Memory Deficits

⊘ Tape Recorded Directives, Messages, and Materials

⊘ Memory Software

Noise Reduction

⊘ Environmental Sound Machines

- Headsets
- Sound Absorption Panels

Sensitivity to Light

- Anti-Glare/Filters for Fluorescent Lights
- Anti-Glare/Radiation Filters for Computer Screens
- Flicker Free/LCD Monitors
- Sun Boxes and Lights

Light Deprivation

- Personal Visors
- Sun Boxes and Lights

For details about each of these products and vendors that have them, go to http://www.jan.wvu.edu/soar/cognitive/index.htm.

Deaf/Hard-of-Hearing Impairments

The deaf/hard-of-hearing impairments category includes people who are completely deaf or have partial hearing in one or both ears. They may be able to communicate through sign language or read lips and may have a slight to severe speech impairment due to hearing loss. They may need hearing protection or noise abatement equipment.

Check this partial list of frequently requested adaptive technology products that SOAR includes on its website for people with hearing impairments:

- Alerting Devices
- Amplified Stethoscopes
- ASR/Voicewriting
- Assistive Listening Devices
- Automated TTY System
- Cellular Telephone Technology
- Cochlear Telephone Patch Cords
- Communication Access Realtime Translation (CART) Services
- Hearing Protection

- Noise Abatement
- Noise Canceling Headsets
- Paging Products and Services
- Personal Paging Devices
- Portable Text Communicators
- Realtime and Off-line Captioning Services
- Telephone Amplification
- Telephone Clarity
- Telephone Flashers
- Tinnitus Maskers/Environmental Sound Machines
- TTYs
- TTY Software
- Vibrating Watches and Alarms
- Video Relay Services
- Video Remote Interpreting Services (VRI)
- Voice Mail Transcription

For details about each of these products and vendors that have them, go to http://www.jan.wvu.edu/soar/hearing/hearingprod.html.

Motor Impairments

Motor impairments include various types of physical disabilities that affect upper limbs, manual dexterity, lower limbs, and muscular coordination of various parts of the body.

Note that, from a clinical standpoint, people who have simply broken a leg or sprained a wrist are considered disabled due to a motor impairment.

A motor impairment can be due to a mild, moderate, or severe brain injury either at birth (such as cerebral palsy) or acquired through a traumatic brain injury.

An accident that damages a person's spinal cord can result in various degrees of motor impairment. Or, a motor impairment can be the result of a disease, such as multiple sclerosis, in which the nerves of the central nervous system (brain and spinal cord) degenerate.

Here is a sample of the frequently requested adaptive technology products that SOAR includes on its website for people with motor impairments:

Alternative Input Devices

- ⊘ Alternative Keyboards
- ⊘ Alternative Mice
- ⊘ Expanded Keyboards
- ⊘ Keyguards
- ⊘ LCD Pen Tablet Displays
- ⊘ Left Hand-Dominant Keyboards
- ⊘ Miniature Keyboards
- ⊘ On-Screen Keyboards
- ⊘ On-Screen Keyboard Software
- ⊘ One-Handed Keyboards
- ⊘ One-Handed Keyboard Software
- ⊘ Optical Character Recognition (OCR)
- ⊘ Speech Recognition Software
- ⊘ Switches
- ⊘ Ten Keypads
- ⊘ Word Prediction/Completion and Macro Software

Anti-Fatigue Matting

Book Holders

Building Access

- ⊘ Elevators
- ⊘ Emergency Evacuation Devices
- ⊘ Stair Lifts
- ⊘ Ramps

Carts

- ⊘ Motorized Carts
- ⊘ Multi-Purpose Carts

Chairs, Cushions, and Stools

- Assist Lift Cushions
- Chairs and Stools for Medical Services
- Ergonomic/Adjustable Office Chairs
- Forward Leaning Chairs
- Large-Rated Chairs
- Nonfluorescent Lighting
- Stand Lean Stools

Doors

- Automatic Door Openers
- Door Handles
- Door Knob Grips
- Force Measurement Gauges

Ergonomic and Other Office Equipment

- Accessible Copiers
- File Carousels
- Forearm Supports
- Headsets
- Money Handling Products
- Mousing Surfaces
- Remote Control Blinds
- Slant Boards
- Typing Aids
- Writing Aids

Lifting Devices

- Compact Lifting Devices
- Page Turners

Software

- Ergonomic Software
- Form Generating Software

⊘   One-Handed Keyboard Software

Tools

⊘   Anti-Vibration Material

⊘   Ergonomic/Pneumatic Tools

⊘   Tool Balancers

Workstations

⊘   Accessible Workstations (Industrial)

⊘   Accessible Workstations (Office)

⊘   Supine Workstations

For details about each of these products and vendors that have them, go to http://www.jan.wvu.edu/soar/motor/index.htm.

Visual Impairments

In North America and most of Europe, legal blindness is defined as visual acuity of 20/200 or less in the better eye with best correction possible. This means that a legally blind individual would have to stand 20 feet from an object to see it (using corrective lenses) with the same degree of clarity as a normally sighted person could from 200 feet.

Visual impairment may be caused by many eye diseases such as age-related macular degeneration or cataracts. Some eye diseases can be treated medically; others cannot.

The following are frequently requested adaptive technology products that SOAR includes on its website for people with visual impairments:

⊘   Anti-Glare/Radiation Filters for Computer Screens

⊘   Braille and/or ADA Signage

⊘   Braille Printers

⊘   Braille Translation Software

⊘   Computer Braille Display

⊘   Closed Circuit TV (CCTV)

⊘   Detectable Warning Surfaces

⊘   External Computer Screen Magnification

- Full Spectrum or Natural Lighting Products
- Keyboard Tops and Labels
- Large Computer Displays
- Low Vision Enhancement Products
- Magnification (Hand or Stand)
- Optical Character Recognition
- Prism Glasses/Bed Spectacles
- Protective Eyewear
- PDAs, Notebooks, and Laptops for Individuals with Vision Impairments
- Screen Magnification Software
- Screen Reading Software
- Spoken Internet and Web Access Software
- Stair Tread/Tape
- Tactile Graphics
- Talking Bar Code Scanner/Reader
- Talking Calculator
- Talking Cash Register
- Talking Coin Sorter
- Talking Color Detector
- Talking Credit Card Terminal
- Talking Global Positioning Systems (GPS) and Maps
- Talking Money Identifier
- Task Lighting
- Telephone Light Sensor

For details about each of these products and vendors that have them, go to http://www.jan.wvu.edu/soar/vision/visionprod.html.

Note that you can search for adaptive technology solutions for specific disabilities (about forty of them) by going to http://www.jan.wvu.edu/soar/disabilities.html. You can also go to Lighthouse International's website (www.lighthouse.org) for information about technology (see http://www.lighthouse.org/services-and-assistance/computers-and-technology/

assistive-technology-training/). You might consider items from the Lighthouse store or get information from a blog about vision-friendly technology at dorriessight.blogspot.com.

FAQ: Guidelines on Reasonable Accommodations for Employees with Disabilities Under the ADA

Knowing the guidelines of "reasonable accommodation" under the ADA is just as important as having a basic understanding of what is available today in workplace adaptive technologies for specific disabilities.

The following information about reasonable accommodations for your employee with a disability is summarized and paraphrased from guidelines offered by JAN at http://www.jan.wvu.edu/links/ADAtam1.html#III and the Equal Employment Opportunity Commission (EEOC) at http://www. eeoc.gov/policy/docs/accommodation.html.

Work-Site Accessibility

Question: Do we have to modify the work site if we do not have an employee with a mobility impairment?

Answer: Under ADA's Title I, you are not required to make your existing facilities accessible until a particular applicant or employee with a particular disability needs an accommodation, and then the modifications should meet that individual's work needs.

You do not have to make changes to provide access in places or facilities that will not be used by that individual for employment-related activities or benefits.

However, private employers that occupy commercial facilities or operate places of public accommodation and state and local governments must conform to more extensive accessibility requirements under Title III and Title II when making alterations to existing facilities or undertaking new construction.

Although the requirement for accessibility in employment is triggered by the needs of a particular individual, you should consider initiating changes that will provide general accessibility, particularly for job applicants, since it is likely that people with disabilities will apply for jobs in the future.

See the EEOC's "Technical Assistance Manual: Title I of the ADA," chapter III, section 3.10 at http://www.jan.wvu.edu/links/ ADAtam1.html#III and "ADA Accessibility Guidelines for Buildings and Facilities (ADAAG)" at http://www.access-board.gov/adaag/ html/adaag.htm.

Question: Do we have to provide accommodations for emergency evacuation?

Answer: If you have an emergency evacuation plan for employees, the plan should include employees with disabilities. If you do not have an evacuation plan for all employees, you must consider accommodations on a case-by-case basis for any employee with a disability who requests accommodations for emergency evacuation.

See "Employer's Guide to Including People with Disabilities in Emergency Evacuation Plans" at http://www.jan.wvu.edu/media/ emergency.html and "Emergency Preparedness and People with Disabilities" at http://www.dol.gov/odep/programs/emergency.htm.

Question: Do we have to provide parking as an accommodation?

Answer: Parking is considered a benefit of employment. Under the ADA, you must make reasonable accommodations that enable employees with disabilities to enjoy equal benefits of employment. So, if you provide parking for all employees, you must provide parking for employees with disabilities unless it would pose an undue hardship to do so.

A tougher question is: Do you have to provide parking for employees with disabilities if you do not provide parking for other employees? There are two ways to look at this issue. First, you could argue that an employer is required to provide reasonable accommodations that eliminate barriers only in the work environment and parking is outside the work environment. Therefore, you would not have to provide parking as an accommodation unless parking is provided for other employees.

Second, you could argue that an employer is required to provide parking as an accommodation because otherwise some employees with disabilities would not be able to access the work site, and, therefore, providing parking is a way to provide equal employment opportunities to employees with disabilities.

Unfortunately, there is no clear answer as of this writing about which argument is correct. See "Parking and the ADA, Act I" at http://www.jan.wvu.edu/corner/vol01iss14.htm and "Parking and the ADA, Act II" at http://www.jan.wvu.edu/corner/vol03iss01.htm.

Question: Do we have to provide transportation to and from work as an accommodation?

Answer: You are required to provide reasonable accommodations that eliminate barriers in the work environment alone, not ones that eliminate barriers outside of the work environment. So, you are not required to provide transportation as a reasonable accommodation for a commute to work unless you generally provide transportation for your employees.

However, if your policy regarding work schedules creates a barrier for an individual whose disability interferes with his or her ability to commute to work, you must modify that policy as a reasonable accommodation unless it would impose an undue hardship. For example, an individual who uses a wheelchair and commutes by public transportation may need a later arrival time in inclement weather.

Job Restructuring

According to the EEOC, job restructuring includes modifications such as reallocating or redistributing marginal job functions that an employee is unable to perform because of a disability and altering when or how a function, essential or marginal, is performed. An employer never has to reallocate essential functions as a reasonable accommodation, but it can do so if it wishes.

Question: How do I determine what job duties are essential?

Answer: JAN put together a publication called "Job Descriptions" (see http://www.jan.wvu.edu/media/jobdescriptions.html) that includes a discussion about how to determine whether a job duty is essential.

The EEOC also provides information about determining essential functions at section 2.3(a) of its "Technical Assistance Manual: Title I of the ADA" (see http://www.jan.wvu.edu/links/ADAtam1.html).

Question: Do I have to provide "light duty" for employees with disabilities?

Answer: The term "light duty" has a number of different meanings in the employment setting. Generally, light duty refers to temporary or permanent work that is physically or mentally less demanding than normal job duties.

Some employers use the term "light duty" to mean simply excusing an employee from performing those job functions that he is unable to perform due to an impairment.

Light duty also may consist of particular positions with duties that are less physically or mentally demanding created specifically for the purpose of providing alternative work for employees who are unable to perform some or all of their normal duties.

You may also refer to any position that is sedentary or is less physically or mentally demanding as light duty.

In the following discussion, light duty refers only to particular positions created specifically for the purpose of providing work for employees who are unable to perform some or all of their normal duties.

As an employer, you do not need to create a light duty position for a nonoccupationally injured employee with a disability as a reasonable accommodation under the ADA. However, you must provide other forms of reasonable accommodation required under the ADA. For example, subject to undue hardship, you must:

- ⊘ Restructure a position by redistributing marginal functions that an individual cannot perform because of a disability or
- ⊘ Provide modified scheduling (including part-time work) or
- ⊘ Reassign a nonoccupationally injured employee with a disability to an equivalent existing vacancy for which he or she is qualified.

You cannot avoid your obligation to accommodate an individual with a disability simply by asserting that the disability did not derive from an occupational injury.

On the other hand, if you reserve light duty positions for employees with occupational injuries (do not create new light duty jobs when needed), the ADA requires you to consider reassigning an employee with a disability who is not occupationally injured to such positions as a reasonable accommodation.

The reason for this is that reassignment to a vacant position and appropriate modification of your policy are forms of reasonable accommodation required by the ADA, absent undue hardship. You cannot establish that the reassignment to a vacant, reserved light duty position imposes an undue hardship simply by showing that you would have no other vacant light duty positions available if an employee became injured on the job and needed light duty.

Note that you are free to determine whether a light duty position will be temporary instead of permanent. For more information, see the EEOC's "Workers' Compensation and the ADA" at http://www.eeoc.gov/policy/docs/workcomp.html.

Modified Work Schedules and Leave

In its publication on reasonable accommodation and undue hardship, the EEOC discusses modified work schedules and leave as accommodations. The information is available at http://www.eeoc.gov/policy/docs/accommodation.html. However, some issues regarding work schedules and leave are not addressed in that guide. Here is how JAN addresses the issues of schedules and leave.

Question: Do I have to change a full-time job to part-time as an accommodation under the ADA?

Answer: Although part-time work is a form of reasonable accommodation, you probably do not have to change an existing full-time job to part-time as an accommodation under the ADA.

According to informal guidance from the EEOC, when an employee is asking to cut his or her hours significantly, then, in essence, that employee is asking for a reassignment to an existing part-time job.

The precise legal rationale will be debated in courts for a while, but, any way you look at it, you fundamentally change a job when you significantly cut the hours (e.g., in half). One argument is that cutting a job's hours in half necessarily entails cutting essential functions if "essential functions" embody the amount of work to be accomplished.

You could also say that you would be cutting the production

standard, which is not simply an hourly standard but also a standard that measures how much should be produced in a full day.

Another legal argument is to say that significantly reducing the hours of a job would be changing a qualification standard of the job—specifically, the ability to work full-time. You should always be able to show that you created a full-time position because there is sufficient work that requires working full-time. As such, the qualification to work full-time meets the business necessity standard, and, as a result, it is not a reasonable accommodation to cut the hours in half.

That is why a request for part-time work by an employee often ends up really being a request for a reassignment to an existing part-time job. If there is only a minimal cut in hours, it might be possible to show that the essential functions, the productivity standard, and/or a qualification standard of the position will not be changed, despite the slight decrease in hours. In this case, you might need to eliminate marginal functions to permit the employee to complete all the essential functions.

Question: If I choose to change a full-time job to part-time, do I have to maintain the employee's full-time pay and benefits?

Answer: No, not under the ADA—unless you maintain pay and benefits for employees without disabilities whose jobs change from full-time to part-time. You should consider whether other laws apply (such as wage and hour laws).

Question: How much leave time must I provide as an accommodation under the ADA?

Answer: Unlike the Family and Medical Leave Act (FMLA), which requires covered employers to provide up to twelve weeks of leave, there is no specific amount of leave time required under the ADA.

Instead, leave time is approached like any other accommodation request: You must provide the amount of leave needed by the employee (unless doing so poses an undue hardship). For additional information about the interplay between the ADA and the FMLA, see "The Family and Medical Leave Act, the Americans with Disabilities Act, and Title VII of the Civil Rights Act of 1964" at http://www.eeoc.gov/policy/docs/fmlaada.html.

Modified Policies

Question: Can I apply a no-fault attendance policy?

Answer: No. If an employee with a disability needs additional unpaid leave as a reasonable accommodation, you must modify your "no-fault" leave policy to provide the employee with the additional leave unless you can show that (1) there is another effective accommodation that would enable the person to perform the essential functions of his position or (2) granting additional leave would cause an undue hardship.

The act of modifying workplace policies, including leave policies, is a form of reasonable accommodation. For more information, see "Reasonable Accommodation and Undue Hardship Under the Americans with Disabilities Act" at http://www.eeoc.gov/policy/docs/accommodation.html.

Question: Can we have a 100 percent restriction-free policy?

Answer: According to informal guidance from the EEOC, requiring an employee to be 100 percent restriction-free can violate the ADA when applied to an employee with a disability.

Although some courts have characterized such policies as per se violations of the ADA, most courts require that the employee meet the definition of disability before being allowed to challenge the policy under the ADA. If an employee does not meet those first two prongs, he may be able to show that his employer regarded him as having a disability, typically by relying on evidence that the employer would not let him return to his regular job or any other job in a class of jobs or broad range of jobs in various classes.

Question: Can I enforce conduct rules?

Answer: You never have to excuse a violation of a uniformly applied conduct rule that is job related and consistent with business necessity. This means, for example, that you never have to tolerate or excuse violence, threats of violence, stealing, or destruction of property. You may discipline an employee with a disability for engaging in such misconduct if you would impose the same discipline on an employee without a disability.

Question: Do I have to modify dress codes or hygiene requirements as an accommodation?

Answer: Most authorities (including the EEOC) treat dress codes and hygiene requirements as "conduct rules" but classify them as the type of conduct rule that must be justified as job related and consistent with business necessity before being enforced. So, if a person with a disability requests modification of a dress code or hygiene requirement as an accommodation, you must consider allowing the modification unless you can show that the dress code or hygiene requirement is necessary for the job at issue.

For information about handling hygiene issues in the workplace, visit http://www.jan.wvu.edu/media/employmenthygienefact.doc. For additional information, see "The Americans with Disabilities Act: Applying Performance and Conduct Standards to Employees with Disabilities" at http://www.eeoc.gov/facts/performance-conduct.html.

Question: Do I have to consider allowing an employee with a disability to work from home as an accommodation?

Answer: Yes. Changing the location where work is performed may fall under the ADA's reasonable accommodation requirement of modifying workplace policies, even if you do not allow other employees to work from home.

However, you are not obligated to adopt an employee's preferred or requested accommodation and may instead offer alternate accommodations as long as they would be effective. For more information about work at home as an accommodation, see "Work at Home/Telework as a Reasonable Accommodation" at http://www.eeoc.gov/facts/telework.html.

Equipment and Services

Question: If we require work equipment, such as steel-toed work boots or stethoscopes, and an employee with a disability needs specialized equipment that costs more than the regular equipment (e.g., customized boots or amplified stethoscopes), do we have to pay the extra cost for the specialized equipment?

Answer: If the equipment or device is a personal-use item, then you do not have to provide it. For example, if an employee has to wear a special type of boot all the time, you do not have to pay for it. Common items that fall into the personal-use category are hearing aids, glasses, and medication. On the other hand, if the boots are necessary only for work and constitute an accommodation, you would have to pay the entire cost of the boots unless it would be an undue hardship to do so.

But there is also a tool-of-the-trade issue here. If the boots constitute a tool of the trade (i.e., the boots are necessary to get the job done), then the employer must pay for the specialized boots as a form of equal treatment if the employer provides the boots for other employees. However, if other employees buy their own boots and they own them, then an employee with a disability can be required to buy his own boots, even if they cost more.

Question: If an employee has a limitation such as a hearing impairment but chooses not to purchase a hearing aid, do we then have an obligation to provide a hearing aid at work?

Answer: The fact that an individual chooses to forego personal-use items at home (e.g., a wheelchair, hearing aids, protective clothing) does not mean that such items become work related because they are needed on the job. The limitations prompting the need for the hearing aids exist on and off the job and, as a result, they remain personal-use items.

However, you may still have to provide a reasonable accommodation, even though you are not obligated to provide personal-use items. For example, you might have to provide an amplified telephone or alternative means of communication for an employee with a hearing impairment who does not choose to use hearing aids.

Question: Do I have to allow an employee with a disability to use personal-need items (e.g., canes, walkers, wheelchairs, hearing aids) or services (personal attendant care, service animals) in the workplace?

Answer: Allowing an employee with a disability to use a personal-need item or service in the workplace is a form of reasonable accommodation, according to the EEOC. For example, it would be a reasonable accommodation for an employer to permit an individual who is blind to use a guide dog at work, even though the employer would not be required to provide a guide dog for the employee.

Question: Do we have to provide personal assistance services (PAS) under the ADA?

Answer: The term "personal assistance services" can include a wide variety of services. The Ticket to Work and Work Incentives Improvement Act defines PAS as "a range of services provided by one or more persons designed to assist an individual with a disability to perform daily living activities on or off the job that the individual would typically perform without assistance if the individual did not have a disability."

Under the ADA, reasonable accommodation can include PAS in the form of work-related assistance, but it generally does not include PAS in the form of personal attendant care at the work site.

Work-related PAS can include task-related assistance at work, such as readers, interpreters, help with lifting or reaching, page turners, a travel attendant to act as a sighted guide to assist an employee with a visual impairment who goes on occasional business trips, and reassignment of nonessential duties to coworkers. For additional information, see "Personal Assistance Services (WPAS) in the Workplace" at http://www.jan.wvu.edu/media/PAS.html.

Question: Do we have to provide personal attendant care for work-related travel?

Answer: According to informal guidance from the EEOC, the ADA does not require you to provide personal attendant care on the job because reasonable accommodation does not require employers to provide personal-need items or services.

However, when an employee travels for work and incurs personal attendant care expenses beyond her usual expenses when not traveling for work, there is a good argument that you must pay the added costs.

Question: What if coworkers voluntarily assist disabled employees with their personal needs? For example, coworkers assist an employee who uses a wheelchair with transferring her from her car into the wheelchair when she arrives at work. Do I have to allow coworkers to assist, or can I prohibit them from doing so?

Answer: According to informal guidance from the EEOC, in general, employers can decide how employees use their time at work. So, you can probably prohibit coworkers from providing personal assistance to employees with disabilities without violating the ADA outright.

However, from a practical standpoint, the EEOC recommends that you take a case-by-case approach and consider allowing coworkers to voluntarily help employees with disabilities when you, as an employer, do not have any liability for resulting injuries and the assistance does not substantially disrupt the workplace.

So, consider allowing coworkers to help an employee with a disability, at least with minor activities, such as taking off and putting on a coat and eating.

When more difficult assistance is needed, such as toileting transfers or administering medications, you may want to make sure that coworkers are properly trained before allowing them to provide this type of assistance.

Remember, under the ADA's reasonable accommodation obligation, you must consider allowing employees with disabilities to have their own personal attendant in the workplace, absent undue hardship.

Question: Is it a reasonable accommodation to provide a job coach?

Answer: Yes. You may be required to provide a temporary job coach to assist in the training of a qualified individual with a disability as a reasonable accommodation, barring undue hardship.

You also may be required to allow a job coach paid by a public or private social service agency to accompany the employee at the job site as a reasonable accommodation. For more information, see "EEOC Enforcement Guidance on the Americans with Disabilities Act and Psychiatric Disabilities" at http://www.eeoc.gov/policy/docs/psych.html.

Question: Do we have to provide accommodations for on-the-job travel such as driving to home visits?

Answer: According to the EEOC, you must consider accommodations such as alternative methods of transportation for work-related travel when driving is not an essential function of the job. For example, an employer must consider alternative transportation for a social worker who cannot drive due to vertigo; the essential function is completing the home visits, not driving.

Question: What guidelines can I use to write an accommodation policy for my company?

Answer: If you want to develop written accommodation policies and procedures, the EEOC, the federal agency that enforces the ADA, provides some useful publications, including:

- ⊘ "Establishing Procedures to Facilitate the Provision of Reasonable Accommodation"
- ⊘ "Internal Accommodation Procedures"
- ⊘ "Practical Advice for Drafting and Implementing Reasonable Accommodation Procedures"

Accommodations for Adaptive Technology: Who Should Pay for What Under What Circumstances

Although disability advocates love to crow that the average cost of accommodations on the job is $50 or less, the fact is that some of the high-tech aids used by some individuals with a disability are on the pricier side of the equation.

Adapting a computer for a person who is blind, for instance, can cost more than the computer itself. And that is just the beginning. It doesn't include other equipment that the employee might need. It would be disingenuous to say otherwise. The cost of accommodations may be higher for your company or for your department than the average investment.

You want to do the right thing, but you also have to be realistic. It would be bad business to use company resources without a return on the investment. That is the "real world."

Before getting into the answers to the question about who pays for what, consider these questions: What does it cost to bring any new worker on board? Do you pay for training? Do you pay for benefits? Do you pay for a workplace, furniture, equipment, supplies, and utilities this worker will need? And do you pay her for her time, talent, and effort?

Would you think twice about any of these costs if you knew you were hiring the person who will best contribute to the bottom line? Probably not.

Peggy works for a company that furnishes her with a car—a benefit designed to persuade her to work for the organization. Furnishing special tools a qualified person with a disability needs for work is a drop in the bucket compared to these very common costs willingly accepted by companies that want the best people working for them.

Now to the funding question. The short answer to "Who pays for it?" in terms of legal responsibility in many jurisdictions is you, the employer. For instance, "Generally, the ADA requires employers to make reasonable accommodations that enable employees with disabilities to enjoy equal employment opportunities," according to JAN.

But let's look at this topic in terms of reality. Who, in fact, is paying for adaptive equipment? To find out who really is picking up the tab for employees with disabilities, we conducted our own informal e-mail poll of eSight Careers Network members.

We asked, "In your personal experience of obtaining adaptive equipment for a job, who has paid for the equipment?" We received ninety-six responses. The results are as follows:

- A state agency, such as vocational rehabilitation: 41 percent
- The employer: 24 percent
- The employee: 20 percent
- Other: 14 percent
- Insurance company: 1 percent
- Family members: 1 percent

Those who selected "other" primarily used this choice to say that it really was a combination—that the government source, the employer, and the worker shared the cost in some way. Others received grants or assistance from private funders.

A fortunately tiny number, two to be precise, revealed that no one paid, and, as a result, they received no accommodation.

Although not scientific, these results appear to be on target with eSight Careers Network over the years. The major source for money for adaptive equipment is a government agency whose mission is to be that source. Next comes the employer, the one who officially should be doing it all. Then another very realistic response is in third place: the blind or visually impaired worker herself.

There are pros and cons to each source. What some believe the law requires and what is realistic are not necessarily the same thing.

Let's say this is the situation confronting you now. You or the person charged with hiring responsibility is sitting across the interview table from a blind or visually impaired applicant for an open position. Let's assume she has the top qualifications for the job, in terms of experience, education, personality, references, and other factors. Add the fact that studies have shown that workers with disabilities are good performers who stay on the job longer and have better than average reliability and safety records. This person could easily be the best addition to your workforce. To do the job, though, she needs some accommodations. Are you going to pass her by? Or work out a creative accommodation solution?

Let's broaden the alternatives listed in our e-mail survey and propose some more funding options for obtaining the adaptive technology she needs.

Funding Options for Adaptive Technology

Employee Brings Her Own Accommodation

All the major producers of adaptive technology for the blind allow their software to be used on multiple computers in multiple locations. For example, if an employee uses a screen reader at home, the same software can be used at work without additional charge. If the employee can bring a software CD from home to be installed on an office computer, the employer just saved $895, hardly an insignificant amount. (This cost is based on the JAWS screen reader, which is the most popular screen reader used by people who are visually impaired.)

If you are not over that sticker shock yet, consider scanning software that allows the worker to read print independently. It costs about $1,000.

In addition to the employee using adaptive software for both home and work purposes, she may have equipment (such as a Braillewriter or magnifiers) that others have purchased for previous jobs or for school that can be brought to the workplace and used there.

So, considering her own equipment in an open and interactive accommodation discussion might lead to options that may show that accommodation expenses for you, as the employer, could be minimal.

Cost Sharing with the Employee

Small employers on extremely tight budgets might consider sharing the cost of software with their employees. Adaptive technology software licenses can be used at work and at home. Sometimes the employee has an older version of the software and an employer-sponsored upgrade is less expensive than buying new.

Other times, the employee may not have the technology needed. If the employee has no technology at home and a purchase is required, she and her employer can both benefit by sharing or splitting the cost of the technology. This may not work for larger employers because the ADA expects more from them. It also may not work if the adaptation can be used only in a work situation.

If the employee is receiving Social Security Disability Insurance benefits, costs for equipment may be applied as a benefit to be received in a month she ordinarily would be ineligible because of wage income. Such additional benefits can be paid while she is being paid a wage, so you, the employer, may actually not incur additional costs.

Sharing Accommodations

If you have more than one employee with a visual impairment on the job, accommodations may be shared. Depending on the job, various pieces of adaptive technology may be used continually or just occasionally. Consider the jobs and the employees involved. Can multiple people use equipment such as scanning systems, Braillewriters, and magnifiers?

Such approaches make the most sense when a customized and tailored access solution for a particular employee isn't necessary.

Tax Incentives

The U.S. government offers two tax incentives for businesses paying for accommodations: a tax credit and a tax deduction.

The tax credit is available for those businesses that for the previous tax year had either revenues of $1,000,000 or less or thirty or fewer full-time workers. The credit can be used to cover a variety of expenditures, including provision of readers for customers or employees, sign language interpreters, adaptive equipment, accessible formats of printed materials, and removal of architectural barriers in facilities or vehicles. The amount of the tax credit is equal to 50 percent of the eligible access expenditures in a year up to a maximum expenditure of $10,250. There is no credit for the first $250 of expenditures. The maximum tax credit, therefore, is $5,000.

The tax deduction available applies to all businesses of any size for accommodation expenses up to $15,000. Unlike the tax credit, the deduction can be used only for the removal of transportation or architectural barriers. Many employers apply this after the fact and don't consider this a true funding source because of the considerable lag time between the expense and the application of the tax benefit. For more about this tax deduction, see "Tax Incentives Packet on the Americans with Disabilities Act" at http://www.ada.gov/taxpack.htm.

In addition, the Work Opportunity Tax Credit is available to employers who hire clients of state or veterans vocational rehabilitation programs or who are recipients of Supplemental Security Income.

Employers can receive a credit equal to $2,400 in wages paid during the first twelve months for each new hire or $4,800 for each veteran hired who is disabled. For more information, see "Tax Incentives" on the JAN website at http://www.jan.wvu.edu/media/tax.html or go to http://www.doleta.gov/business/incentives/opptax/.

State and Veterans Vocational Rehabilitation Programs

The U.S. federal government funds states and the Veterans Administration to operate vocational rehabilitation programs for people with disabilities. These programs can pay the entire cost of equipment and technology used on the job.

However, as one might expect when government bureaucrats are involved in something, the process can be complicated and lengthy, and the rehabilitation agency might only agree to pay part of the cost. Some employers report some success, if they have the right relationship with people who can get them through the process. It is a mixed bag and success with this program often depends on the people involved.

Public and Private Sources

In addition to government rehabilitation programs, there are numerous private foundations and other organizations that can be called upon to make grants or loans to fund accommodations. The Small Business Administration, economic development programs, charities, and other institutions include specific or general funding for employment of people with disabilities. The JAN lists several sources, including Delta Foundation, Southern Rural Development, and Abilities Fund on its website (http://www.jan.wvu.edu/links/Funding/GeneralInfo.html).

These sources may not present your best option for help paying for accommodations, however, since the process can be lengthy and convoluted. Many of these programs also favor small-business owners with disabilities instead of employers of people with disabilities. Nevertheless, they are worth checking.

Paying for It Yourself

The final funding option is to bite the bullet and pay for the adaptive technology as the employer. You can justify this through the mandates of the ADA.

In addition, there are accommodation obligations tied to equipment purchases for employees with disabilities if you receive federal funds or are a federal contractor. Size of the employer, revenues, and cash flow are given consideration in determining an employer's obligation—which is why smaller employers may be able to justify a position in which an employee shares some of the cost of the technology.

Whatever the situation, with today's adaptive technology employing a worker who has a disability is possible and entirely feasible for even the smallest and most budget squeezed of employers. Consider the total accommodation and stipulate what works best for you, the employer, and the employee, and then decide who should fairly take responsibility for what.

When a Worker with a Disability Tries to Put One Over on You

Being manipulated by an employee with a disability can occur under a variety of circumstances.

Is an employee who uses a wheelchair demanding shorter hours because of transportation problems? Is someone with medical problems taking a lot of time off for doctor appointments but not making the time up? Does an employee appear to feel that rules around dress or behavior do not apply to him? Have you made accommodations but the worker still is not performing up to the appropriate level?

Remember, the "reasonable accommodations" guideline under the ADA does not require you to provide the accommodation the employee requests but only whatever will enable him to do the work. He may be expecting exactly what he requests, but if another tool will do what the employee needs with the same results and efficiency, you probably are not obliged to provide it.

When you start to have doubts about whether a person with a disability is being truthful with you about an accommodation or about an access need he has, take a step back and think about it. Try to get some further information about his particular condition, bearing in mind that he may not share the exact characteristics of the example descriptions about his particular disability you find during your research.

It is not necessary just to take a disabled person's word for it when he says he needs some special conditions. You can ask for supporting evidence.

It may be that it's only your perception that the problem is disability related. The worker, regardless of the existence of a disability, may be unable to perform the work simply because he is unprepared, unqualified, undermotivated, poorly trained or equipped, or not motivated by his direct supervisor in your company. Address these issues first—not your assumptions about the disability.

Here are five tips Jim Hasse has collected over the years:

1. Talk directly to the individual who has raised the issue. It could be a miscommunication. Once you have visited with the person, you may be able to find out more about the real issue (or if there is an issue at all).

2. Keep discussion about the employee to a minimum when the person in question is not present or is not totally informed about outside discussions. There is a tendency to patronize the person with a disability when he is "discussed" without having equal opportunity to contribute in such discussions.

3. Watch for resentment among coworkers. There may be other workers who regard reasonable accommodations as "special treatment," which they then resent. Nip that in the bud by being open and honest with everyone concerned. Be willing to negotiate—but only what is truly fair.

4. Avoid taking into consideration what nondisabled coworkers say. They may be "ratting" on the disabled person. Their own fear and prejudice could be at work, trying to get the employee with a disability to leave.

5. Be willing to admit you may have made a wrong hiring decision. If you have hired a person with a disability and clearly see that that person does not fit the job or your company, clarify and restate your expectations in terms of job performance and interpersonal relationships for the individual and then give him respectful, positive, nonpunitive ways to stay or choose not to stay.

FAQ: Guidelines on Confidentiality for Employees with Disabilities Under the ADA

The following questions and answers about information and confidentiality under EEOC and ADA guidelines are based on information

provided by the New York Lawyers for the Public Interest, Inc.
(NYLPI), 151 West 30th Street, 11th Floor, New York, NY 10001-4007
(telephone: 212-244-4664; fax: 212-244-4570). NYLPI's website is at
www.nylpi.org.

This paraphrased information is only an overview and should not be
regarded as legal advice. Consult your legal counsel about specific situations you may face as an employer.

Question: Can I ask an employee for medical or psychiatric information about his or her disability?

Answer: No, under most circumstances. However, there are some
important exceptions to this rule:

After Extending a Conditional Offer of Employment

You may require a medical and/or psychiatric examination or ask
questions related to the employee's physical or mental disability. You
are allowed to do this *only if you require all entering employees in the
same job category to be subject to the same inquiries or examination,
regardless of disability.*

While the inquiries or examination do not need to be related to the
job, if you use the results of these inquiries or examination to screen
out an individual because of disability, you must prove that the
exclusionary criteria are job related and consistent with business
necessity and cannot be met with "reasonable accommodation."

After Hiring an Employee

You can ask an employee to volunteer information about whether she
has a disability for affirmative action–reporting purposes. However,
it's up to her whether or not to provide this information to you.

You may ask an employee about her disability if she requests a "reasonable accommodation" to carry out the responsibilities of the job.

You are allowed to ask for medical or psychiatric information when
an employee is returning to work after being absent for a disability-
related reason and you want to know that she is able to return safe-
ly to work and perform the requirements of the job.

As of this writing, you may ask an employee about her disability when
she is having difficulty with her job *and* you have a reasonable basis for
believing that a disability is affecting her ability to perform the essen-

tial functions of her job or to work without posing a direct threat to herself or others. But check the current ADA and EEOC positions on this issue at http://www.jan.wvu.edu/links/ADAtam1.html#III and at http://www.eeoc.gov/policy/docs/accommodation.html.

Question: Can I ask an employee to see a doctor employed or hired by my company?

Answer: Yes, in all of the aforementioned situations except for the affirmative action situation. When you ask an employee to see a doctor hired and compensated by your company for reasonable accommodation purposes, any medical examination must be job related and consistent with "business necessity" (which means the examination must be limited to determining the existence of a disability and the need for reasonable accommodation).

Question: Can a doctor hired by my company talk to an employee's private physician about his or her medical condition or history?

Answer: That's reasonable and legal to do so, but the employee's doctor must have permission from the employee before discussing her medical condition or history. A savvy employee will permit your company's doctor to discuss only information about her current condition and abilities—not her *entire* medical or psychiatric history.

Question: If an employee asks for a reasonable accommodation, can I ask for specific information about her disability?

Answer: Yes, if the disability in question and the need for reasonable accommodation are not obvious or you have not already received enough information to show that an ADA disability is involved, you can ask for more specific information.

Note that you cannot ask for documentation when the disability and the need for reasonable accommodation are obvious or when the employee has already provided sufficient information to establish the existence of an ADA disability and the need for reasonable accommodation.

Question: Exactly what am I legally allowed to ask?

Answer: You may ask an employee to provide medical or psychiatric documentation that she has a disability and document why the accommodation she is requesting is needed for her disability or because of her disability.

In requesting documentation, you need to state the specific information you require about the disability, the resulting functional limitations, and the need for reasonable accommodation (all narrowly tailored information).

Question: Can I ask for and obtain an employee's entire medical or psychiatric record?

Answer: No. But you may ask an employee to sign a limited release, which allows you to ask a set of specific questions of her health care professional.

An employee may refuse to provide the medical or psychiatric release you request, if she believes that information is irrelevant to her current ability to do the job. You may generate an EEOC complaint, if, upon that refusal, you do not provide a reasonable accommodation or allow the employee to return to or remain at her job.

Question: Do I have to keep medical or psychiatric information about an employee confidential?

Answer: Yes. You must collect and maintain such information on separate forms and in separate medical files, apart from the usual personnel files. However, there are five limited exceptions to the ADA confidentiality requirements:

1. Supervisors and managers may be told about necessary restrictions on the work or duties of the employee and about necessary accommodations.

2. First aid and safety personnel may be told if the disability might require emergency treatment.

3. Government officials investigating compliance with the ADA must be given relevant information on request.

4. Employers may give information to state workers compensation offices, state Second Injury Funds, or workers compensation insurance carriers in accordance with state workers compensation laws.

5. Employers may use the information for insurance purposes.

(As previously noted, please note that the information in this chapter as well as the rest of this book is not presented as legal advice but as guidelines from experts and expert sources.)

How to Prevent a Disability Discrimination Lawsuit

Preventing discrimination against disabled people in your company's staffing requires a great deal of self-examination. You must look at everything—from your hiring practices to the language in your documentation to the work environment (in terms of both physical and interpersonal conditions). This self-examination can prevent a less than comfortable examination by a court of law.

10 Percent Discrimination

Almost 10 percent of working adults with disabilities faced job discrimination in the early 1990s, despite ADA protections, according to Jae Kennedy, Ph.D., and Marjorie Olney, Ph.D., CRC, who were both professors of community health at the University of Illinois at the time of their study. In a September 2001 article for the journal *Rehabilitation Counseling Bulletin,* Kennedy and Olney estimate that the 10 percent rate translates to about 1.6 million people who believed they experienced discrimination "due to their health, impairment or disability status."

Their estimates come from a supplement to the 1994–1995 National Health Interview Survey, an ongoing survey of U.S. households by the Centers for Disease Control. The supplement provided "an unprecedented level of detail on disability-related issues," Kennedy said. "And, as far as I'm aware, these are the first nationally representative estimates of workplace discrimination for persons with disabilities."

The authors' study was based on responses from 9,843 adults with disabilities who were currently working or had worked at least some time during the previous five years (1989–1994). Respondents were asked if, during those years, they had been refused employment, a promotion, a transfer, or access to training programs because of an ongoing health problem, impairment, or disability.

Preventative Steps

Here are some initial steps you can take in your effort to eliminate the opportunity for discrimination in your company's employment practices.

⊘ **Know the law.** If you are under the jurisdiction of U.S. law (or that of another country) that protects the rights of disabled employees, it is important that you acquaint yourself thoroughly with it and with the case law stemming from it.

- ⊘ **Obtain appropriate counsel.** A law firm that specializes in employment law can identify problem areas and recommend solutions.

- ⊘ **Review your job descriptions.** Make sure you can identify essential functions as distinct from those that can be handled cooperatively or with adaptive equipment.

- ⊘ **Examine your hiring procedures.** Make sure your job applications do not call for information referring to physical or mental capacities that cannot be shown to be directly related to the job the applicant seeks. Make sure interviews or tests are accessible (i.e., people with a range of disabilities can access them from a physical as well as an informational standpoint).

- ⊘ **Use medical examinations fairly and respectfully.** Uniformity (a policy that applies to all employees with a particular job classification) is the key concept here.

- ⊘ **Codify decision making.** Create a well-documented and adhered-to procedure for hiring decisions and use it for all hiring—not just deciding whether to hire a person with a disability.

- ⊘ **Train personnel, especially interviewers and supervisors, about disabilities and the law.** Such awareness training is most effective when it eventually covers a wide range of disabilities and involves trainers who can speak from experience because they, themselves, have a disability. Awareness training also needs to be conducted within a wide range, vertically and horizontally, of your workforce.

- ⊘ **Conduct employee evaluations on a strict schedule.** By applying the same standards to all workers and informing them of problems and disciplinary actions according to established procedures, you demonstrate that you have evaluated the complaining employee objectively. Also provide a clear grievance procedure. Conduct exit interviews no matter what the reason for the worker's departure.

These are just some of the ways you can start lawsuit-proofing your human resources policies and procedures. Contact your attorney, your local human rights commission, or your state's Business Leadership Network for more in-depth information.

Documentation Is the Key

Documenting the accommodation plans you and your employee work out together, including before-and-after evaluations, is one tool for lessening the possibility of a discrimination suit. Broadening your documentation to include how you have improved policies and practices and any other proactive efforts can help protect you, too. Consult your attorney for guidance about what and how to document your inclusion initiatives.

It is important to understand the legal concept of "discrimination." If you or your representative refuses to hire a disabled job applicant or neglects to promote (or decides to fire) a disabled employee, it is not necessarily discrimination. If you refuse to hire or promote him or fire him because of his disability and cannot show that the disability truly prevented him from doing the job, then it is discrimination.

The act is not what determines the discrimination; the motivation for the act is the discrimination. Careful documentation can be the lynchpin in your defense—that your decision was sound and unrelated to an intention to discriminate.

Your legal obligation as an employer is to provide for the mechanical or strategic bridge that provides the pathway for inclusion. The nuances of this requirement depend on where you are. The ADA uses the qualifiers "reasonable accommodation" and "undue hardship." These "outs" actually add considerably to the importance of good documentation about your inclusion efforts. Courts make decisions about your goodwill efforts by examining what steps you have taken to promote and fulfill your obligation for inclusion.

By being solution oriented, you can avoid a discrimination lawsuit. But keep records of what you've tried, what you and the worker have negotiated, what resulted, and how you measured those results. A true good-faith effort will reveal itself in the records you keep.

For further information, see "The ADA: Your Responsibilities as an Employer" at http://www.eeoc.gov/facts/ada17.html.

Curtis Bryan and Randy Hammer Make Blindness Irrelevant in Serving Customers

Here's a success story that spans a decade.

Curtis Bryan, manager of client services for CIS at Illuminet in Olympia, Washington, says it was easy to provide adaptive technology for Randy Hammer, when he hired him to serve the telecommunication company's customers.

"He was the first person I called," says Bryan in an interview for eSight in 2002. Charged with developing a new department to analyze and coordinate changes made in key software and systems, Bryan picked up the phone in the spring of 2000 and called someone he had worked with at Weyerhaeuser, a lumber and paper titan in the Pacific Northwest. This young man was Randy Hammer, who had impressed Bryan with his superior teamwork skills and ability to learn quickly.

The fact that Hammer was blind was, says Bryan, "irrelevant."

At that time, Illuminet, a publicly traded company headquartered in Olympia, was providing advanced nationwide signaling and specialized network database services to communications carriers as well as prepaid wireless services through its subsidiary, National Telemanagement Corporation in Dallas, Texas.

Illuminet needed top-flight workers, and Hammer was a top-flight worker. Hammer, who became blind as a child, was happy to make the move to an exciting company in a location that was also a better commute.

No Concerns About Adaptive Technology

Bryan had himself been aware of some of the developments in making computers accessible for those with disabilities, but he had not seen them at work until he met Randy Hammer. The young graduate from Evergreen State College had appeared in the University of Washington's DO-IT videos, which highlight motivated college students with disabilities who are using technology to advance their career goals. Hammer had also switched from MicroTalk's ASAW to new software, Henter-Joyce's JAWS for Windows, which was more compatible with Weyerhaeuser's in-house software. JAWS is a speech output application that works with a wide variety of screen configurations.

Bryan had seen for himself how readily, with this tool, Hammer could equal or better any other worker, so he had no concerns when he asked Hammer if he wanted to work at Illuminet.

"The expense was minimal," Bryan admits. "Nothing we would even worry about. In fact, we'd ordered it before Randy even started working here."

The only barrier these two ran into was that the software arrived during Hammer's second day on the job. But, Hammer says, "I just downloaded the JAWS for Windows demo from Henter-Joyce's website to use on my first day. I was able to get to work right away."

Illuminet purchased the access software for about $1,500 and added a software maintenance agreement. "The computer," Hammer adds, "already had the sound card you use with JAWS for Windows."

Bryan says he wishes other employers knew how easy this was. He adds, "Our building was 10 years old [at that time], so it was already wheelchair accessible. We have been successful in accommodating other disabilities as well. With Randy, the only other thing we needed to do was go to less paper and more electronic communications, but we were doing that anyway."

Hired for His Capability

Describing Randy Hammer, Bryan says, "Randy shines! He is a wonderful employee and earns all the kudos he gets. He was hired for his capability more than his experience. When I wanted to hire him and some were concerned that he may not have had the experience he would need, I told them that he is the quickest learner I've ever met. He has a natural aptitude for serving our customers."

Bryan can't say if being blind helped Hammer develop his skills or if he comes by them naturally, but he credits Randy's success to other qualities as well: memorization, organizational ability, and troubleshooting skills. "He has a different perspective on problems because, at least in part, he uses slightly different tools."

Illuminet and Hammer learned to solve unanticipated issues. When asked to provide drawn charts for reports, Hammer turned to Bryan for help. "I was glad to do it," Bryan says. "And I tried to make sure all our charts had good accompanying text so Randy could use them."

Hammer himself was a resourceful worker when other challenges came up. When he needed to help others within Illuminet, he ran into the barrier that JAWS for Windows was not installed on everyone's computer. But he had so much experience doing support via the telephone that having a coworker just read the screen was all he needed.

Fast forward to 2010.

Bryan continues to work in information technology services in the Seattle area.

Hammer is manager of systems administration and support, directly supervising a six-person technical support team at Transaction Network Services, the parent company of Illuminet.

After bouncing between people and project supervision and finally settling on people management as his track, Hammer gives this decade-wide perspective: "The technology that we have today is vastly improved from when I started working at Illuminet in April 2000. There are very few barriers technologically to a visually impaired employee with today's software."

What to Remember from This Example

Bryan's experience in hiring Hammer demonstrates the three main recommendations members of eSight Careers Network said they wanted to pass along to you as an employer—once they knew some of their blog entries would be included in this book. Here are their tips (in priority order):

1. **Focus on individual abilities.** Focus on how an individual job candidate can be an asset to your organization instead of that person's disability. Since no two people are alike, assumptions about their abilities and disabilities are often misleading. So, evaluate both ability and disability on an individual basis.

2. **Look at core attributes.** Hire job candidates who have learned to live well with their disabilities and, in the process, have developed a personal sense of creativity, adaptability, and flexibility—attributes that can spark problem solving, interdependency, and innovation in your organization.

3. **Allow for career growth.** Gear your recruitment efforts toward job candidates with disabilities only when you have a sincere intent to address their career aspirations and provide them the same opportunities for accessible training, career development, and internal advancement you provide those who do not have disabilities.

The fact that Hammer is blind was irrelevant in Bryan's mind when he hired him. Bryan chose Hammer for his organizational ability, troubleshooting skills, and customer orientation. Hammer appears to have an opportunity to grow in his career at Illuminet because Bryan recognized that he had superior teamwork skills and the ability to learn quickly (important attributes in a rapidly changing business sector).

Here are two key questions for you as a human resources executive or hiring manager:

1. If you substitute the word "differences" for the word "disabilities" in the three inclusive recruiting strategies just given, do you change the meaning of any of these guidelines?
2. If you see substantial overlap between these three recommendations and the priorities in your company's diversity policy statements, is there any reason why disability should not be a part of your company's diversity initiative?

These three recommendations stand alone as just good recruiting, hiring, placement, and development principles.

As eSight Careers Network member Barney Mayse urges, "Let's grow beyond the idea that diversity is just about culture and skin color." By doing so, you'll have an opportunity to have first dibs on recruiting the top job candidates with talent, persistence, skill, and authenticity in a relatively untapped pool of job seekers with disabilities.

QUICK TIPS FROM THIS CHAPTER

⊘ Self-Esteem and Workplace Performance

As one of the pillars of emotional intelligence, self-esteem provides a capacity for regeneration—an attribute that gives top-notch job candidates with disabilities the resiliency to cope effectively with personal vulnerability. That resiliency is invaluable in job candidates because it can help your work group continue to succeed. For more information, see "Passport to Self-Esteem Is Easier Than You Might Think" at http://www.odt.org/SEP%20Press%20Release.htm.

⊘ Paternalism in the Workplace

Maturity, respect, credibility—all three are in jeopardy for both the individual with a disability and your corporate culture when paternalism is allowed to grow, largely because of lack of awareness and misinformation.

For another view of paternalism, see "Court Says ADA Does Not Require Companies to Hire Those with Health Risks" at http://www.accessiblesociety.org/topics/ada/echazabal1.htm.

⊘ Validating an Employee as an Equal Member of Your Team

When you hire an employee with a disability, you may forget the basics of supervision and leadership and try to accommodate that person in ways that are inappropriate. That sets up unrealistic expectations for the organization, for the person with the disability, and for that person's colleagues. For more information, see "Effective Interaction: Communicating with and About People with Disabilities in the Workplace" at http://www.dol.gov/odep/pubs/fact/ effectiveinteraction.htm.

⊘ Choosing the Right Mentor

Hiring managers may be concerned about hiring individuals with disabilities because of a potential drain on company time and resources when the new employee has real or perceived limitations. Assigning mentors to these newly hired people directly addresses that concern. For more about why employees with disabilities need mentors, see "Restricted Access: A Survey of Employers About People with Disabilities and Lowering Barriers to Work" at http://www.heldrich.rutgers.edu/ uploadedFiles/Publications/Restricted%20Access.pdf.

⊘ Helping an Employee with a Disability Grow in His Job

You and your employee with a disability may have a mutual interest. Someone who is "different" has a larger than usual stake in how well you perform as a leader. And he can be your bellwether. The extra time you may be required to spend in helping him perform well in his job and as a member of your team may actually provide you with an opportunity to showcase your skills—and grow—as a leader. For more information, see "Managing Diverse Employees with Disabilities" at http://www.icdri.org/Employment/managingdivers.htm.

⊘ Removing Barriers to Achievement

Most obstacles to achievement among employees with disabilities occur unintentionally—even in companies with genuinely inclusive philosophies. Many times the barrier is simply an oversight, a "Gee, I never thought of that!" Never let your assumptions or lack of access block achievement. For more information, see "Survey of Employer Perspectives on the Employment of People with Disabilities" at http://www.dol.gov/odep/documents/survey_report_jan_09.doc.

⊘ Adaptive Technology for Specific Disabilities

Adaptive technology is available today for making each type of disability an irrelevant factor in how a person can perform in the workplace. See the JAN's "For Employers," a service of the U.S. Department of Labor's Office of Disability Employment Policy, at http://www.jan.wvu.edu/empl/index.htm.

⊘ Guidelines for Reasonable Accommodation Under the ADA

Title I of the ADA outlines specific guidelines for work-site accommodation, job restructuring, modified work schedules and leave, modified policies, and equipment and services. See the JAN's "Employers' Practical Guide to Reasonable Accommodation Under the American with Disabilities Act (ADA)" at http://www.jan.wvu.edu/Erguide/index.htm.

⊘ Who Should Pay for What Under What Circumstances

There are at least seven general options for funding the adaptive technology a new employee with a disability may need. That means with today's adaptive technology employing a worker who has a disability is possible and entirely feasible for even the smallest and most budget squeezed of employers. Consider the total accommodation and stipulate what works best for you, the employer, and the employee, and then decide who should fairly take responsibility for what. For more information, see "Accommodation" at http://www.jan.wvu.edu/topics/accommo.htm.

⊘ When You Are Being Manipulated

When you start to have doubts about whether a person with a disability is being truthful with you about an accommodation or about an access need he has, take a step back and think about it. For more information, see "Accommodation Requests" at http://www.jan.wvu.edu/Erguide/Three.htm#B.

⊘ Guidelines for Information and Confidentiality Under the ADA

You may require a medical and/or psychiatric examination or ask questions related to a new employee's physical or mental disability.

However, you are allowed to do this *only if you require all entering employees in the same job category to be subject to the same inquiries or examination, regardless of disability*. For more information, see "Medical Exams and Inquiries" at http://www.jan.wvu.edu/topics/medexinq.htm.

⊘ Preventing a Disability Lawsuit

Documenting the accommodation plans you and your employee work out together, including before-and-after evaluations, is one tool for lessening the possibility of a discrimination suit. Broadening your documentation to include how you have improved policies and practices and any other proactive efforts can help protect you, too. Consult your attorney for guidance about what and how to document your inclusion initiatives. For more information, see "Seven Essential Elements of Quality Disability Documentation" at http://ahead.org/resources/best-practices-resources/elements.

⊘ Making Blindness Irrelevant in Servicing Customers

In hiring Randy Hammer, Curtis Bryan followed the three recommendations eSight Careers Network members would like to pass along to you as an employer: (1) focus on individual abilities, (2) look at core attributes, and (3) allow for career growth. For more information, see "Business, Disability and Employment: Corporate Models of Success Manual" at http://www.worksupport.com/research/printView.cfm/578.

Suggestion for Job Interview Topic

Your company can be a corporate model of success in terms of attracting and hiring talented people with disabilities. What's the telltale sign that you have "arrived"? You routinely ask this question of all job candidates during your interviewing process:

"How do you see yourself achieving your career goal within our company?"

It's nothing new. But, in exploring that question with applicants (nondisabled and disabled alike), you open a dialogue that focuses on individual abilities, core attributes, and career growth. And that shows that you and your company are prepared to embrace differences among the individuals within your workforce because that diversity adds value to what you offer your customers.

Appendix A

▲

Comprehensive Resource List for Hiring People with Disabilities

"Able & Willing" is a captioned video of stories about people with disabilities and businesses working together to create successful mentorships, internships, and long-term employment opportunities.

http://www.ableandwilling.net/

"Accessibility Case Studies" showcases organizations that have integrated accessible technology solutions into their technology plans to help individuals with various types of impairments maintain productivity on the job. They feature best practices and lessons learned as well as examples of why it makes good business sense to provide accessible technology in the workplace.

http://www.microsoft.com/enable/casestudy/default.aspx

ADA Title II tutorial (Project of the DBTAC National Network of ADA Centers)

www.adacourse.org/title2

"ADA Toolbox"

http://www.mmb.state.mn.us/ada-toolbox

"ADA: Your Responsibilities as an Employer"

http://www.eeoc.gov/facts/ada17.html

Asia & Pacific Disability Forum (APDF)

http://www.normanet.ne.jp/~apdf/index.html

"Survey of Employer Perspectives on the Employment of People with Disabilities" is a report that provides findings from the most extensive survey in history of employers' actions and attitudes toward employing people with disabilities.

http://www.dol.gov/odep/documents/survey_report_jan_09.doc

"Best Practices of Private Sector Employers" is a report from the U.S. Equal Employment Opportunity Commission that highlights noteworthy business practices by which employers are complying with their equal employment opportunity obligations and diversity objectives.

http://archive.eeoc.gov/abouteeoc/task_reports/prac2.html

"Circle of Champions: Innovators in Employing All Americans"

http://www.dol.gov/odep/newfreedom/coc2007/brochure.htm

"Defining Your DDQ: Disability Diversity Quotient"

http://www.disability-marketing.com/newsletter/
2006-03-article-ddq.php4

Definition of Disability by Deborah Kaplan, director of the World Institute on Disability

http://www.accessiblesociety.org/topics/demographics-identity/
dkaplanpaper.htm

Department of Veterans Affairs, Vocational Rehabilitation & Employment Service helps employers across the country fill workforce needs with trained, educated, and experienced disabled veterans. It provides recruitment assistance based on employers' specific qualification requirements, and candidates are skilled, committed workers who are prescreened for specific employment opportunities. Through the service, employers also gain access to resources to assist with recruitment, retention, and succession planning strategies.

http://www.vba.va.gov/bln/vre/

Disability & HR: Tips for Human Resource (HR) Professionals
This website contains resources, articles, and checklists for HR professionals.

http://www.ilr.cornell.edu/edi/hr_tips/home.cfm

HR Checklists: Disability Nondiscrimination and Best Practices

http://www.ilr.cornell.edu/edi/hr_tips/list.cfm

Disability Employment 101 is a publication that addresses how to find qualified workers with disabilities and highlights what various businesses have done to successfully integrate individuals with disabilities into the workforce. Jointly developed by the U.S. Department of Education and the U.S. Chamber of Commerce, it provides information about Vocational Rehab Agencies and Disability and Business Technical Assistance Centers as well as checklists and other resources to aid employers as they prepare to employ people with disabilities.

http://www.ed.gov/about/offices/list/osers/products/
employmentguide/index.html

Disabled Peoples' International (DPI)

http://www.dpi.org/

Diversity World

http://www.diversityworld.com/Disability/newsletter.htm

Equality and Human Rights Commission (United Kingdom)

http://www.equalityhumanrights.com/

"Diverse Perspectives: People with Disabilities Fulfilling Your Business Goals"

http://www.dol.gov/odep/pubs/fact/diverse.htm

"Diversifying Your Workforce: A Four-Step Reference Guide to Recruiting, Hiring, & Retaining Employees with Disabilities"

http://www.pueblo.gsa.gov/cic_text/smbuss/diversify/workforce.pdf

The DRM Regional Resources Directory lists disability organizations by state.
http://www.disabilityresources.org/DRMreg.html

"Effective Interaction: Communicating with and About People with Disabilities in the Workplace"

http://www.dol.gov/odep/pubs/fact/effectiveinteraction.htm

Employer Assistance & Resource Network (EARN) is a free, confidential service from the U.S. Department of Labor's Office of Disability Employment Policy that connects job seekers and employers seeking qualified candidates with disabilities. By using EARN, employers gain access to a nationwide network of employment service providers who work with people with disabilities looking to join or return to the workforce. EARN also offers technical assistance to employers on issues relating to hiring and employing individuals with disabilities.

http://www.earnworks.com/

"Employer's Accommodation Process"

http://www.ilr.cornell.edu/edi/hr_tips/list_1.cfm?c_id=62&view_all=true

"Employers and the ADA: Myths and Facts"

http://www.dol.gov/odep/pubs/fact/ada.htm

"Employer's Guide to Hidden Disabilities"

http://www.muhlenberg.edu/careercenter/emplguide/cognitive.html

"Employment Checklist for Hiring Persons with Disabilities"

http://www.dol.gov/odep/pubs/ek96/chcklist.htm

"Employment Laws: Disability & Discrimination"

http://www.dol.gov/odep/pubs/fact/laws.htm

"Employment Laws: Overview & Resources for Employers"
    http://www.dol.gov/odep/pubs/fact/overview.htm

European Disability Forum (EDF)
    http://www.edf-feph.org/

"Focus on Ability: Interviewing Applicants with Disabilities"
    http://www.dol.gov/odep/pubs/fact/focus.htm

Frequently Asked Questions for Employers from Earnworks.com
    http://www.earnworks.com/BusinessCase/faqs.asp

Government publications and fact sheets about accommodations, disability and workplace culture, discrimination in the workplace, emergency preparedness, employment laws and legal issues, employment options, recruitment and retention, and tax incentives for employers
    http://www.dol.gov/odep/pubs/publicat.htm

Inclusion International (II)
    http://www.inclusion-international.org

"Interaction with State and Federal Legislation"
    http://www.ilr.cornell.edu/edi/hr_tips/list_1.cfm?c_id=63&view_all=true

"It Takes Ingenuity and Persistence to Succeed, Disabled Workers Say"
    http://nexxstepsolutions.com/_WpBlog/?p=3

"The Job Accommodation Process: Steps to Collaborative Solutions"
    http://www.dol.gov/odep/pubs/misc/job.htm

"Making It Easy to Do the Right Thing" (booklet and DVD)
    http://diversitynz.com/diversityworks-trust/past-projects/hdc-dvd/

Marketing Course: Reaching Out to Customers with Disabilities
    http://www.ada.gov/reachingout/intro1.htm

"Maximizing Productivity: Accommodations for Employees with Psychiatric Disabilities"

http://www.dol.gov/odep/pubs/fact/psychiatric.htm

"Myths and Facts About Workers with Disabilities"

http://www.doleta.gov/disability/htmldocs/myths.cfm

"Opening Doors to All Candidates: Tips for Ensuring Access for Applicants with Disabilities"

http://www.dol.gov/odep/pubs/fact/opening.htm

"Performance Management and Opportunities for Promotion and Training"

http://www.ilr.cornell.edu/edi/hr_tips/list_1.cfm?c_id=61&view_all=true

"Personal Assistance Services in the Workplace"

Basic fact sheet about personal assistance services in the workplace prepared by the U.S. Department of Labor's Office of Disability Employment Policy.

http://www.dol.gov/odep/pubs/ek97/personal.htm

"Recruitment, Pre-Employment Screening, Testing, and Orientation"

http://www.ilr.cornell.edu/edi/hr_tips/list_1.cfm?c_id=60&view_all=true

"Return on Investment" is a video about ROI.

http://www.earnworks.com/BusinessCase/videos/roi.html

"Sample ADA Policies, Forms and Checklists" (Job Accommodation Network)

http://www.jan.wvu.edu/links/adapolicies.html

State governors' committees on employment of people with disabilities. Each state typically has a governor-appointed board, committee, commission, or council that provides leadership to its efforts to improve employment opportunities for individuals with disabilities. Employers may contact these committees for information about state-specific resources available to help them recruit and retain qualified individuals with disabilities.

http://www.dol.gov/odep/state/state.htm

"The State of Disability in America: An Evaluation of the Disability Experience by the Life Without Limits Project" (United Cerebral Palsy)

http://www.ucp.org/uploads/StateofDisability.pdf

"Tax Incentives for Providing Business Accessibility"

http://www.dol.gov/odep/pubs/fact/tifpba.htm

Think Beyond the Label is an online source of expert tools and resources for businesses looking to evolve their workforce.

http://www.thinkbeyondthelabel.com/Default.aspx

Thinking Outside the Box: Creative Solutions for Accommodating Disabilities is a resource tool for accommodating employees with a disability.

http://www.totb.ca/english/index.asp

Title III compliance checklist (from the Job Accommodation Network)

http://janweb.icdi.wvu.edu/media/IIIChecklist.html

UN disability statistics

http://unstats.un.org/unsd/demographic/sconcerns/disability/

UN focal point on disability

http://www.un.org/disabilities/

U.S. International Council on Disabilities (USA)

http://www.usicd.org/

Value of Employees with Disabilities: What Businesses Say

http://www.earnworks.com/BusinessCase/index.asp

Vocational Rehabilitation (VR) state agencies help individuals with
disabilities obtain and maintain employment. Thus, they also assist
employers in identifying qualified, job-ready candidates with
disabilities to fill their workforce needs. Each state has a
designated person tasked with building and maintaining employer
relationships. In addition to recruitment assistance, state VR
agencies can provide services such as work evaluation and
assessment for and provision of assistive technology and other
workplace accommodations.

http://www.ed.gov/rschstat/research/pubs/vrpractices/busdev.html

Workforce Recruitment Program (WRP) helps employers identify
qualified college students with disabilities for summer work
experience and, in some cases, full-time employment. Jointly
coordinated by the Office of Disability Employment Policy and
the U.S. Department of Defense, WRP establishes partnerships
with other federal agencies that commit to provide summer jobs
as well as a staff recruiter for the program. Each year, recruiters
personally interview about 1,500 students and compile a database
of their qualifications that is available to these agencies, as well
as private employers, at no cost.

http://www.dol.gov/odep/programs/workforc.htm

Appendix B

▲

About eSight Careers Network

As the global, cross-disability online community addressing disability employment issues, eSight Careers Network (www.esight.org) is a service of Lighthouse International.

Founded in 1905, Lighthouse International is a leading nonprofit organization dedicated to fighting vision loss through prevention, treatment, and empowerment. It achieves this through clinical and rehabilitation services, education, research, and advocacy.

Lighthouse International's website, *www.lighthouse.org*, offers information for employers, job seekers, and small businesses as well as a range of information on vision health, special venues, and other material for people who are visually impaired as well as their friends and families.

The purpose of the interactivity through eSight is to build knowledge about what works best in managing a career from a disability perspective. eSight is working to extend that dialogue to include key leaders within disability-friendly companies.

Examples of that eSight dialogue are summarized in four "Swimming in the Mainstream" (SiM) articles (made possible by a grant from the American Express Foundation):

1. "Breaking Accessibility Barriers"
    (http://www.esight.org/View.cfm?x=1751)

2. "Creating a Level Recruiting Field"
    (http://www.esight.org/View.cfm?x=1777)

3. "Telltale Signs of Inclusion"
    (http://www.esight.org/View.cfm?x=1761)

4. "Unique Confidence-Building Experiences"
    (http://www.esight.org/View.cfm?x=1770)

Each article includes snippets of member comments from eSight's SiM blog. Participants discussed one disability employment issue each month, and eSight staff writers summarized each month's discussion into a concise article for employers.

Blog participants quoted in the articles were linked to another eSight gathering place where they can post their "offering" statements (how they can help an employer in a particular job sector) for prospective employers to browse.

In 1998, eSight was first conceived as one of several services (including computer training, disability awareness training, and residential housing) The Associated Blind, Inc. offered to individuals with visual impairments in New York City.

An initial business plan for the site was prepared in 1999, and content development began in 2000 with a team of freelance, part-time writers under the direction of a content developer. The full-time staff for the site also included a technical director, a webmaster, and a membership services director.

An in-house team of international student interns created the site's infrastructure, and a team of individuals who are blind developed the design specifications so every detail on eSight is accessible for users of speech (screen-reading) software.

The site development team created editorial applications so content could be created and published from anywhere in the world.

eSight was officially launched in October 2000, using Cold Fusion and a relational database to create dynamic, customized pages.

There have been five phases in the development of eSight since 2000:

1. **Content Development.** Between 2000 and 2002, five part-time freelancers generated content, which now includes more than 1,300 extensively researched feature articles.

2. **Interactive Functionality.** In 2002 and 2003, eSight began offering members the opportunity to share ideas through dialogue boards; post replies to articles; and use a send-this-article-to-a-friend tool as well as real-time, private text chat and real-time idea sharing with an exclusive "Blindstorming" tool. In 2003, eSight began offering toll-free eSight Phone Conferences in which participants can listen to as well as question guest speakers.

3. **Syndicated Content.** In July 2004, eSight launched the eSight Disability Employment Web, a Real Simple Syndication (RSS) service for providing other websites a link to eSight content that rotates each day seven days a week.

4. **Online Training.** During 2005, eSight developed an accessible instructional platform, and, in 2006, started offering its first online course, "Online Networking as a Job Search Tool," through the eSight eLearning Center.

5. **Book Publishing.** In October 2010, AMACOM published *Perfectly Able: How to Attract and Hire Talented People with Disabilities,* which features dozens of personal experience observations in submissions from more than fifty individuals with disabilities who participated in eSight discussions focused on dignity from a disability employment perspective.

In 2003, The Associated Blind, Inc. refocused all of its resources on eSight Careers Network. In 2008, The Associated Blind, Inc. became a part of Lighthouse International, a leading nonprofit organization that fights vision loss through prevention, treatment, and empowerment.

In addition to the extensively researched articles written by individuals with a disability and with real-world employment experience, eSight provided phone conferences, online professional development seminars, job postings, an eSight newsletter, step-by-step Career Management Guides, 100 interactive forums, profiles of disability-friendly companies, book reviews, scholarship notices, and internship information.

Here are comments from four individuals about how they use eSight:

"As an eSight eLearner, I've been supported in various ways:

- ⊘ I was helped to improve and develop knowledge and experience of job searching and online networking;

- ⊘ I was helped to acquire practical skills in facilitating and participating in online discussions;

- ⊘ Finally, I was helped to expand the list of professional contacts and strengthened my own position as a job seeker with disability."   —Vladimir

"I am a blind information technology professional and owner of a new small business. I have found eSight extremely valuable in the success of my career, both in the quality of the articles and the exchanges between blind people like myself."   —D.S.

"[I am] an instructor [and] eSight has been invaluable in our weekly Job Readiness classes. The audio files have been especially useful in stimulating discussion and brainstorming sessions. Thank you for the information, ideas, and variety!"

—S.C.

"You provide me with an opportunity to voice my opinion and see those of others. . . . Through your articles, job coaching tips, and career advice, you have pushed me to ultimately making that step and start the search for a more suitable job."

—Kerry

eSight Careers Network is a service of Lighthouse International. For more information about eSight, go to www.esight.org. For more information about Lighthouse International, go to www.lighthouse.org.

Appendix C

▲

eSight Careers Network Article Links

Portions of the following eSight Careers Network articles appear in the text of this book. Here are links to the full articles.

"Self-Determination: New Opportunities, New Responsibilities," http://www.esight.org/view.cfm?x=303.

"Overview: The Traits of Self-Esteem," http://www.esight.org/view.cfm?x=554.

"Three Constructive Approaches to Disability Employment," http://www.esight.org/view.cfm?x=1603.

"Dissension, Reconciliation: Do Unemployed Blind People Resent Those with Jobs?," http://www.esight.org/view.cfm?x=802.

"Creating a Level Recruiting Field," http://www.esight.org/view.cfm?x=1777.

"Everything You Always Wanted to Know About Blind Employees but Were Reluctant to Ask," http://www.esight.org/view.cfm?x=565.

"Share the Load: You Don't Have to Be the Weakest Link due to Your Disability," http://www.esight.org/view.cfm?x=483.

"Hire People Who Resolve 'Easy Mark' Situations for Themselves," http://www.esight.org/view.cfm?x=1840.

"What to Expect from a Job Candidate Who Has Emotional Intelligence About Disability," http://www.esight.org/view.cfm?x=265.

"How to Validate a Visually Impaired Employee as an Equal Member of Your Team," http://www.esight.org/view.cfm?x=216.

"Creative Survivors Add Elasticity to Your Workforce," http://www.esight.org/view.cfm?x=1827.

"Has Disability Made You a Workaholic?," http://www.esight.org/view.cfm?x=597.

"The Icing on the Cake: Tax Breaks for Hiring Those with Disabilities," http://www.esight.org/view.cfm?x=382.

"Assessing Applicants: When to Seriously Consider Experience from Volunteer Work," http://www.esight.org/view.cfm?x=629.

"How to Decide What to Do as a Volunteer, Part I," http://www.esight.org/view.cfm?x=16.

"How to Decide What You Can and Want to Do as a Volunteer, Part II," http://www.esight.org/view.cfm?x=79.

"Tapping Job Candidates Who Have Transformed Vulnerability into Authenticity," http://www.esight.org/view.cfm?x=1785.

"Weed Out Paternalism in the Workplace," http://www.esight.org/view.cfm?x=1815.

"How to Foster a Work Environment That Values Employees with Diversity," http://www.esight.org/view.cfm?x=523.

"Use Leadership to Help an Employee with a Disability Grow in His Job," http://www.esight.org/view.cfm?x=611.

"Clear the Way to Achievement for Your Visually Impaired Employees," http://www.esight.org/view.cfm?x=1139.

"Choose the Right Mentor for a New Employee Who Is Visually Impaired," http://www.esight.org/view.cfm?x=320.

"Target Job Candidates with Disabilities Who Are Risk Takers," http://www.esight.org/view.cfm?x=1860.

"Workplace Interdependence and Employees with Disabilities," http://www.esight.org/view.cfm?x=348.

"Disability Awareness: Essential to Any Diversity Program," http://www.esight.org/view.cfm?x=106.

"Two Trends Show Why Diversity Needs to Include Disability," http://www.esight.org/view.cfm?x=698.

"Telltale Signs of Inclusion," http://www.esight.org/view.cfm?x=1761.

"How to Put Diversity Values into Practice," http://www.esight.org/view.cfm?x=228.

"Choosing the Right Disability Awareness Trainer for Your Organization," http://www.esight.org/view.cfm?x=192.

"Use Job Fairs to Recruit Visually Impaired Candidates, Enhance Corporate Success," http://www.esight.org/view.cfm?x=193.

"Make Sure Job Postings Reach Job Candidates with Disabilities," http://www.esight.org/view.cfm?x=401.

"Making Blindness Irrelevant Through Accommodations to Effectively Serve Customers," http://www.esight.org/view.cfm?x=122.

"Webliography for Locating Job Candidates with Disabilities," http://www.esight.org/view.cfm?x=636.

"How to Recruit Qualified Job Candidates with Disabilities on College Campuses," http://www.esight.org/view.cfm?x=1344.

"Best Practices for Interviewing a Blind or Print Impaired Job Candidate," http://www.esight.org/view.cfm?x=113.

"Accommodations for Adaptive Technology: Who Should Pay for What Under What Circumstances," http://www.esight.org/view.cfm?x=600.

"Uh-Oh, Busted: How to Lessen the Impact of a Discrimination Lawsuit," http://www.esight.org/view.cfm?x=775.

"Worker with a Disability Trying to Put One Over on You? Here's What to Do," http://www.esight.org/view.cfm?x=880.

Index

▲